KING ALBERT'S
BOOK

*This book is sold
for the benefit of the
Daily Telegraph Belgian Fund*

Albert

KING ALBERT'S BOOK

A TRIBUTE TO THE BELGIAN KING AND PEOPLE FROM REPRESENTATIVE MEN AND WOMEN THROUGHOUT THE WORLD

THE DAILY TELEGRAPH
IN CONJUNCTION WITH
THE DAILY SKETCH THE GLASGOW HERALD
AND HODDER AND STOUGHTON

KNIGHTS

MANUFACTURING·COMPANY·LTD

PHOTO·ENGRAVERS·DESIGNERS·PHOTOGRAPHERS·PRINTERS &c

THE COMPLETE PRESS

BY TEMPLE BAR IN THE CITY OF LONDON:

INTRODUCTION TO KING ALBERT'S BOOK

THE immediate object of this Book is to offer, in the names and by the pens of a large group of the representative men and women of the civilised countries, a tribute of admiration to Belgium, on the heroic and ever-memorable share she has taken in the war which now convulses Europe, and at the same time to invoke the world's sympathy, its help and its prayers for the gallant little nation in the vast sorrow of its present condition.

With nothing to gain by taking up arms, with no territory to annex, no commerce to capture, no injury to revenge, having neither part nor lot in any European quarrel, desiring only to be left alone that she might pursue the arts of peace, Belgium found herself suddenly confronted by the choice of allowing her soil to be invaded by a powerful neighbour on his way to destroy his enemy, or of protecting her independence as a separate nation by the whole strength of her armed resistance.

Although one of the smallest and least aggressive of the countries of Europe, the daughter among the nations, Belgium, true to her lofty political idealism, chose the latter part, not counting the cost, only realising that a ruthless crime was about to be committed, and drawing the sword, after the sword had been drawn against her, in defence of her honour, her national integrity, her right to be mistress in her own house, her historic heritage of freedom and all the spiritual traditions of her race.

In doing this during the past fateful months, Belgium has fought not only her own battle but also the battle of France, the battle of Great Britain and the battle of Freedom. By her brave stand against incalculable odds she has added a new and inspiring chapter to the heroic annals of humanity and perhaps lifted to a higher level the future destinies of man.

But she has paid a terrible penalty. Her beautiful country has been laid waste. Her harvests, which were ripe for the gathering, have been trodden into the earth. Her villages have been given up to the flames. Her cities have been made to resound with the screams of shell and the cries of slaughter. Her historic monuments, venerable with the associations of learning and piety, have been razed to the ground. And, above all, Death has taken an awful toll of her manhood on the field of battle, while multitudes of her surviving people, the very young, the very old, the very weak, the very poor, all innocent and all helpless, have been driven forth on the verge of winter from their smoking, blackened and outraged homes into an exile in foreign lands from which there can hardly be any hope that many of them will return.

No more woeful and terrible spectacle of a country in utter desolation ever came from earthquake, eruption or other convulsion of Nature in her wrath than has been produced in Belgium by the hand of man. A complete nation is in ruin. A whole country is in ashes. An entire people are destitute, homeless and on the roads. A little Kingdom, dedicated to liberty, has " kept the pledge and died for it."

As Belgium has thus become the martyr nation of the war, however great the sacrifices which the other Allies have had to make, it seems reasonable to expect that in view of her limitless and undeserved sufferings, the deepest feelings of human nature will be stirred to an infinite pity, and that in the present dark hour of her utmost need the world will see that it is not more important that the material succour of food and clothing should be found for the bodies of her stricken and impoverished people than that comfort and solace should be offered to their souls. Therefore this book is published as the united voice of the world's gratitude to Belgium for her unexampled heroism, and of its sympathy with her in the heavy price she has to pay in discharging the sublime duty which Destiny laid upon her of fighting by our side for the liberties of all.

Especially it has been intended that the present volume should address itself, as far as possible, to the King of the Belgians, who, from his first moving appeal to Great Britain and to France, to help him to resist the gigantic and unconscionable ambition which was preparing to stalk over his country, down to the last agony of his dauntless stand behind the fortresses of Antwerp, has by his matchless courage in Council and on the battlefield, where he makes common cause with his soldiers in the trenches, displayed some of the noblest energies of the human character, and sustained those highest traditions of Kingship which, among free nations, unite the people to the throne.

Such is the aim and character of this book, and if so high an object has been in some measure achieved, it has only been by the ready and whole-hearted co-operation of the leaders of thought, of art and of action who are prominent throughout the world for their love of justice and freedom. There are many thousands of such leaders in every country, fully capable of interpreting, each in his or her own way, the immense emotion which now fills the heart of humanity at the spectacle of Belgium's sorrows ; but the exigencies of space in a single volume have made it necessary to limit the number of contributors whom it has been possible to invite to join in this world's tribute to the martyr nation.

With the utmost care, and not without many misgivings about illustrious names which well merited inclusion, a list was compiled of princes, statesmen, churchmen, authors, artists, and composers of all civilised countries, except the countries of our enemies, in the hope that each in his own medium, whether of word or picture or song or story, might be impelled, according as the spirit moved him, to present his view of Belgium's sacrifice and of the measureless calamity which has befallen her.

The result is now offered to the public in the present volume, which it is hoped to publish in various editions, and as nearly as possible simultaneously, in most of the countries of the authors, especially France, Russia, Italy, and America, thus making it a work of international interest, calculated to be a moral inspiration to posterity and to take its place as one of the luminous pages in the world's history.

Never before, perhaps, have so many illustrious names been inscribed within the covers of a single volume, but KING ALBERT'S BOOK has a significance which even transcends its distinction. Out of the storm of battle a great new spirit of brotherhood has been born into the world, calling together the scattered and divided parts of it, uniting them in a single mind, a single sentiment, a single

6

purpose, so that here, in love of justice and in hatred of oppression, speaking in many voices and many tongues but from only one soul, which enkindles the earth as with a holy fire, men and women of all civilised countries have drawn closer and clasped hands.

Nor is that everything. In sight and witness of this World-league of some of the spiritual leaders of mankind, who labour for and live by peace, and in memory of this Covenant of princes, statesmen, soldiers, sailors, teachers, preachers, and artists of the great and historic races, signed on the desecrated altar of a little nation's liberty, is it too much to hope that the peoples they represent may never again, from any narrower or less noble aims, draw the sword against each other as long as the world may last?

So be it. God grant so may it be.

But meantime it is perhaps enough that as sons and daughters of many lands, sufferers ourselves by a fratricidal war, we should bring to Belgium, in this solemn moment when her heart is cruelly and almost incurably wounded, the expression of our love, our sympathy, and our unbounded admiration, as the spiritual message of the civilised world to the suffering millions of her people, in the midst of the ruin and desolation which still lie heavy upon her even at this sacred Season when the holiest aspirations of humanity are towards peace on earth and good-will to men.

Belgians, in the person of your heroic young Sovereign we salute you. The statesmanship, the learning, the wisdom, the genius of the world lay their tribute at your feet.

HALL CAINE

Christmas 1914

The Editor of KING ALBERT'S BOOK on his own behalf and on behalf of the proprietors of the " Daily Telegraph " and its associate newspapers, the " Daily Sketch " and the " Glasgow Herald," makes grateful acknowledgment of the services of Mr. G. Ralph Hall Caine as general organiser, of Mr. Ridgwell Cullum as editorial assistant, of Miss Florence Simmonds and Mrs. Marie Conor Leighton as French and Italian translators, and of Mr. Desmond McAuliffe as compiler of the Index.

He also desires to thank Professor Fitzmaurice-Kelly, Dr. Hagberg Wright, Mr. J. S. Cotton, Dr. Henry Bradley (Oxford), and Mr. Edmund Gosse for valuable help in the translation of contributions in the lesser-known languages, as well as The Complete Press for the admirable craftsmanship displayed in the engraving, the beautiful typographical page, and the printing, and also Mr. J. E. Hodder-Williams, head of Messrs. Hodder and Stoughton, for his own and his firm's valuable services as general publishers of KING ALBERT'S BOOK.

The Editor feels that it would be presumption on his part to thank the illustrious contributors, the Belgian people and the universal sentiment of the world will assuredly do that, but he trusts he may be permitted to express his personal gratitude to his own distinguished colleagues, the artists, composers, and men and women of letters in many countries, whose spontaneous and whole-hearted response to his request have made it possible for him to produce this memorable book.

INDEX TO CONTRIBUTORS

9

INDEX TO CONTRIBUTORS

INDEX TO CONTRIBUTORS

II

INDEX TO CONTRIBUTORS

END OF THE INDEX TO CONTRIBUTORS

10. Downing Street,
Whitehall. S.W.

The Belgians have won for themselves the immortal glory which belongs to a people who prefer freedom to ease, to security, even to life itself. We are proud of their alliance and their friendship. We salute them with respect & with honour. Belgium has deserved well of the world. She has placed us under an obligation which, as a nation, we shall not forget. We assure her to-day in the name of this United Kingdom, and of the whole Empire, that she may count to the end on our whole-hearted and unfailing support.

H. H. Asquith.

13

By THE ARCHBISHOP OF CANTERBURY

CAPABLE historians, men of insight and research, will set themselves, long hence, in the calmer air which distance lends, to tell afresh, for old and young, the beginnings of this dark and devastating war. Then the story of Belgium's steadfastness to her plighted word of honour, and her tireless resistance to high-handed wrong—a resistance sustained with unconquerable courage in face of ruthless and overwhelming force—will become one of the golden pages of the world's story. And the contemporary witnesses of the ennobling fidelity thus shown by the people of a little land do well to record at the moment, as in this book, their appreciation of a valour which was tested by a sterner strain than even Thermopylæ or Sempach knew, and remained unshaken and unsullied to the end. God grant to these men and women, and to their children yet unborn, the grace and power to garner hereafter, for the common good, the fruits of this devotion to the cause of liberty and of good faith, and of whatsoever makes life worthier of our Christian heritage.

Randall Cantuar:

By H. H. AGA KHAN

I DEEM it a great privilege to be associated with this tribute to King Albert, the heroic monarch of the martyr nation. The Moslems of India and the British Empire, 100 millions in all, have watched with ever-deepening admiration the unflinching stand of the Belgian King and people against the unprovoked attack of a terrible foe. Had Belgium been guided by considerations of material good and immediate interest she would have accepted the Kaiser's promise not to molest or injure if he was allowed an undisputed passage to the French frontier for his troops. But this easy and inglorious course was not contemplated even for a moment. Belgium unhesitatingly chose the path of honour and duty and made an irreparable sacrifice of material good for moral glory. This undying record of a great refusal has appealed to the best traditions and sentiments of Moslems in India, whose history affords many stirring examples of readiness to lose all, even life itself, for honour and duty. I can assure King Albert and his glorious people that the Moslems of the British Empire fall behind no other nation in their profound and sincere sympathy with them in the countless sorrows and sacrifices which constitute the imperishable glory of Belgium.

Aga Khan

By EDMOND ROSTAND

Belgique, c'est ton front que l'Aurore préfère !
Ceux-là sont dévolus aux ténèbres, qui n'ont
Mis l'obus le plus grand dans le plus grand canon
Que pour mieux empêcher l'Avenir de se faire !

" Trahissez l'Idéal et traitons une affaire,"
Siffle un Bethmann-Hollweg plus double que son nom.
" Non ! " dit un Roi sublime. Et, butant sur ce non,
Le cheval d'Attila tout d'un coup se déferre.

" On s'en tire," a dit le Bethmann, " comme l'on peut."
Mais le Monde, admirant qu'un pays soit en feu
Pour avoir cru que c'est comme on doit qu'on s'en tire,

Luttera tant qu'un seul Barbare fera tort,
A ton voile, Maline, à ta couronne, Sire,
D'un seul point de dentelle et d'un seul fleuron d'or !

Edmond Rostand

By THE Rt. Hon. ARTHUR J. BALFOUR

I AM asked to speak of Belgium. Is it of Belgium as she is, or of Belgium as she will one day be ? If the first, my theme would be the greatest of national tragedies, but also the noblest. Nothing that can heighten our sympathy or move our admiration is wanting. The weakness of the victim, the justice of her cause, the greatness of her sufferings, and her unconquerable soul, have moved the wonder and pity of the world. And when we turn from the victim to the oppressor, the tragic horror deepens. We see wrong heaped on wrong, and treachery on treachery. Faithless in designing his schemes, brutal in executing them, he has ruthlessly trampled under foot all laws but the law of the strongest. He knows, it seems, no other. But the drama is not going to end with the triumph of evil. We are witnessing no irremediable tragedy. Happier days are yet to come. Wrongs have indeed been done which nothing can right ; sufferings endured which nothing can repay. Yet the time will surely come, and come soon, when Belgium's wounds will heal, when morally and materially greater than before, she will pursue in peace her high destiny, strong in the memories of an heroic past, and in the affectionate esteem of all who love liberty and admire valour.

Arthur James Balfour

15

By HIS EXCELLENCY M. PAUL CAMBON

EN luttant avec héroïsme pour leur indépendance nationale et en s'imposant noblement les plus douloureux sacrifices pour la défense du droit, le peuple Belge et son Roi ont mérité la reconnaissance et l'admiration du monde civilisé, et ils se sont acquis une gloire impérissable.

TRANSLATION
By their heroic struggle for national independence and their noble acceptance of the most terrible sacrifices in defence of Right, the Belgian King and people have earned the admiration and gratitude of the civilised world, and have won imperishable glory.

Paul Cambon

By THE COUNT DE BENCKENDORFF

SI, par l'héroïsme déployé à la défense de son indépendance, la Belgique s'est acquise l'admiration du monde, c'est de la reconnaissance que lui doivent tous les peuples auxquels importe le maintien de l'ordre social, sur lequel repose la civilisation.

Sans hésiter, elle s'est faite champion de la condition première à ce maintien, la sainteté des conventions humaines et des traités, sans laquelle le principe de l'état moderne s'effondre.

A sa gloire impérissable, la Belgique est restée également fidèle aux traditions les plus reculées de ses peuples, et aux devoirs plus récents que la loi des nations lui impose.

TRANSLATION
If, by the heroism displayed in the defence of her independence, Belgium has won the admiration of the world, all other nations owe her gratitude, that is, all nations which value the maintenance of social order, on which civilisation is based.
Without hesitation, she has played the part of champion of the first condition of such maintenance—the sanctity of human obligations and of treaties, without which the principle of the modern State would collapse.
To her everlasting glory, Belgium has remained faithful to the most ancient traditions of her people, and to the more modern duties that the law of nations has imposed upon her.

By HIS EXCELLENCY KATSUNOSKE INOUYE

THE indomitable courage and patriotic ardour with which Belgium has been exerting herself to defend her liberty and independence against the wanton invasion of her territory by a powerful enemy has created the greatest admiration throughout the world. In Japan, where chivalry and patriotism reigns, Belgium's heroic defence has greatly aroused the sympathy of her people, and we join in the hope that her flag, adorned anew with glory, will in no distant future be floating again triumphantly throughout her dominion.

K. Inouye

By THE EARL OF ROSEBERY

IT is a privilege to write about the Belgians and their King, who have proved once more that Kingship is not dead, and that heroism still survives. A short time ago a young prince ascended the throne of this happy and peaceful kingdom, the home of industry, manufacture, and commerce, the garden of the Continent, at the gates of which stood a guardian angel armed with the sword of Europe. It might well seem that a career of secure prosperity lay before him and his subjects, who, to use an old Border phrase, were " dreading harm from no man, but only wishing to live in God's peace and the King's." In an instant all this fair prospect was blackened. Prussia, which had twice solemnly guaranteed the independence of the little kingdom, suddenly poured her hosts into it, not as might be supposed to protect, but to destroy that independence. She thought, no doubt, that the Belgians would bow to the necessity of such overwhelming odds and submit to the invaders. She mistook her men. King Albert and his people protested with arms in their hands. For the moment they stemmed the torrent. Liége successfully resisted the enemy till overwhelming artillery pounded its forts to powder. Inch by inch the Belgians, headed by the King, resisted, but the mass of invaders irresistibly rolled over them. Brussels the capital and Antwerp the citadel had to be successively abandoned. At last, almost all the kingdom was submerged, the Government had to retire to France, the King to his unbroken army. Meanwhile the German legions like a horde of barbarians had ravaged, plundered, and destroyed the country they had sworn to protect. The rage of being baffled had apparently maddened them. For the King and his Belgians at the cost of all they cherished had retarded the march of the invaders and nullified their plans. For the moment, Belgium, all mapped out, as it was, for Prussian cannon, and swarming with Prussian spies, was the bulwark of Europe and of public law. Not the resistance at Thermopylæ to the millions of Xerxes was more splendid, and Thermopylæ only involved the sacrifice of a handful of men, while this has cost a country and a nation.

There have been three Kings of the Belgians. The first, Leopold, steered the little kingdom with exquisite skill through dangers from within and from without until he was hailed as the Nestor of Europe. The second energetically sustained and developed the commerce and manufactures of his realm with extraordinary success. But the third, Albert, has already eclipsed his predecessors and ranks with William the Silent, the indomitable champion of the Low Countries.

And when the Belgians return, to what will they return? The bare, ruined remains of their smiling country. Her fields ravaged, her villages burned, her ancient monuments, the glory of Europe as well as of Belgium, destroyed. For long years, perhaps for ever, Belgium will remain a monument of infamy. War is a ruthless devouring monster at best. But there is chivalrous war and there is devilish war, and the devastation of innocent Belgium will long subsist as the capital example of the devilish. She has suffered much in the past, she has often been the theatre of conflict, she has been the scene of great battles under Marlborough, she contains the field of Waterloo. But she did not know what were the fiendish possibilities of warfare till she was invaded by a treacherous friend. There has been no desolation like it since the Thirty terrible Years which plunged Germany into ruin. But nearly three centuries have elapsed since then, centuries of culture, especially of German culture, in which we hoped that we had progressed far from the possibility of the recurrence of such horrors. We were wrong. German culture had taken a quick turn, and left civilisation, honour, and chivalry far behind. The fruits of that culture are mines sown broadcast in the ocean to destroy indiscriminately enemy, neutral, or friend, and bombs to fall on peaceful cities to kill women and children. " By their fruits ye shall know them." The Prussians indeed have abandoned the Christian God, and substituted the worship of a Pagan deity which they call Force or Might; Might to supersede Right and all other moral forces. Of this squalid idol they are fortunate enough to hold the permanent proxy; before this Moloch, if they worship anything, their chiefs bow the knee. Its motto is Hate. Its angels are Fury, Destruction, and Rapine. It has apparently no honour, no faith, no reverence. In its name they ravage, massacre, and plunder. Before its shrine they burn their treaties as incense. By its aid they hoped to subdue the world. Belgium was the first victim. But the harrying and devastation of Belgium was only an incident. France crushed, Russia humbled, Holland annexed were, it would seem, only the milestones on a triumphant march to the real, supreme object, the humiliation and destruction of the British Empire. Even that might not be the ultimate aim, for, with Europe prostrate, the liberties and prosperity of America would alarm the jealousy of the tyrant and call Moloch once more into requisition.

How our practical and prosaic nation has earned this stealthy and masked but determined hostility it is not easy to guess. And it is impossible to believe that every German participates and approves of all that has been done in their name. But in war criticism and dissent are always criminal, and always silent.

The desolation of Belgium was, then, it appears, only an incident in this subterranean policy. That consideration is but little solace to a ruined nation. Their reward was to have been to become a Prussian province, with all the liberty, independence, and happiness that that position involves; to be in fact a second Posen or Alsace. But, as things are, their only consolation, bleak for the moment, but eternal, can be that they have been the vanguard in a battle of emancipation for the human race, that they stood forth alone and nailed to the flagstaff the simple assertion of Right as against Might, that they have immortalised themselves and will stand eternally as heroes. History will pay homage for all time, as we now, to the King and the nation who sacrificed all but honour to preserve their own independence and safeguard the liberties of Europe.

18

Rosebery

By RUDYARD KIPLING

THE OUTLAWS *

> Through learned and laborious years
>   They set themselves to find
> Fresh terrors and undreamed-of fears
>   To heap upon mankind.
>
> All that they drew from Heaven above
>   Or digged from earth beneath,
> They laid into their treasure-trove
>   And arsenals of death,
>
> While, for well-weighed advantage sake,
>   Ruler and ruled alike
> Built up a faith they meant to break
>   When the fit hour should strike.
>
> They traded with the careless earth,
>   And good return it gave ;
> They plotted by their neighbour's hearth
>   The means to make him slave.
>
> When all was readied to their hand
>   They loosed their hidden sword
> And utterly laid waste a land
>   Their oath was pledged to guard.
>
> Coldly they went about to raise
>   To life and make more dread
> Abominations of old days,
>   That men believed were dead.
>
> They paid the price to reach their goal
>   Across a world in flame,
> But their own hate slew their own soul
>   Before that victory came.

Rudyard Kipling

By THE RT. HON. SIR EDWARD GREY, BART.

THE wrongs done to Belgium have brought home to us that we must spare nothing and if need be must spend everything to secure justice for her and freedom for us all.

What had the Belgians done that their country should be invaded and ravaged ? What provocation had a people given who threatened no one and wanted nothing, but to be let alone, to govern themselves, to cultivate their own land and to develop peaceful commerce ?

Love of liberty and independence is not crushed by oppression and force, but set off by courage and suffering becomes an inspiration to its own generation and is exalted to an imperishable place in history.

E. Grey.

By LORD HARDINGE, VICEROY OF INDIA
By Telegraph from Delhi

NO nation has regarded with greater abhorrence than India the series of crimes committed by Germans against their peaceful Belgian brothers. With the deep sympathy, felt for them by the people of India in this hour of sorrow, is coupled their admiration of the gallant resistance of their army against the heaviest odds. May they be comforted by the thought that their sacrifice will not have been in vain when the oppressors of the weak have been finally overthrown. India will never rest till Belgium's wrongs have been avenged.

By SIR REGINALD WINGATE
By Telegraph from Khartoum

ON behalf of the inhabitants of the Sudan, irrespective of race or creed, I offer our respectful and united homage to Belgium's King, to the gallant Belgian people and to Belgium's dead, who, in a materialistic age, have vindicated the supremacy of an ideal and thereby have testified that the age of heroes is indeed not past.

I have the honour of personally knowing His Majesty who came to the Sudan shortly after his accession, stayed with us for a few days, and visited portions of the districts south of Khartoum.

In the many talks I had with him, I was particularly struck with his high ideals of Kingship and Government—not only of his own Belgian subjects—but of the vast areas of the Congo Free State, in the advancement of which he takes a most humane and absorbing interest, and which, under his direction, have made such sensible strides in the direction of true civilisation and progress.

20

HER MAJESTY QUEEN MARY
By JOHN LAVERY, R.S.A.

By THOMAS HARDY
SONNET ON THE BELGIAN EXPATRIATION

I dreamt that people from the Land of Chimes
Arrived one autumn morning with their bells,
To hoist them on the towers and citadels
Of my own country, that the musical rhymes

Rung by them into space at measured times
Amid the market's daily stir and stress,
And the night's empty starlit silentness,
Might solace souls of this and kindred climes.

Then I awoke : and lo, before me stood
The visioned ones, but pale and full of fear ;
From Bruges they came, and Antwerp, and Ostend,

No carillons in their train.   Vicissitude
Had left these tinkling to the invaders' ear,
And ravaged street, and smouldering gable-end.

Thomas Hardy.

By THE MARQUESS OF CREWE

SALUTING with deep respect the gallant Belgians and their noble Sovereign, we reflect that never in the world's history has any nation, with so slender a pretence of reason, been subjected to outrage so cruel and so deliberate as that which has lately stirred the blood of civilised mankind. Those who begin by tearing up a solemn engagement have not far to descend in the moral scale before they lay an innocent country waste ; but as an English poet wrote when Lombardy was likewise trampled by a foreign oppressor :

And though the stranger stand, 'tis true,
By force and fortune's right he stands ;
By fortune, which is in God's hands,
And strength, which yet shall spring in you.

Crewe

By CARDINAL BOURNE

IN all history it must be difficult to find an attack more brutal or less provoked than that made in August of this year upon the Belgian people. But, amid the untold sorrow of the weeks that have passed since then, the world has been privileged to witness a wonderful outburst of courage and heroism which, like the cause that has so purposelessly evoked it, is unparalleled in the history of the nations. And the bravery of the Belgian people has been centred and carried to its highest expression in the person of their undaunted sovereign, Albert the First, King of the Belgians. No tribute, therefore, could be more acceptable to our Allies, who indeed have made themselves at the cost of immense suffering the very saviours of European civilisation, than that which recognises in their King the inspiring force of a resistance to injustice which has won the admiration of the world.

By none is that tribute paid more gladly than by the Catholics of England. To them in the sad days of religious strife and persecution Flanders gave a generous hospitality, which with willing hearts they endeavour to repay to-day. We recall how, in 1561, when the ancient Universities of our country banished from their halls those who ventured still to maintain the old allegiance to the Holy See, it was at Louvain that the exiles found a new home of learning, and set up therein two houses, to one of which they gave the name of Oxford, and the other they called Cambridge.

In more recent happier times it is in Belgium that so many of our fellow-countrymen have seen for the first time in action the living practice of the Catholic Faith. It is to Belgium again that, often first among foreign lands, they have turned their steps, when they have been brought to understand and to accept anew the authority in spiritual things of the Apostolic See of Rome. Belgium, too, has sent to us successive generations of devoted priests who, in town and country, have laboured with us in gathering in the harvest that has been so plentiful since the second spring.

For these reasons, and for many others on which the grateful memories of individuals may dwell, we join in offering to His Majesty King Albert the tribute of our thanks and praise, of our deepest sympathy, and of our fervent prayer that the Divine Ruler of us all may soon restore peace to the Belgian nation, and grant it renewed life and national prosperity far excelling all that the past has known.

Francis Cardinal Bourne
Abp. of Westminster

By THE EARL OF HALSBURY

HIS MAJESTY THE KING OF THE BELGIANS

"HE has honour and courage—qualities that eagle-plume men's souls and fit them for the fiercest sun that ever melted the weak waxen minds that flutter in the beams of gaudy power."

Halsbury

By THE MARQUESS OF LANSDOWNE

I AM invited to add a few words to the tribute of admiration which the compilers of this book desire to lay at the feet of the King of the Belgians. On August 27, when both Houses of Parliament passed unanimously a resolution conveying to His Majesty their sympathy and admiration, I uttered the words which are quoted below. They were but a feeble expression of my sentiments and of the sentiments of those who listened to them, but they were at all events spontaneous and sincere, and all that has happened during the two months which have since elapsed has only served to intensify the feelings which prompted them.

Lansdowne

All who are lovers of liberty, all who can appreciate the virtue of self-sacrifice, all who are able to admire patriotism and who entertain respect for treaty obligations, must feel that Belgium has rendered to the civilised world a signal service by what she has done. If she had been inspired by less glorious ideals, if her standard of honour had been less high, it might have been easy for her to evade these responsibilities and to escape the terrible penalties which have fallen upon her through her observance of them. She might have urged that this dispute had arisen over a question which was far removed from her and her interests. She might have dwelt upon her own comparative weakness as compared with the strength of the Great Powers who are engaged in this colossal struggle. She might have urged that events were moving so rapidly that there was not time for her friends to range themselves at her side when the struggle began. She might have dwelt upon the ruinous consequences to herself and to her people of allowing the first act of this drama to be played upon Belgian soil. But she did none of these things. She never faltered in her sense of what she owed to her own position as an independent State. When the bribe was offered to her she knew how to thrust it on one side. She advanced two simple propositions—first, that to accept the German proposal meant the sacrifice of her honour as a nation ; second, that she felt able, in case her territory was violated, to defend her own neutrality. My Lords, no simpler, no more dignified rejoinder could, I venture to say, have been given to the inducements which the German Government did not hesitate to dangle before Belgium as the price of her dishonour.

We know how gallantly Belgium did defend the neutrality of her soil. She has emerged from the struggle bruised but indomitable.

And I venture to think that she has come out of this, the first phase of a great war, with a halo of reputation of which any mighty Empire might well be proud. If we had been merely disinterested spectators of these events the conduct of Belgium would have claimed our applause and our admiration. But we are not mere spectators. We are the comrades in arms of Belgium, we are her allies, we are associated with her in this vast enterprise, in which our country

23

has so tremendous a stake, and therefore it is that we have to offer to Belgium not merely our admiration, but our gratitude, for the great achievement which she has accomplished.

The noble Marquess dwelt in eloquent words upon the price which the people of Belgium have had to pay for these great achievements. It has indeed been a terrible price. We can, at any rate, offer to them the whole-hearted sympathy of our people. And I will take upon myself to say this : whatever else may happen during the course of the war—and it is a war in which there will be no doubt stirring episodes and great feats of arms—nothing can happen which will more affect public opinion in this country than the conduct of Belgium in this short period of time. Whatever else is forgotten, that episode will remain graven upon the hearts of the people of this country. I believe there is not a man or woman within it who does not pray that in the fullness of time we may be able to give practical proof by our deeds of the gratitude, the sympathy, and the admiration which in feeble words we are seeking to express this evening.

By THE Rt. Hon. SIR ROBERT BORDEN
By Cable

FOR the crime of defending its territories against unprovoked invasion by a Power pledged to hold them inviolate, Belgium has, with supreme fortitude, endured sufferings and sacrifices almost surpassing the imagination and moving all humanity to an infinite compassion.

As long as the Love of Liberty shall endure, as long as the character and greatness of a nation shall be measured by its ideals, the valour and heroism, the faith and devotion of the Belgian People and of their King shall dwell in the memory of men, and shall be the exemplar and inspiration, not of Belgium alone, but of the world.

By JOHN REDMOND

THE Irish nation has many strong and tender ties with Belgium. We owe her a debt of gratitude for the past, and there is no nation in the world which has been more profoundly touched than Ireland by the extraordinary gallantry of the Belgian people and their brave Sovereign. We Irishmen are all glad to know that men of our race have been at the front helping Belgium to defend her integrity and independence, and Ireland sends to King Albert an expression of her deepest sympathy and admiration.

THE WALLS OF OLD ENGLAND (BUDE).
By Sir E. J. Poynter, P.R.A.

By ALFRED NOYES
THE REDEMPTION OF EUROPE

. . . donec templa refeceris.

Under which banner ?   It was night
      Beyond all nights that ever were.
The Cross was broken.   Blood-stained might
      Moved like a tiger from its lair ;
And all that heaven had died to quell
Awoke, and mingled earth with hell.

For Europe, if it held a creed,
      Held it through custom, not through faith.
Chaos returned, in dream and deed.
      Right was a legend ; Love—a wraith ;
And That from which the world began
Was less than even the best in man.

God in the image of a Snake
      Dethroned that dream, too fond, too blind,
The man-shaped God whose heart could break,
      Live, die, and triumph with mankind.
A Super-snake, a Juggernaut,
Dethroned the highest of human thought.

The lists were set.   The eternal foe,
      Within us as without grew strong,
By many a super-subtle blow
      Blurring the lines of right and wrong
In Art and Thought, till nought seemed true
But that soul-slaughtering cry of New !

New wreckage of the shrines we made
      Thro' centuries of forgotten tears . . .
We knew not where their scorn had laid
      Our Master.   Twice a thousand years
Had dulled the uncapricious Sun.
Manifold worlds obscured the One ;

25

Obscured the reign of Law, our stay,
      Our compass through this darkling sea,
The one sure light, the one sure way,
      The one firm base of Liberty ;
The one firm road that men have trod
Through Chaos to the Throne of God.

Choose ye, a hundred legions cried,
      Dishonour or the instant sword !
Ye chose.   Ye met that blood-stained tide.
      A little kingdom kept its word ;
And, dying, cried across the night,
Hear us, O earth, we chose the Right !

Whose is the victory ?   Though ye stood
      Alone against the unmeasured foe ;
By all the tears, by all the blood
      That flowed, and have not ceased to flow ;
By all the legions that ye hurled
Back, thro' the thunder-shaken world ;

By the old that have not where to rest,
      By lands laid waste and hearths defiled ;
By every lacerated breast,
      And every mutilated child,
Whose is the victory ?   Answer ye,
Who, dying, smiled at tyranny :

Under the sky's triumphal arch
      The glories of the dawn begin.
Our dead, our shadowy armies march
      E'en now, in silence, through Berlin ;
Dumb shadows, tattered blood-stained ghosts,
But cast by what swift following hosts ?

26

And answer, England ! At thy side,
  Thro' seas of blood, thro' mists of tears,
Thou that for Liberty hast died
  And livest, to the end of years !—
And answer, Earth ! Far off, I hear
The pæans of a happier sphere :

The trumpet blown at Marathon
  Resounded over earth and sea,
But burning angel lips have blown
  The trumpets of *thy* Liberty ;
For who, beside thy dead, could deem
The faith, for which they died, a dream ?

Earth has not been the same since then.
  Europe from thee received a soul,
Whence nations moved in law, like men,
  As members of a mightier whole,
Till wars were ended. . . . *In that day,*
So shall our children's children say.

Alfred Noyes

By EARL CURZON OF KEDLESTON

WHATEVER the future may have in store for Belgium, her name and that of her heroic Sovereign, King Albert, will for ever shine out in history for the noble stand which they have made on behalf of her own independence, of international honour, and of the liberties of mankind.

For her fortitude she has paid the penalty of a suffering unequalled in modern history, inflicted by an enemy, to whose cruelty ancient history scarcely affords a parallel.

Nevertheless Belgium by her conduct, and still more by her example, has rendered a priceless service to humanity, for she has once more taught the world the sublime truth that national honour is preferable to national security, and that, though the body may be destroyed the spirit is immortal. For the moment a crown of thorns has been pressed down upon her temples, but Europe, nay, the civilised world, will see to it that she is healed of her grievous wounds ; and some day, let us hope before long, she will live again in the recovered prosperity of her people, and the admiring gratitude of mankind.

Curzon of Kedleston

27

By THE RT. HON. WINSTON S. CHURCHILL

AT this moment when their cities are captive, their country under the yoke, their government and army forced into exile, the Belgian nation is exerting an influence upon the destinies of Europe and of mankind beyond that of great States in the fullness of prosperity and power; and from the abyss of present grief and suffering Belgium looks out with certainty to a future more brilliant than any which she could ever have planned.

Winston S. Churchill

By FREDERIC HARRISON

IT was the chief glory of ancient Athens, even when it was acknowledged by the civilised world to stand first in poetry, art, eloquence, and grace, that the men of Athens had been " the first to withstand and defeat the terrible Mede in battle." So, the men of Belgium have been the first to defy and stem the torrent over France of the German host which thought itself invincible and went forth to domineer in Europe.

History tells us that if the millions of Xerxes could have crushed Greece the higher civilisation of mankind would have been arrested. Just so, modern civilisation would have been set back if the Kaiser's millions had been suffered to make their procession along the Meuse in triumph and could have reached Paris according to the time-table of Potsdam. France, Britain, Europe owe an imperishable debt to Belgium, that her heroic constancy and valour prevented this monstrous catastrophe even at the cost of their lives, their homes, and their children.

It is the first duty of the Allies to restore the noble people who sacrificed themselves for us—for peace—for freedom—for humanity.

In all modern history there is no example of a martyrdom by a whole nation—so cruel—so generous—so valiant. When France, Britain, Russia shall have crushed out this conspiracy against humanity, when militarism is extinct in Germany—extinct for ever in the world—whatever may have been the victories and the achievements of the Allies—still for all time the heroism of the Belgian people who " first bore the brunt of the terrible Mede " (as the orators would say at Athens) will stand highest in the record of valour.

Frederic Harrison

By VISCOUNT ESHER

I SHOULD not have ventured to write in KING ALBERT'S BOOK were it not that my father-in-law's name, " Sylvain Van de Weyer," stands with that of Lord Palmerston at the head of the " scrap of paper," so contemptuously scorned by the German Chancellor.

The Belgian patriots of 1830 who offered the throne to King Leopold would have gloried in the steadfast valour of his grandson, and in the immortal sufferings of the nation they helped to call into being.

Esher

By THE CARDINAL ARCHBISHOP OF PARIS

C'EST de toute mon âme que j'offre mon hommage à la vaillante nation Belge et à son magnanime Souverain, Sa Majesté Albert Iᵉʳ.

Mis en demeure de fouler aux pieds la foi jurée ou de subir une invasion sanglante et ruineuse, le Roi des Belges et son peuple ont répondu : " Plutôt la mort que la souillure ! " Pour résister à la violence inique et barbare dont ils sont victimes, ils ont lutté et luttent encore avec un courage que rien n'abat, ils supportent sans défaillance les pires calamités. Honneur à eux !

Leur héroïsme est digne de toute admiration, et leurs souffrances méritent toute sympathie. Soldats tombés en grand nombre sur les champs de bataille, innocents massacrés, villes et villages incendiés, monuments détruits, populations exilées : tous les malheurs font de la Belgique une nation martyre, et excitent la compassion de tous les nobles cœurs.

Nulle part cette sympathie ne saurait être plus vive qu'en France.

En se sacrifiant pour défendre son honneur et son indépendance, la Belgique a barré le chemin à l'envahisseur qui voulait écraser la France. Par là elle s'est acquis des droits impérissables à la reconnaissance de tous les Français. Ceux-ci ne seront point ingrats.

Avec les Belges et avec les Anglais, nos glorieux alliés, nos armées combattront jusqu'au bout pour chasser l'envahisseur. Nous aurons à cœur de venir largement en aide à nos frères en détresse. Enfin nous supplierons le Dieu des justices de prendre en mains la cause de ce peuple, si fidèle au Christ et à son Eglise, et de lui rendre, avec un territoire libéré et un patrimoine de gloire agrandi, la paix et la prospérité.

Léon-Ad. Card. Amette

TRANSLATION by Florence Simmonds

From the depths of my soul I offer my homage to the valiant Belgian nation and to her magnanimous Sovereign, His Majesty Albert I.

Faced with the alternative of spurning their pledged word or submitting to a bloody and ruinous invasion, the King of the Belgians and his people replied : " Death before dishonour ! " In their resistance to the iniquitous and barbarous violence of which they are the victims, they have struggled and are still struggling with unconquerable courage—they endure the worst calamities without flinching. All honour to them !

Their heroism is worthy of the highest admiration and their sufferings claim the sympathy of the whole world. Soldiers fallen in vast numbers on the field of battle, innocent creatures massacred, towns and villages burnt to the ground, monuments destroyed, populations exiled : such are the horrors that have made Belgium the Martyr Nation, and stirred the compassion of all noble hearts.

In no country is this sympathy deeper than in France. By sacrificing herself in defence of her honour and independence, Belgium blocked the invader's passage when he aimed at crushing France. By so doing she has earned imperishable rights and the gratitude of all French people.

They will not be ungrateful.

With the Belgians and the English, our glorious Allies, our armies will fight to the end to drive out the invader. We shall make it a point of honour to come generously to the assistance of our brothers in distress. Finally, we shall pray to the God of Justice to uphold the cause of a people so faithful to Christ and to His Church, and to grant them peace and prosperity in a free land with an increased patrimony of glory.

By PIERRE LOTI

Deux Pauvres Petits Oisillons de Belgique

UN soir, dans une de nos villes du sud, un train de réfugiés belges venait d'entrer en gare, et les pauvres martyrs un à un descendaient lentement, exténués et ahuris, sur ce quai inconnu, où des français les attendaient pour les recueillir. Traînant avec eux quelques hardes prises au hasard, ils étaient montés dans ces voitures sans même se demander où elles les conduiraient, ils étaient montés dans la hâte de fuir, d'éperdûment fuir devant l'horreur et la mort, devant le feu, devant les indicibles mutilations et les viols sadiques,—devant tout ce qui ne semblait plus possible sur la Terre, mais qui couvait encore, parait-il, au fond des piétistes cervelles allemandes, et qui tout à coup s'était déversé, sur leur pays et sur le nôtre, comme un dernier vomissement des barbaries originelles. Ils n'avaient plus ni village, ni foyer, ni famille, ceux qui arrivaient là sans but, comme des épaves, et la détresse effarée était dans les yeux de tous. Beaucoup d'enfants, de petites filles, dont les parents s'étaient perdus au milieu des incendies ou des batailles. Et aussi des aïeules, maintenant seules au monde, qui avaient fui sans trop savoir pourquoi, ne tenant plus à vivre mais poussées par un obscur instinct de conservation ; leur figure, à celles-là, n'exprimait plus rien, pas même le désespoir, comme si vraiment leur âme était partie et leur tête vidée.

Deux tout petits, perdus dans cette foule lamentable, se tenaient serrés par la main, deux petits garçons, visiblement deux petits frères, l'aîné, qui avait peut-être cinq ans, protégeant le plus jeune qui pouvait bien en avoir trois. Personne ne les réclamait, personne ne les connaissait. Comment avaient-ils compris, trouvés tout seuls, qu'il fallait monter dans ce train, eux aussi, pour ne pas mourir ? Leurs vêtements étaient convenables et ils portaient des petits bas de laine bien chauds ; on devinait qu'ils devaient appartenir à des parents modestes, mais soigneux ; sans doute étaient-ils fils de l'un de ces sublimes soldats belges, tombés heroïquement au champ d'honneur, et qui avait dû avoir pour eux, au moment de la mort, une suprême pensée de tendresse. Ils ne pleuraient même pas, tant ils étaient anéantis par la fatigue et le sommeil ; à peine s'ils tenaient debout. Ils étaient incapables de répondre quand on les questionnait, mais surtout ils ne voulaient pas se lâcher, non. Enfin le grand aîné, crispant toujours sa main sur celle de l'autre, dans la peur de le perdre, prit tout à coup conscience de son rôle de protecteur et trouva la force de parler à la dame à brassard penchée vers lui :

" Madame," dit-il, d'une toute petite voix suppliante et déjà à moitié endormie, " Madame, est-ce qu'on va nous coucher ? " Pour le moment, c'était tout ce qu'ils étaient capables de souhaiter encore, tout ce qu'ils attendaient de la pitié humaine : qu'on voulût bien les coucher. Vite on les coucha, ensemble bien entendu, et ils s'endormirent aussitôt, se tenant toujours par la main et pressés l'un contre l'autre, à la même minute plongés tous les deux dans la tranquille inconscience des sommeils enfantins. . . .

30

Une fois, il y a longtemps, dans la mer de Chine, pendant la guerre, deux petits oiseaux étourdis, deux minuscules petits oiseaux, moindres encore que nos roitelets, étaient arrivés je ne sais comment à bord de notre cuirassé, dans l'appartement de notre amiral, et, tout le jour, sans que personne du reste cherchât à leur faire peur, ils avaient voleté là de côté et d'autre, se perchant sur les corniches ou sur les plantes vertes.

La nuit venue, je les avais oubliés, quand l'amiral me fit appeler chez lui. C'était pour me les montrer, et avec attendrissement, les deux petits visiteurs, qui étaient allés se coucher dans sa chambre, posés d'une patte sur un frêle cordon de soie qui passait au-dessus de son lit. Bien près, bien près l'un de l'autre, devenus deux petites boules de plumes qui se touchaient et se confondaient presque, ils dormaient sans la moindre crainte, comme très sûrs de notre pitié. . . .

Et ces pauvres petits belges, endormis côte à côte, m'ont fait penser aux deux oisillons perdus au milieu de la mer de Chine. C'était bien la même confiance et le même innocent sommeil ; — mais des sollicitudes beaucoup plus douces encore allaient veiller sur eux. . . .

Pierre Loti

TRANSLATION by Florence Simmonds

TWO POOR LITTLE BELGIAN FLEDGLINGS

At evening in one of our southern towns, a train full of Belgian refugees ran into the station, and the poor martyrs, exhausted and bewildered, got out slowly, one by one, on the unfamiliar platform, where French people were waiting to receive them. Carrying a few possessions caught up at random, they had got into the carriages without even asking whither they were bound, urged by their anxiety to flee, to flee desperately from horror and death, from unspeakable mutilation and Sadic outrage—from things that seemed no longer possible in the world, but which, it seems, were lying dormant in pietistic German brains, and had suddenly belched forth upon their land and ours, like a belated manifestation of original barbarism. They no longer possessed a village, nor a home, nor a family ; they arrived like jetsom cast up by the waters, and the eyes of all were full of terrified anguish. Many children, little girls whose parents had disappeared in the stress of fire and battle ; and aged women, now alone in the world, who had fled, hardly knowing why, no longer caring for life, but moved by some obscure instinct of self-preservation.

Two little creatures, lost in the pitiable throng, held each other tightly by the hand, two little boys obviously brothers, the elder, who may have been five years old, protecting the younger, of about three. No one claimed them, no one knew them. How had they been able to understand, finding themselves alone, that they too must get into this train, to escape death? Their clothes were decent, and their little stockings were thick and warm ; clearly they belonged to humble but careful parents ; they were, doubtless, the sons of one of those sublime Belgian soldiers who had fallen heroically on the battle-field, and whose last thought had perhaps been one of supreme tenderness for them.

They were not even crying, so overcome were they by fatigue and sleepiness ; they could scarcely stand. They could not answer when they were questioned, but they seemed intent, above all, upon keeping a tight hold of each other. Finally the elder, clasping the little one's hand closely, as if fearing to lose him, seemed to awake to a sense of his duty as protector, and, half asleep already, found strength to say, in a suppliant tone, to the Red Cross lady bending over him : " Madame, are they going to put us to bed soon ? " For the moment this was all they were capable of wishing, all that they hoped for from human pity : to be put to bed.

They were put to bed at once, together, of course, still holding each other tightly by the hand, and nestling one against the other, they fell at the same moment into the tranquil unconsciousness of childish slumber.

Once, long ago, in the China Sea, during the war, two little frightened birds, smaller even than our wrens, arrived I know not how, on board our iron-clad, in our admiral's cabin, and all day long, though no one attempted to disturb them, they fluttered from side to side, perching on cornices and plants.

At nightfall, when I had forgotten them, the admiral sent for me. It was to show me, not without emotion, the two little visitors, who had gone to roost in his room, perched upon a slender silken cord above his bed. They nestled closely together, two little balls of feathers, touching and almost merged one in the other, and slept without the slightest fear, sure of our pity. And those little Belgians sleeping side by side made me think of the two little birds lost in the China Sea. There was the same confidence, and the same innocent slumber ; — but a greater tenderness was about to watch over them.

31

By THE RIGHT HON. DAVID LLOYD GEORGE

IT has been the privilege of little nations at different periods in the history of the world to render some signal service to civilisation. That duty Belgium has now been called upon to render to European civilisation, and nobly has she answered the call.

It is her heroism that has forced Prussian Junkerdom, its character, and its designs, into the light of day. As long as it intrigued against France, Russia, or Britain, it might have continued to take cover under some plausible, diplomatic pretext ; but to assail Belgium it had to come into the open, where its arrogance, its brutality, and its aggressiveness became manifest to the world. It was Belgian valour that exposed the sinister character of Prussian militarism, and when that menace is finally overthrown the most honourable share in the triumph will be due to Belgian sacrifice.

This unfortunate country is now overwhelmed by the barbarian flood ; but when the sanguinary deluge subsides Belgium will emerge a great and a glorious land which every lover of liberty will honour, and every tyrant henceforth shun.

By EARL KITCHENER OF KHARTOUM

I SINCERELY hope that this book may accomplish its twofold object of bearing further testimony to our admiration of the courage and devotion to duty shown by King Albert and his Army, and of securing material help and comforts for the Belgians who have suffered so terribly at the hands of an invading enemy.

By FRIDTJOF NANSEN

IT is a great privilege to have obtained such an opportunity as this book affords of expressing the deepest sympathy of the citizen of a small nation for the gallant people and the noble King and Queen of Belgium.

It is needless to say that one's heart goes out to this people whose fate is the most cruel tragedy of modern history. But words seem weak and of little value when one thinks of the distress of a splendid people who have fought so nobly and sacrificed so much for their freedom and their country.

32

RESURGAM
By Frank Dicksee, R.A.

By WILLIAM WATSON
To His Majesty King Albert

Receive, from one who hath not lavished praise
    On many Princes, nor was ever awed
    By Empire such as grovelling slaves applaud,
Who cast their souls into its altar-blaze,—
Receive the homage that a freeman pays
    To Kinghood flowering out of Manhood broad,
    Kinghood that toils uncovetous of laud,
Loves whom it rules, and serves the realm it sways.
For when Your people, caught in agony's net,
    Rose as one dauntless heart, their King was found
Worthy on such a throne to have been set,
    Worthy by such as They to have been crowned ;
And loftier praise than this did never yet
    On mortal ears from lips of mortals sound.

William Watson

By THE Hon. JOSEPH H. CHOATE

UNDER the gallant lead of the heroic Belgian King, his down-trodden and afflicted people have been fighting for liberty, and to maintain the plighted faith of nations, which guaranteed it to them. Those who were guilty of an awful breach of faith, confessed their crime while in the act of committing it, and pleaded necessity, to absolve them from all law, a plea which the whole civilised world refuses to accept.

For their bold stand for right and duty, the Belgians, guiltless of all offence, have been overwhelmed by numbers, trampled in the dust, and reduced to starvation, their homes destroyed, their whole country devastated and converted into a human slaughter-house.

In this sad plight, they have deserved and are receiving the sympathy and the helping hand of people of every civilised nation in this hour of their dire distress.

I am glad to know that my countrymen are sending material relief to the sufferers, and with it the hearts of our people go out to them and their brave King, in human sympathy, unfeigned and unrestrained.

As neutrals, by international law and by our own law, our hands are tied and will remain so. But our hearts go whither they list.

Joseph H Choate

By SIR WILLIAM RAMSAY

EVERY scientific man who is not a Teuton (and I hope and trust many who are of German race) deplores the barbarity, incredible if it were not true, with which Belgium has been treated. We had hoped that the universality of the spread of science, both pure, and applied to industry, would have made it impossible for any nation to revert to barbarism, and to destroy what it has taken so many centuries to create. The scientific achievements of the Belgians has always stood on the highest plane ; to quote only two instances, taken from my own subject, the name of Stas, in pure science, and of Solvay, in applied science, are among the most illustrious in their particular spheres, which the world has ever produced.

We can only extend to the Belgians our most heartfelt sympathy, and assure them, in the person of their Sovereign, that we shall spare no effort, when the time comes, to aid Belgium to regain that place among the nations which she has filled with so much credit in the past. Complete restitution of all she has lost will be impossible ; but much can, and no doubt will be done to recompense her for having, alone and unaided, repelled for a time successfully the invasion of barbaric hordes, and enabled the progressive races of Europe to repel the incursions of those who would subject them to an era of retrogression in Arts, Science, and Literature.

William Ramsay

By THE HON. WILLIAM H. TAFT

THE heart of the world should go out to the poor people of Belgium. Without being in any respect a party to the controversies of the war, their country has been made the battle-ground of the greatest, and in some respects the most destructive war in history. Any movement to relieve their distress has my profound sympathy.

Wm H Taft

By SIR W. B. RICHMOND, R.A.
" THE CROWN OF PEACE "

Sweet Peace rises out of the flames of War which give way to her benign Beauty : she brings with Her an immortal crown which she presents to a Brave King and People who have saved Europe from Barbarian hordes by their sacrifice and heroism.

DEDICATED TO THE GREAT KING OF THE NOBLE BELGIANS, WHO HAVE SAVED EUROPE FROM THE BARBARIANS.

In respect,

W. B. Richmond

MOTHERLESS
By Sir Luke Fildes, R.A.

By ARNOLD BENNETT
THE RETURN

TWENTY years ago I learnt one day by chance that the first-class return fare from London to Ostend by steamer was only half a guinea. I had always imagined that "the Continent" could only be visited by rich people, —certainly not by clerks. For me it was a region beyond the borders of my hopes for ages to come. The fact that the cost of reaching the Continent from London was much less than half of the cost of reaching my own home in the Midlands struck me such a blow in the back as wakes up a man dozing on the high-road and sends him staggering forward on his way.

At the earliest opportunity I boarded the Ostend steamer, somewhere near London Bridge, and saw, first, the marvels of the Port of London. I had lived in London several years and never realised that it was a port—to say nothing of being the largest port in the world. I next realised, tossing in the small steamer at sea, that Great Britain really was an island—a fact with which I had hitherto been only intellectually familiar, from enforced study of a school geography. These were remarkable experiences, but they were naught in comparison with the sensation of first seeing a foreign land. I descried a lighthouse, a long line of pale hotels, and the grandiose outlines of the Kursaal. I said to myself with awe :

"That is the Continent !"

It seemed fabulous, dream-like, impossible. The steamer touched the quay, threw out ropes, and was moored. I stepped ashore. I was on Belgian soil, the first foreign soil my feet had ever touched. I saw strange architecture, strange costumes ; I heard strange sounds and strange languages. Everything was romantic. Even the tramcar was inexpressibly romantic ; the postmen with their little horns were fantastic, and the cafés each a quaint paradise of good cheer. I was so moved by the sheer romance of the affair that I could not speak. I said to myself :

"I actually am on the Continent."

I could hardly believe it. It was too good, and too astounding, too overwhelming, to be true.

Yet it was true. And after a time I grew somewhat accustomed, though never entirely accustomed, to the feeling—though since then I have lived on the Continent for many years.

My emotion as I first walked about in Ostend (looking no doubt a queer enough uncouth gaping English figure) was one of the emotions that I could not conceivably forget, one of the major formative emotions of my whole life. And therefore, among all the cities and countries of the Continent Ostend and Belgium hold a unique position in my souvenirs. I have gone to Belgium frequently since then. I have entered by sea at Antwerp, and by train from Paris, and I have sailed right into Bruges in my yacht—and each time I have had the same thrill, recalling my first visit.

From Ostend, on that first visit, I went to Bruges, and there understood for the first time what a historical city of art could be. Bruges was to me

C*

37

incredible in its lofty and mellow completeness. It was a town in a story; its inhabitants were characters out of unread novels; its chimes were magic from the skies. It had not a street that was not a vision. Even the railway-station at Bruges had some of the characteristics of a cathedral. . . Thence to Ghent, where the same kind of wondrous picturesqueness was united to the spectacle of commerce . . . Thence to Brussels—the capital. What boulevards, what parks, what palaces, what galleries, what cafés, and above all what restaurants! The symmetry and the elegance of the civic organism! England held nothing like it. I had imagined nothing like it. " A continental capital ! " I felt as though I could live in Brussels for ever. . . . Thence to Malines, of the unequalled carillon. Thence to Antwerp, a kind of complementary and utterly different sister-capital to Brussels. . . . Thence southwards to Roulers with its industry, and the unique Ypres, with its cloth-hall and its ramparts. . . . Thence to Namur, with the first glimpse of the Meuse ! . . . . Thence to Dinant, with its cliffs and its tower, and on to little Anseremme, where one could have a bed and four meals and a bathe in the Meuse for four francs a day ! . . . The whole country was a museum of architecture, art, and history. It was full of the amenities of civilisation. Everywhere were parks and music. In each town was an opera, and galleries containing masterpieces.

In twenty-four days—and nights—I saw it all, with a most ridiculous inexpensiveness, and on the evening of the twenty-fourth day I embarked at Ostend again. I hated to leave Belgium. The prospect of plain, unpoetic England was offensive to me. But I had to go. And when I reached London, strange to say, I began to perceive what a wonderful place London was. Belgium has taught me to appreciate London. Moreover there was a peculiar feel about London and England. It was the feel of the city to its own citizen, and of the country to its native.

And now, what I imagine is the ultimate return, by Ostend, by Zeebrugge, by Antwerp, and by the trains from the south, of exiled Belgians into Belgium ! Their thrill will far outdo the thrill of the eager ingenuous tourist. I imagine their gaze from the sea towards the whiteness of Ostend, and from the Scheldt towards the steeples of Antwerp. They will pass through emotions—at once tragic and triumphant, terrible and exquisite— such as fate has accorded to no other people in the modern age. Confronted by ruin and desolation, appalled by the immense task of reconstruction that lies before them, saddened by the recollection of indescribable woe, impoverished and bereaved but not enfeebled, they will be heartened by the obstinate courage which through every disaster has kept them a nation, and by the living splendid hope of the future. Not into a museum will they be entering, but into a house and an environment which their ancestors and they themselves created, and of which they profoundly comprehend the secret significance, and which, however defaced and blackened, they will slowly restore again to the full expression of the soul of a nation. . . .

38

And I seem to be already present at a great, unexampled, sacred occasion of solemn rejoicing in Brussels, and to stand amid silent crowds on the pavement of the Boulevard Anspach, while the young veterans of the Belgian army go by, and the cannons, and the flags, and then the youthful King, with his Queen, a crowned monarch who has earned a nation's affection perhaps more nobly than a nation's affection ever was earned before. And there is a vast deafening cheer, that shakes the tears out of the eyes. And in every chastened and bursting heart lies like a miraculous solace the new-proved conviction that righteousness prevails.

Arnold Bennett

By SIR JOSEPH LARMOR

THE Belgian nation has sacrificed herself without measure, not only for the sake of her own independence, but to assert the right of the States of Europe each to pursue her own national development, free from the pressure of an iron mould imposed by ruthless foreign domination. In the Middle Ages Flanders was a centre of art and learning and industry, in a Renaissance which vied with the revival in Italy. She has now enhanced her right to the possession of her great monuments of the past by a new renown. The burning light of her patriotism, now shining upon the world, has created a new and unwavering faith in the nobility of her destiny, which the tragedy of her present misfortunes will keep ever bright. We can look forward with confidence to a renewed and transfigured Belgium, occupying in the future, under her heroic dynasty, an honoured place in the family of the free nations of Europe.

Joseph Larmor

By MADELEINE LUCETTE RYLEY

TO THE VICTORS BELONG THE SPOILS !

The Victor true is he who conquers fear,
Who knows no time save now—no place but here.
Who counts no cost—who only plays the game,
To him shall go the prize—Immortal Fame !

> *To the Illustrious Ruler and his Gallant Little Nation, whose heroism and bravery are surely unparalleled in the whole of our World's History, I bow my head in respectful homage.*

Madeleine Lucette Ryley

39

By THE RT. HON. A. BONAR LAW

IN July of this year there was no part of the world more peaceful and prosperous than the little country of Belgium. There the monuments of ancient art, of learning and of piety stood out in bold relief in the midst of an industrial development which was scarcely equalled, which was nowhere surpassed in any country in the world.

In a moment, almost without warning, this smiling garden of industry was turned into a scene of bitterest desolation, not by a convulsion of nature but by the cruelty of man. In a struggle which was not sought by them, which no forbearance or wisdom on the part of their rulers could have averted, the Belgian people, by what they have done and by what they have endured, have won for themselves immortal fame.

But for the unexpected and heroic resistance of the small Belgian Army, the German hosts would have hurled themselves against the French Army before it had been mobilised. Belgium averted a terrible disaster to us and to our Allies, but at what a cost to herself? She is for the moment a nation without a fatherland; but the soul of the nation is living still, is living in her brave soldiers, is living in King Albert, who has shown to the modern world what can be done by a Hero-King.

As a nation we long for a successful end to this terrible war, which is filling with mourning so many of our homes, but it can never end till the wrongs of Belgium have been avenged and expiated.

A Bonar Law

By ADMIRAL LORD CHARLES BERESFORD

THE conscience of the whole civilised world is shocked at the odious barbarities perpetrated on the gallant Belgian nation by the ruthless, cowardly, and savage action of Germany in her efforts to smash Belgium's independence.

The Belgians have been fighting a battle for liberty, humanity, and civilisation; they have also been fighting a battle for the French as well as the British, and though thousands of her best have been killed and wounded, and her civil population, including women and children, have been driven from their homes and martyred in the cause of their country, her youth are still fighting for justice and freedom.

When this wicked war is over, the first duty of the allies must be to enforce every compensation that is possible from the brutal nation that has ravaged Belgium.

Germany has scorned the laws of God and man; her fiendish savageries have proved that German militarism is a disgrace to humanity.

Sympathy, respect, and admiration for Belgium is universal and international in the cruel wrongs she has suffered for the cause of liberty and the rights of small States.

Charles Beresford

THE CROWN OF PEACE
By Sir W. B. Richmond, R.A.

POUR LA PATRIE
POEM BY
VICTOR HUGO
MUSIC BY
ANDRÉ MESSAGER

41

Tou-te gloi-re près d'eux passe et tombe é-phé-mè-re.

Et, com-me fe-rait u-ne mè-re, Et,

com-me fe-rait u-ne mè-re, La voix d'un peuple en-tier les berce en leur tcm-

-beau, . . La voix d'un peuple en-tier les berce en leur tom-beau, . . les

berce en leur tom-beau. . . .

By FLORA ANNIE STEEL

SUNRISE

THE shells had been shrieking and screaming all day long; but now that the dusk had fallen they were silent.

So on this All Souls' night the moon could rise, still, silvery, serene over the ruined village. And the cold, remote radiance softened the charred glow of still burning rafters to cool glimmerings, and made the little trails of smoke rising from them show like incense seeking the star-strewn sky.

Carven stones heaped high in weird shapeless piles showed where for countless generations the village church had stood; and high amongst these rose the stone Crucifixion let into the wall behind the altar, which a generation of men, long since past and gone, had hewn out of a solid block. So it stood still erect, a sorrowful figure to which those countless generations of patient people had brought their hopes, their fears, their sins, their successes, and their failures.

The altar itself was shattered, but the steps remained, and on them—seeking the shelter of a high piled heap of *débris* from the tower—lay three figures. One was crumpled up face downwards almost as it had first fallen. Another with helpless loose-hanging arm sate limply on the top step. The third had crawled to the very foot of the Cross and lay restfully its head upon a splintered stone.

All was still as the grave. Then suddenly, waveringly, came a man's voice: " It's a long, long way to Tipperary."

The chant ended in a sort of sob, as the seated figure on the top step rose to its feet unsteadily.

" I seed 'im move," murmured the Englishman, " an' I 'oped he was a deader." So he stood, looking down on the crumpled figure. " Must be beastly oneasy," he continued. " Lordy! ain't 'e like the bumbadeer arter 'e got one from Charpenteer." Then he paused; so after a space looked back and called out:

" Hi! you there, Frenchy! Wake up, Jacko, and give a h'arm with this German bloke, there's a decent chap."

The man who rested his head on the splintered altar-stone sate up, showing himself a long-limbed, broad-shouldered Breton, kindly but uncomprehending. The gestures of the other, however, were sufficient added to the explanation: " 'E ain't comfy, see you, Jacko! and 'e ain't got long t'er be comfortable; so let's 'eft 'im up."

Jean the Breton nodded at John the Englishman and half crawled, half limped, down the steps to lend an aid. Together the two wounded men dragged the third to more fitting rest, where on his back he could breathe easier, for he was shot through the lungs; but in the process the helmet he had worn fell off and rolled, glinting and clanking, into the shadows.

" 'E mieuox comm' ça," remarked Jean the Breton approvingly in his *patois*.

" Beastly unbecomin' things, 'elmets," said John the Englishman in his.

43

But Johan the German only opened his blue eyes on his enemies and drew in a long gasping breath. They none of them understood each other's speech, but something older than the Tower of Babel had given them comprehension and was to give them more.

For something else besides the helmet had fallen from its place in that laborious journey up the altar steps. The wounded German had torn his tunic open in his first agonised fight for breath and from it had slipped a cheap locket attached to a cheap chain, and holding a cheap photograph cheaply coloured—the photograph of a fair-haired baby.

" By gum ! Ain't it like my kid," muttered John the Englishman, and from his khaki tunic he drew another cheap locket.

And Jean the Breton, not to be outdone, followed suit in his blue coatee. So there in the still, silvery, serene moonlight showed three fair-haired, blue-eyed baby faces, framed in tawdry pinchbeck ; but the faces were the faces of immortality—the symbol of the race.

" Mon p'tit fils," murmured Jean the Breton fondly. " Mon p'tit Jean."

" Hello ! Jacky my boy," chirruped John the Englishman, trying to hide the ache in his heart under a smile.

But Johan the German only rolled his head from side to side and his lips moved as if he would have said " Vater." Perhaps he was thinking of his country. Perhaps his dying ear had become more acute to the sounds that matter, and he was forestalling the little wailing cry which after a space rose fitfully among the ruins, " Faster ! Faster ! Faster ! Faster ! "

The cry of a child !

Yes ! the wail of a sturdy little Flemish fellow of two, who came totteringly over the scattered stones with his bare feet. He wore a quaint little night garment ; so, in the hurry of flight, he must have been left behind asleep. But now, awake, his insistent " Faster ! Faster ! Faster ! " was like the cry of a plover luring danger from her nest.

In the next five minutes John the Englishman's wounded arm forgot itself, and Jean the Breton's splintered knee and wrist secured solace, but Johan the German's wistful eyes were all he could place at the service of the little lad, until as the pitiful wailing would not cease, a trembling hand pointed waveringly to a haversack, and once again the unwritten unspoken word brought comprehension. The little Flamand munching away contentedly at a concentrated German sausage ration gave his name shyly with a smile as " Jan—pi'ou' Jan."

" Mon p'tit gars—mon Jean," murmured the Breton ecstatically, and fell to dreaming of a cottage among apple orchards.

" Kids is terrible similar ! " pronounced the Englishman with awe in his voice, and fell to dreaming of a tenement-flat high up among the chimneys. But the German's dazed mind could not get beyond a vague insistent dream, and his blood-stained lips moved as if he would have said " Vater." He was evidently going fast, and all things worth having in this life—love and loyalty—were bound up in that word.

44

Still with one final effort he pointed to the thick overcoat which they had spread over him and motioned they should wrap the drowsy child in it.

They did not say him nay ; he was too far gone for that.

" But I ain't agoin' to disturb you, sonny," said John the Englishman cheerfully. " There's room of a little un beside you—so creep in, Jackie."

" Ses prières ? " expostulated Jean the Breton ; he was a devout Catholic.

" N'oublies pas tes prières, mon p'tit Jean."

And the little fellow understanding the man's clasped hands murmured something sleepily. No one understood the words, but their spirit—the spirit of father and son—was in the hearts of the listeners.

And one of them saw further to that spirit than the others, gave a long gasp, and lay still.

" He's off, pore chap," said John the Englishman, " but let be—— Creep in, sonny—you'll both rest the better mayhap."

Jean the Breton looked at the dead face that lay so close to the child's and crossed himself as he murmured the dimittance prayer which sends a soul to find freedom.

After that the moon, still, silvery, serene, shone on a silent group about the feet of the Christ with its eternal message of forgiveness, of reconciliation, of immortal fatherhood and sonship.

So the silent night passed, till in the east the blood-red glow of dawn heralded another dreadful day, and incarnadined the crown of thorns upon the Sorrowful Brow.

And almost with the glow came the shriek, the scream of the first shell fired by the advancing Germans as a precaution lest the village should have been reoccupied during the night.

It did not disturb the sleepers. The ears of one were deaf to strife for ever, and the child, in childhood's deep dreamless sleep, slept on. The two others lying either side, used to long days and nights of such hellish devilish tumult, only stirred, and, half conscious, threw each a protecting arm across the dead man and the child.

The swift crackle passed, the sharp resounding explosion was over ere it could be realised, sending out a fierce rain of scattering shrapnel.

After that there was no sound save the soft breathing of little Jan as he lay secure beneath dead protecting arms, his head pillowed on his dead enemy's heart.

And as the child slept the sun rose and turned the incarnadined crown of thorns upon the bowed head of the Son of Man into a crown of gold.

F. A. Steel

By VISCOUNT BRYCE

ALL honour to the Belgian King and the Belgian People. No king and no nation, not even the oldest and the strongest nation, has shown more dignity and gallantry than Belgium, which is among the youngest and the smallest in area of European States.

When Belgium was erected into a kingdom in 1832, many doubted whether a real nation could be formed by linking together the Flemish element and the Walloon element, races that had different characteristics and spoke different languages. But Belgium has grown to be a truly united nation, consolidated by a fervent patriotism. She has produced many men of literary and artistic genius, poets and jurists and scholars and men of science, painters who have renewed the great traditions of Rubens and Vandyck. The principles of constitutional liberty have taken root and flourished among her citizens, and her annals have been adorned by not a few capable and high-minded statesmen. Her peasantry, laborious and resourceful, have brought her soil to a wonderful pitch of productiveness, while a skill and enterprise have made some among her manufacturing industries second to none in Europe. Peace and prosperity have reigned such as these regions had not seen since the days of Duke Philip the Good, nearly five centuries ago.

All this peace and prosperity have been suddenly and ruthlessly torn from her. Her fields have been laid waste, her cities burned. Treasures of Art have been destroyed and the people have been reduced to poverty or driven forth as helpless refugees. All this Belgium has suffered because she refused to forfeit her independence and betray the pledge of neutrality she had given, a pledge which was the very foundation of her independence. Confronted by armies ten times their strength, her King and people risked everything for Honour, and everything save Honour they have lost. But Honour is the greatest thing. It has won for them the admiration of the world. It will be a glorious memory to them and their children when freedom and independence, peace and prosperity, have been restored, as they must be, and we trust soon will be, restored.

We in Britain salute the gallant King and the gallant Army which still fights heroically on, reduced to less than one-third of its strength. We sorrow at their sufferings. We will not rest till those sufferings are ended and the invader has been expelled. And we thank them for the example they have set to all Europe and to the generations yet to come. History records no finer example since Thermopylæ of untarnished fidelity and undaunted courage.

Bryce

By HENRYK SIENKIEWICZ
By Telegraph

LES malheurs passent, la gloire reste et immortalise. Honneur à l'héroïque nation et à son héroïque Souverain.

By PAUL HERVIEU

IL etait, une fois, un Roi et une Reine . . .

Oui, ce sera le conte des fées le plus émouvant qui se puisse écrire, et le plus édifiant, que la très véridique histoire de S.M. le Roi Albert Ier et de S.M. la Reine Elisabeth !

Cette noble quiétude dans le dévouement aux tâches quotidiennes, cette pureté familiale dans laquelle ils vivaient . . .

Tout à coup, l'intervention du Diable, avec ses offres et ses menaces . . .

Les souverains et le Peuple de Belgique communiant aussitôt dans le sentiment de l'honneur et de l'héroïsme.

L'invasion scélérate, et l'innombrable légion d'esprits infernaux qui crachent le soufre, déversent les trombes de fer, font pleuvoir le feu ; et les demeures des cités se transformant en colonnes tronquées de cimetières ; et des innocents devenus partout des suppliciés ; et le Roi et la Reine qui n'ont plus pour royaume qu'une dune sur le rivage et autour d'eux les restes vaillants de leur armée ;

Enfin ! Enfin ! Ce revirement du sort que souhaite ardemment toute l'humanité digne de ce nom, et que l'autre même sent aujourd'hui s'approcher d'une marche sure.

A cet endroit du conte, à ce passage de haute légende, oh ! comme les mains des enfants battront, dans leur amour inné de la justice ! Et le visage des honnêtes parents rira d'approbation et de conscience satisfaite.

Et ceux qui, dans l'avenir, mettront, a contempler les Armes royales, la pieuse admiration qui siéra, y verront apparaître une Rose triomphante, accompagnant le Lion de Belgique, pour l'immortelle union de S.M. la Reine Elisabeth dans la gloire de S.M. le Roi Albert Ier.

Paul Hervieu

TRANSLATION by Florence Simmonds

Once upon a time there lived a King and a Queen . . . Indeed, it would be the most touching and edifying fairy-tale imaginable, this true story of H.M. Albert I and H.M. Queen Elisabeth !

It would tell of their quiet and noble devotion to their daily tasks, of the purity of their happy family life . . .

Suddenly, the Devil would intervene, with his threats and his offers . . .

Then we should hear of the Sovereigns and the people of Belgium agreeing at once in their sense of honour and heroism.

Then the dastardly invasion, and the innumerable host of infernal spirits breathing out sulphur, belching torrents of iron, and raining fire ; city dwellings transformed into the shattered columns of cemeteries ; innocent creatures tortured and victimised ; and the King and Queen with their kingdom reduced to a sandhill on the shore, and the remnant of their valiant army round them.

And at last, at last ! That turn of the tide which all humanity worthy of the name desires so ardently, and which even the baser sort now sees to be surely approaching.

At this point in the story, at this page of the legendary tale, how the children would clap their hands, with all that love of justice innate in children, and how the faces of worthy parents would beam with the approval of satisfied consciences !

And in the future, those who contemplate the Royal Arms with the pious admiration due to them, will see a blooming Rose side by side with the Lion of Belgium, typifying the immortal share of H.M. Queen Elisabeth in the glory of H.M. Albert I.

By ADMIRAL LORD FISHER OF KILVERSTONE
" THE Lord God of recompences shall surely requite."

Jeremiah, chap. 51, *verse* 56.

" One poor girl of nineteen was found stripped, outraged and dead."

Special Correspondent of THE TIMES (*Oct.* 25, 1914).

By VISCOUNT GLADSTONE
THE best tribute to King Albert and his gallant Belgians from all to whom opportunity falls, lies in personal effort and service to relieve multitudes of men, women, and children who are suffering because of Belgium's heroic sacrifice for Liberty and International Justice.

By NORMAN ANGELL
BELGIUM has done this great service for all of us : she has shown how great a little country may be and how little a great one may become. She has shown that the real nobility of patriotism is not a matter of wide territory and political power and does not need to be nourished by these things ; while the action of Germany towards Belgium has shown that power and size may well destroy all that makes patriotism worth while.

By ELLA WHEELER WILCOX
BELGIUM

> *Ruined? Destroyed? Ah no ; though blood in rivers ran*
>> *Down all her ancient streets ; though treasures manifold*
>> *Love-wrought, time-mellowed, and beyond the price of gold*
> *Are lost, yet Belgium's star shines still in God's vast plan.*

> *Rarely have kings been great, since kingdoms first began ;*
>> *Rarely have great kings been great men, when all was told.*
>> *But, by the lighted torch in mailèd hands, behold*
> *Immortal Belgium's immortal king, and man.*

48

THE HARVEST MOON
By Sir E. A. Waterlow, R.A.

By ARISTIDE SARTORIO

UNO scrittore tedesco ha reso noto, come i soldati dell' impero germanico portino nello zaino Faust e Zaratustra. Il bagaglio è significativo, perché Mephistofeles é il nonno di Zaratustra e questi derivò dall' avo quell' indole filosofica, sprone ad ogni violenza e che, fatta scuola in Germania, sappiamo rinsaldì ora così la disciplina della soldatesca imperiale.

Evidentemente i soldati non si trovano sui campi di battaglia per fare un corso di letteratura, e si inspireranno ai concetti morali dei " Vade mecum," anzichè a quelle bellezze estetiche che rendono immortali quei capolavori e, come lo provano duramente oggi i belgi, lo proveremmo noi italiani, qualora gl' imperi centrali uscissero vittoriosi dalla lotta immane ; essi costringerebbero l'Italia al vassallaggio ed il nostro paese sarebbe, con tutta probabilità, annientato, derubato, distrutto. Liberati dall' incubo dell' alleanza, noi italiani abbiamo assistito sdegnati allo strazio del Belgio, paese neutrale, paese d'arte, di coltura e d'industria, con il quale fin dalla rinascenza avemmo contatti spirituali, e che, come noi, guadagnò la sua indipendenza a prezzo di enormi sacrificì.

Ma le ossa di Friedrich Nietzsche, che si corrucciò vendendo la Germania addormentata in un sogno pacifista, dovevano esultare nella tomba, scavata poco lontano da quella dell' olimpico Goethe ; arrivò l'epoca della violenza conquistatrice ; ora noi sappiamo come la civiltà tedesca cammini oltre i confini con Mephistopheles e Zaratustra animatori. E così, come Mephistopheles, al soldo dell' imperatore beniamino di Dio, inventava le sorprendenti armi guerresche, il genio tedesco appresta quei terribili ordigni di guerra contro i quali né le fortezze, né le città, né i monumenti, né le scuole resisteranno più. E così, come Faust fattosi sognatore umanitario, attendeva l'investitura delle terre guadagnate con l'aiuto diabolico, 94 professori tedeschi proclamano al mondo civile il buon diritto della conquista imperiale, sulla quale riverserebbero il superfluo della loro coltura.

Mephistopheles, dice il poema, bruciò la casa, la chiesa ed il giardino di due poveri vecchi, i quali infastidivano l'espandersi del felice regno di Faust. I due vecchi, insieme ad un ospite, morirono arrostiti, quali neutri di numero tre.

Ma sarebbe desiderabile sapere il giudizio del vecchio buon Dio su quegli aviatori che, sorvolando le città, vi uccidono donne, vecchi e fanciulli, perchè il caso non fu contemplato né da Mephistopheles, né da Zaratustra. Faust li deve vedere dal paradiso. Il dottore, in procinto di morire, si pentì ; ascese ai piedi del trono di Maria Vergine, e lì trovò quella preclara intelligenza di Gretchen, che nel frattempo aveva uccisa la madre, soffocato il figlio dell' amore ed era morta pentita.

Esaltati da queste edificanti letture, i soldati tedeschi devono considerarsi quali arcangeli, contro quelle Fiandre cattoliche, che elaborarono la loro morale, contemplando la virtù nelle immagini sante dell' arte latina.

Ma sia benedetto e glorificato il tuo sacrificato, o Belgio eroico, né spento, né vinto ! Ti sei levato contro l'imperialismo barbaro invadente nel nome della scienza e della coltura ; Salve tu nei secoli o Belgio eroico !

49

Qualche cosa di bestiale minaccia la gloria del mondo : Che il tuo sangue rinsaldi, come un battesimo, la nostro fede nella civiltà latina, e ci sospinga contro il torpido ed oscuro impero, che pare scaturito dalle oscure caligini dell' Asia primordiale o del medio evo europeo !

Aristide Sartorio

TRANSLATION by Florence Simmonds

A German writer has informed us that the soldiers of the Empire carry Faust *and* Zarathustra *in their knapsacks. These possessions are significant, for Mephistopheles was the grandfather of Zarathustra, and the latter inherited from his ancestor that philosophical temper which incites to every kind of violence. It has created a school in Germany, and as we know, is now a factor in the discipline of the Imperial soldiery.*

It is obvious that soldiers do not come to the battlefield to take a course of literature ; they find inspiration in the moral axioms of their vade mecum *rather than in the æsthetic beauties that make these masterpieces immortal. The Belgians have had dire proof of this, and we Italians would have a like experience, if the central European Empires should issue victorious from the ruthless conflict. Italy would become their vassal, and in all probability our country would be plundered, ravaged, and annihilated. Delivered from the incubus of the alliance, we Italians have looked on with indignation at the torture of Belgium, a neutral country, a land of art, of culture and of industry, with which we have had spiritual relations since the period of the Renaissance, a land which like our own won her independence by immense sacrifices. But the bones of Friedrich Nietzsche, who raged at the sight of a Germany sunk in pacifist slumber, must exult in the grave where they lie not far from those of the Olympian Goethe ; the epoch of conquering violence has begun ; we know now that German culture, inspired by Mephistopheles and Zarathustra, regards no boundaries ; thus, as Mephistopheles, at the behest of the Emperor, that Benjamin of the Almighty, invented astounding military weapons, so the Teutonic genius has prepared those terrible engines of war which neither fortresses, cities, public buildings, nor schools can withstand. And just as*

Faust in the guise of a humanitarian dreamer, awaited the possession of territories acquired by diabolical aid, so 94 German professors proclaim to the civilised world the equity of Imperial conquest, on the victims of which they propose to pour out the superfluity of their culture.

Mephistopheles, says the poem, burnt the church, the house, and the garden of two poor old people, which obstructed the expansion of Faust's happy kingdom. The two old people, together with a guest, were roasted alive (three neutrals !)

But it would be well to know the judgment of the God of Ages upon those aviators, who, flying over cities, murder women, old men, and children, for such a case was not dealt with either by Mephistopheles or Zarathustra. Faust must behold them from his place in Paradise. The doctor repented at the approach of death ; ascending to the steps of the Virgin's throne, he found there the noble intelligence of Gretchen, who in the meantime had killed her mother, strangled her child, and died repentant.

Exalted by this edifying reading, what archangels the German soldiers must consider themselves compared with those Catholic Flemings, who have elaborated their morality, contemplating virtue in the sacred images of Latin art ! Blessed and glorified be thy sacrifice, O heroic Belgium, neither quenched nor vanquished ! Thou didst rise against Imperial barbarism, invading thee in the name of science and culture. Hail to thee throughout the ages, heroic Belgium !

Brutality menaces the glory of the world. May thy blood, like baptismal waters, revive our faith in Latin civilisation, and spur us on against the dark and heavy Empire, that might well have issued from the gloom of primordial Asia or the mediæval ages of Europe.

By ALICE MEYNELL
THE HEROIC LANGUAGE

When our now living languages are " dead,"
Which in the classes shall be treasurèd ?
    Which will the masters teach ?
Kepler's, and Shakespeare's, and thy word, thy phrase,
Thy grammar, thou heroic, for all days,
    O little Flemish speech !

Alice Meynell

By SIDNEY LOW

" FROM THE BODY OF THIS DEATH "

> She is not dead !   Although the spoiler's hand,
>   Lies heavy as death upon her ; though the smart
>   Of his accursèd steel is at her heart,
> And scarred upon her breast his shameful brand ;
> Though yet the torches of the Vandal band,
>   Smoke on her ruined fields, her trampled lanes,
>   Her ravaged homes and desolated fanes,
> She is not dead but sleeping, that wronged land.
>
> O little nation, valorous and free,
>   Thou shalt o'erlive the terror and the pain ;
> Call back thy scattered children unto thee,
>   Strong with the memory of their brothers slain,
> And rise from out thy charnel-house, to be
>   Thine own immortal, radiant Self again.

Sidney Low

By SIR ARTHUR PINERO

TO ALBERT THE BRAVE

ENGLAND honours and salutes you, Sir. Inspired by your true patriotism, your splendid courage, your heroic soul, Little Belgium has become for all time Great Belgium. Betrayed, outraged, exiled, you and your people prove yourselves to be unconquerable. Such a spirit cannot be quenched. Beside it, the flames lighted by your barbarous enemy show pale and impotent.

Sir, the pangs of Belgium's rebirth are terrible ; but the shrieks of travail reach the ears of a just Heaven. The hour is at hand when the cries of agony shall die down ; when the rich meadows of your new-born kingdom shall respond to the caress of the sun with a smile like the smile of an infant ; when you shall lead the remnant of your indomitable army back in triumph to witness the glory of your country's re-creation. Till that moment, whatever her fortunes in other fields, England will know no rest, no contentment, not one particle of gladness.

Arthur Pinero

By SIR WILLIAM CROOKES

ONE'S sympathy with and admiration of the gallant Belgian nation and their valiant King are only to be paralleled by the horror and detestation one feels for their universal enemy—the modern Huns.

To express my feelings I would go to the Bible or to Shakespeare for an apt quotation, and I do not think the following words from Isaiah (ch. 14), can be improved on as a prophetic statement of the depth of the modern catastrophe and of prospective comfort to the afflicted ruler :

> *In the day that the Lord shall give thee rest from thy sorrow, and from thy trouble, and from the hard bondage wherein thou wast made to serve, thou shalt take up this parable against the King of Babylon, and say, How hath the oppressor ceased ! the golden exactress ceased ! The Lord hath broken the staff of the wicked, and the sceptre of the rulers, He who smote the peoples in wrath with a continual stroke, he that ruled the nations in anger, is persecuted and none hindereth.*

William Crookes.

By SIR CHARLES LUCAS

THE cause of Belgium is the cause of all who hold that nations have a right to live. Terrible are the sufferings of this present time, but coming generations will stand up and call the land and the people blessed.

C. P. Lucas

By G. W. PROTHERO

" MY tongue hath sworn ; unsworn remains my mind."

This is the motto Germany has chosen for herself ; it is not the motto of Belgium—or of England.

G. W. Prothero

By H.H. THE RANEE OF SARAWAK

WORDS cannot express the immense feeling of admiration and sympathy I feel for the King and his people in this frightful calamity which has overtaken them—a feeling that, outside Germany, must be paramount in the hearts of men and women all over the world.

Margaret Sarawak

By SIR WILFRID LAURIER
By Telegraph

YOUR own Introduction to KING ALBERT'S BOOK is a most eloquent tribute to the heroism of the King and people of Belgium. No other words are needed from me. My share will be to assist as far as in my power may lie the diffusion of the book among the Canadian people.

JUSTICE
By Solomon J. Solomon, R.A.

By JOHN GALSWORTHY

REVEILLE

IN my dream I saw a fertile plain, rich with the hues of autumn. Tranquil it was, and warm. Men and women, children, and the beasts worked and played and wandered there in peace. Under the blue sky and the white clouds low-hanging, great trees shaded the fields ; and from all the land there rose a murmur as from bees clustering on the rose-coloured blossoms of tall clover. And, in my dream, I roamed, looking into every face, the faces of prosperity, broad and well-favoured—of people living in a land of plenty, of people drinking of the joy of life, caring nothing for the morrow. But I could not see their eyes, that seemed ever cast down, gazing at the ground, watching the progress of their feet over the rich grass and the golden leaves already fallen from the trees. The longer I walked among them the more I wondered that never was I suffered to see the eyes of any, not even of the little children, not even of the beasts. It was as if ordinance had gone forth that their eyes should be banded with invisibility.

While I mused on this, the sky began to darken. A muttering of distant winds and waters came travelling. The children stopped their play, the beasts raised their heads ; men and women halted and cried to each other : " The River—the River is rising ! If it floods, we are lost ! Our beasts will drown ; we, even we, shall drown ! The River ! " And women stood like things of stone, listening ; and men shook their fists at the black sky, and at that travelling mutter of the winds and waters ; and the beasts sniffed at the darkening air.

Then, clear, I heard a Voice call : " Brothers ! The dyke is breaking ! The River comes ! Link arms, brothers ; with the dyke of our bodies we will save our home ! Sisters, behind us, link arms ! Close in the crevices, children ! The River ! " And all that multitude, whom I had seen treading quietly the grass and fallen leaves with prosperous feet, came hurrying, their eyes no longer fixed on the rich plain, but lifted in trouble and defiance, staring at that rushing blackness. And the Voice called : " Hasten, brothers ! The dyke is broken. The River floods ! "

And they answered : " Brother, we come ! "

Thousands and thousands they pressed, shoulder to shoulder—men, women, and children, and the beasts lying down behind, till the living dyke was formed. And that blackness came on, nearer, nearer, till, like the whites of glaring eyes, the wave crests glinted in the dark rushing flood. And the sound of the raging waters was as a roar from a million harsh mouths. But the Voice called : " Hold, brothers ! Hold ! "

And from the living dyke came answer : " Brother ! We hold ! "

Then the sky blackened to night. And the terrible dark water broke on that dyke of life ; and from all the thin living wall rose such cry of struggle as never was heard.

But above it ever the Voice called : " Hold ! My brave ones, hold ! " And ever the answer came from those drowning mouths, of men and

women, of little children and the very beasts : " Brother ! We hold ! "
But the black flood rolled over and on. There, down in its dark tumult,
beneath its cruel tumult, I saw men still with arms linked ; women on their
knees, clinging to earth ; little children drifting—dead, all dead ; and the
beasts dead. And their eyes were still open facing that death. And above
them the savage water roared. But clear and high I heard the Voice call :
" Brothers ! Hold ! Death is not ! We live ! " And, fronting the edge
of the flooding waters, I saw the shades of those dead, with arms yet linked,
and heard them crying : " Brother ! We hold ! " . . .
Then came oblivion.
When once more I dreamed, it was light. The plain was free of darkness,
free of waters. The River, shrunk and muddied, flowed again within its
banks. And Dawn was breaking ; but the stars were still alight.
At first it seemed to me that only trees stood on that plain ; but then, in the
ground mist fast clearing, I saw the forms of men and women, children,
beasts ; and I moved among them, looking at their faces—not those broad
and prosperous faces whose eyes were banded with invisibility, but grave
with suffering, carved and strong. And all their eyes, lifted to the sky,
were shining.
While I stood thus watching, the sun rose, and heaven brightened to full
morning. And, amazed, I saw that the stars had not gone in, but shone
there in the blue, crystals of immortality.
And above the plain, clad in the hues of spring, I heard the Voice call :
" Brothers ! Behold ! The Stars are lit for ever ! "

By MILLICENT GARRETT FAWCETT

THE Belgian people have given the world an example of heroic courage
and self-devotion which will rank in history with the great deeds of all time.
Let no one say that Belgium, devastated and martyred as she is, has ceased
to exist. Her nationality is stronger, her vitality is more intense than it has
ever been. Every Belgian, man, woman, and child, bears himself proudly
to-day because of his nationality.

> *Unto each man his handiwork, unto each his crown*
> *The just Fate gives :*
> *Whoso takes the world's life on him, and his own lays down*
> *He, dying so, lives.*

It should be the very first concern of the Allies at the end of the war to see
that Belgium remains a free and independent nation.

54

By THE Rt. Hon. EARL ROBERTS OF KANDAHAR

MY admiration for the part Belgium has played in the war now being waged against aggression, dishonourable contempt of Treaty obligations, falsehood, and injustice, knows no bounds. I feel most strongly that Great Britain owes Belgium a deep debt of gratitude which it will be difficult to repay. Inspired by the noble example of their King, the Belgians arrested the first onslaught of the Germans, and thus gave us time to ward off the punishment we so richly deserve for our neglect to prepare to defend our own interests. Little Belgium has shown to the great nations of the earth that a brave and united people, daring everything and prepared to suffer anything in the sacred cause of liberty, can resist successfully overwhelming numbers for a long time, and materially help towards victory in the end. In the terrible struggle still raging, to the Belgians must be awarded the palm for freely and fearlessly offering themselves as the first bulwark against the invading hordes of Germany. Glorious has been their stand, and priceless the time and the advantage gained thereby. No acknowledgment of their splendid example can be too liberal. No admiration too lavish, no compensation for the loss and misery they have endured, too generous.

They have fought heroically for a sacred principle against frightful odds. They have suffered up to the limit of human endurance. God grant that there may be yet in store for them a bright and prosperous future, and a permanent place in the van of Civilisation and Freedom.

Roberts

By MAURICE HEWLETT

FROM ENGLAND

> *O MEN of mickle heart and little speech,*
> *Slow, stubborn countrymen of heath and plain,*
> *Now have ye shown these insolent again*
> *That which to Cæsar's legions ye could teach,*
> *That slow-provok'd is long-provok'd.   May each*
> *Crass Cæsar learn this of the Keltic grain,*
> *Until at last they reckon it in vain*
> *To browbeat us who hold the Western reach.*
>
> *For even as you are, we are, ill to rouse,*
> *Rooted in Custom, Order, Church, and King ;*
> *And as you fight for their sake, so shall we,*
> *Doggedly inch by inch, and house by house ;*
> *Seeing for us too there's a dearer thing*
> *Than land or blood—and that thing LIBERTY.*

Maurice Hewlett.

By SIR OLIVER LODGE

THE world is the richer for the experience of the past few months, and Belgium has inscribed its name on an eternal roll of honour—the roll of those who have died in holding a pass against overwhelming odds.

Humanity blesses the heroic struggle for freedom of the Belgian nation ; for without their aid the face of Europe would have been changed past redemption, and the Earth might have been subject to a brutal and intolerable dominance. We have witnessed in our own generation one of the classical contests of the world ; and the tale will go down to remote posterity—a tale of deep infamy and lofty honour—relating how at this time the powers of evil were frustrated, and how the holiest cause emerged, stricken but victorious,—triumphing as always through grievous pain.

By CLAUDE MONET

TRÈS honoré de l'occasion qui m'est offerte, de pouvoir crier toute mon admiration à l'héroïque Belgique, et d'adresser très respectueusement la même admiration au noble et vaillant roi de la nation Belge.

Vive la Belgique ! Vive les Alliés ! Vive la France !

TRANSLATION
I feel myself greatly honoured by the opportunity given me to express all my admiration of heroic Belgium, and to offer a like admiration to the noble and valiant King of the Belgians.
Long live Belgium ! Long live the Allies ! Long live France !

By SIR JAMES CRICHTON-BROWNE

BELGIUM

BELGIUM, a stripling Knight in the shining armour of Truth and with the flashing blade of Right, withstood the first fierce onslaught of the monstrous and fire-belching Dragon that has grown up in Central Europe and uncoiled itself to devour the world. Scorched, wounded, trodden on, the stripling has never blanched nor quailed but has given pause to the Dragon and time to the strong men to awake from slumber in which, but for him, they might have been smitten down. When, amidst the execrations of mankind, the Dragon is driven back to his lair and chained there for a thousand years, then, for all that time, will women, with tears in their eyes, tell their children of the stripling's agony and men with stiffened sinews recall his valiant deeds.

Laud and homage to Belgium ! bravest of the brave, lealest of the leal, and loving care and succour too, that healing and solace may come to him.

56

ST. GEORGE AND THE DRAGON
By Briton Rivière, R.A.

By EDMUND GOSSE

THE BELGIAN POETS

ONE by one, like the apparitions that rose and pointed at Macbeth, the arts and sciences, the amenities and the pieties of Belgium defile in a blood-boltered line, and accuse their murderer of foul and treacherous offences. To a single phantom I would speak to-day. While others call for vengeance on Germany for other wickedness, I would speak in anger and pity of a murdered literature. Incredible as it sounds, a literature, the articulate imagination of a people, may be destroyed. After the battle of the White Mountain, the flourishing and genial literature of Bohemia was annihilated by the Austrians, and it lay in ashes for one hundred and fifty years. Such, if Germany had her brutal will, would be the fate of poetry and prose in the Low Countries to-day, and although the inevitable hour of reckoning and restitution cannot for ever be delayed, at the present moment her enemies have succeeded in silencing the written voice of Belgium. If they have not silenced it, at least they have dispersed it on the wings of the wind. It has no longer an abiding-place within its own borders ; it sounds, so far as it still sounds at all, in the piteous murmurs of an exile.

Modern literature in Belgium is a creation of our own times. It dates from 1880, when a generation of young men started it under the leadership of a youth who lived but nine years more to witness the progress of his work, Max Waller, whose name will always demand the honour due to precursors. Waller founded a review, *La Jeune Belgique*, in which his most brilliant contemporaries, tired of the nullity of the intellectual life of their forbears, developed ideas and forms of expression which translated for the first time the peculiar emotions and graces of the Flemish temperament. They chose the French language for their expression, and they all were in sympathy with the Latin genius, although they were careful never to denationalise themselves, and never to abandon the vehement or mystical attributes proper to the country of their birth. In less than thirty-five years, Belgium has placed herself in the forefront of the creative literary nations of Europe. This is not the place, nor mine the hand, to analyse or describe the achievements of Belgian literature. But it is manifest to every one that it is in poetry that its success has been most eminent. In the few words which I am privileged to say here, I will attempt no more than to bend in affection and homage towards our admirable and stricken brethren, the poets of Belgium. Two of them, through a merciful Providence, have been spared by an early death from drinking the bitter cup. We name in honour the harbinger of the brilliant company, the ecstatic CHARLES VAN LEERBERGHE, whose pen was dipped in moonlit dew, whose ethereal genius translated into verse all that was most delicately in harmony with the spirit of the old Flemish illuminators, whose pictures of Paradise seem painted by an inspired monk on the vellum fly-leaves of a missal. We name GEORGES RODENBACH, in whom the melancholy of Flanders, above all the grey beauty of Bruges, found so tender an interpreter.

But chiefly to the living we proffer our reverent and indignant sympathy. Driven from their homes, their books scattered, their manuscripts burned, they are but as beautiful autumn leaves in the blast of the Teuton war-gods. We greet the noble EMILE VERHAEREN, the first of the living poets of Europe. In him the religious intensity of Belgium has taken a different expression from that of the mystics. He has not shrunk, in his abundant and various yet eminently consistent productive work, from celebrating many sides of the national character. He blows through bronze and he breathes through silver, and if we would understand the life and soil of Belgium, *toute la Flandre*, we must go to this inspired and multiform mind for our instruction. Thirty-five years ago, three young men who were students at the Collège Sainte-Barbe at Ghent, determined to devote their lives to the creation of a poetical drama in Belgium ; they were Van Leerberghe, Le Roy, and Maeterlinck. The whole world has submitted to the fascination of MAURICE MAETERLINCK. A Parisian admirer unwisely introduced him as " the Belgian Shakespeare." He is, on the contrary, the one and only Belgian Maeterlinck. We greet with emotion other names, less universally recognised. Brussels is the mother of ANDRÉ FONTAINAS, whose enchanted gardens are like the backgrounds of Rubens' pictures. From Antwerp MAX ELSKAMP has brought his idylls of a peaceful Flanders. Let me not forget that Liége has sent us the tender and tremulous ALBERT MOCKEL, nor that Louvain, till the hour of her desecration, was proud of the accomplished talent of ALBERT GIRAUD.

If I name no more, it is due to ignorance or lack of space. Our protest is not in favour of these great names alone, but of the whole intellectual civilisation of Belgium, so flourishing and so vivid in the peace of a month or two ago, now humiliated and trampled like an autumn rose under the hoof of a bull.

Edmund Gosse

By ANDREW CARNEGIE

ASSUREDLY the people of Belgium have shown themselves worthy descendants of their ancestors whom Julius Cæsar honoured thus : *Omnium fortissimi sunt Belgæ*. King Albert has proven himself possessed of courage, which is one of the essentials of high character, which Farquhar thus describes :

> *Courage the highest gift, which scorns to bend*
> *To mean devices for a sordid end.*
> *Courage—an independent spark from Heaven's bright throne,*
> *By which the soul stands raised, triumphant, high, alone.*

Andrew Carnegie

58

By HENRI BERGSON

Le *Daily Telegraph* veut bien me demander mon sentiment sur la Belgique et sur le Roi Albert. Je cherche en vain, je ne trouve pas de mots pour exprimer mon admiration. Je m'incline en proie à une émotion profonde et je salue respectueusement.

Un petit peuple s'est trouvé tout à coup en présence d'une des plus formidables armées de la terre. On lui demandait simplement la permission de passer ; on lui rendrait, disait-on, son territoire intact ; on respecterait son indépendance. L'eût-on fait ? Je ne sais, mais ce petit peuple était libre de le croire. Et s'il eût déclaré qu'il cédait à la force, qu'il acceptait l'inévitable, nous l'aurions plaint, nous n'aurions pas osé le blâmer. Mais non ! il a résisté à ce qui paraissait irrésistible ; il a fait par avance le sacrifice de tout ce qu'il avait et de tout ce qu'il était : ses villes et ses villages, sa fortune et sa vie, il a tout donné à une idée, à la conception héroïque qu'il s'était faite de l'honneur. Gloire à lui ! gloire à son roi !

J'ai dit, j'ai enseigné pendant longtemps que l'histoire était une école d'immoralité. Je ne le dirai plus, après l'exemple que la Belgique vient de donner au monde. Un acte comme celui-là rachète les plus grandes vilenies de l'humanité. Il fait qu'on se sent plus fier d'être homme.

Sera-t-il permis à un professeur de philosophie d'ajouter qu'on se sentira plus fier, désormais, d'être philosophe ? Le roi Albert s'est adonné aux études philosophiques. Leur doit-il quelque chose de sa force d'âme et de son généreux idéalisme ? Je le voudrais, car la philosophie recueillirait alors quelque chose de sa gloire. Deux fois, au cours de l'histoire, elle a brillé sur un trône ; et, les deux fois, elle aura été associée à la plus haute vertu. Elle inspira jadis le stoïcisme de Marc Aurèle. Elle sourit aujourd'hui avec amour à l'héroïsme simple et sublime du Roi Albert.

H. Bergson

TRANSLATION by J. S. C.

The Daily Telegraph *has been pleased to ask of me to say what I feel about Belgium and King Albert. I have searched in vain to find words adequate for expressing my admiration : I can only bow my head, a prey to profound emotion, and offer a respectful homage. A small nation found herself suddenly confronted by one of the most formidable armies in the world. They asked of her merely permission to pass through ; they would restore to her, so they said, her territory untouched ; they would respect her independence. Would they have done so ? I know not, but the small nation was free to believe them. And if she had declared that she yielded to force and accepted the inevitable, we might have pitied but we should not have dared to blame. Far otherwise ! She has resisted what seemed irresistible ; she has sacrificed at once all that she had, all that she was : her towns and her villages, her wealth and her life, she has given all for an idea, for the heroic belief that it was done for honour. Glory to her ! Glory to her king ! I have said and I have taught for long that history was a school of immorality. I shall say so no more, after the example that Belgium has just given to the world. A deed like this redeems the worst meannesses of mankind. It makes one feel more proud of being a man.*

May it be permitted to a professor of philosophy to add that it makes one feel more proud henceforth of being a philosopher ? King Albert has followed philosophical studies. Is it to them that he owes something of his strength of soul and his noble idealism ? I could wish so, for philosophy would then share in his glory. Twice in the course of history has philosophy shone from a throne, and on both occasions it will have been associated with the highest virtue. In ancient times philosophy inspired the stoicism of Marcus Aurelius. It smiles lovingly to-day on the simple and sublime heroism of King Albert.

59

HAIL!
A HYMN TO BELGIUM

POEM BY
JOHN GALSWORTHY

MUSIC BY
FREDERIC H. COWEN.

N.B.—If it is desired to sing this as a simple Hymn, the Melody of the 3rd verse should be omitted and the words sung to the opening eight bars, as in the 1st and 2nd verses.

ter-ror,   yet with eyes un - dazed,— Smiled on at Hope— ye sweet-hearts: Hail!.. Maids of

Bel - gium ! Sweet-hearts, Hail !   4. Land   of Bel - gium ! earth and sky For ev - er-more shall

tell thy tale. The morn - ing comes ! Thou shalt not die !   Hail ! Thou Sad Im - mor - tal : Hail !

Hail ! Thou Sad Im - mor - tal :   Hail !

61

By EDEN PHILLPOTTS

To Belgium

Champion of human honour, let us lave
Your feet and bind your wounds on bended knee,
Though coward hands have nailed you to the tree
And shed your innocent blood and dug your grave,
Rejoice and live ! Your oriflamme shall wave
While man has power to perish and be free—
A golden flame of holiest Liberty,
Proud as the dawn and as the sunset brave.

Belgium, where dwelleth reverence for right
Enthroned above all ideals ; where your fate
And your supernal patience and your might
Most sacred grow in human estimate,
You shine a star above this stormy night,
Little no more, but infinitely great.

By MARY CHOLMONDELEY

Polydore in England

WHEN Polydore came to stay with us he did not come alone. He was accompanied by Nestor Maria and René and Achille and poor Jan, who was not a soldier at all, but had been wounded while lending a hand in the trenches.

But somehow the others only formed a background to Polydore. Polydore invariably met the eye first, from the moment when a jaded Red Cross official handed him and his companions over to us at a roadside station. It was Polydore who advanced to meet us, the others making a little bunch behind him. Polydore, with his dusky complexion and round, grey, impassive, unwinking eyes, amazed at nothing, at once constituted himself as spokesman of the party, interpreter and expert on matters of etiquette. Possibly he may have felt that this position was his due as he was the only one of the contingent in full Belgian uniform. Dark blue coat, wide light blue trousers, and peaked cap. Nestor Maria and Achille wore English sweaters with their blue trousers. Jan, of course, had no uniform, only a weird English cheap suit rather too tight in the waist.   None of them except Polydore had a peaked cap. But all five were wound up in enormous woollen comforters.

62

All five had been seriously wounded, and had come to us to recruit after being discharged from the hospital at E——. But though René and Achille were lame they were in the best of spirits, as were Nestor Maria and Polydore himself, though still somewhat pallid and worn-looking. Only Jan never smiled and hardly spoke a word. He had no news of his old mother, last heard of at Ostend.

Our guests had brought no luggage with them, except a packet of English picture post cards presented to Polydore in hospital, and one pipe among the five.

They obeyed Polydore's directions implicitly, why, I know not. When they retired to their carefully tucked-up beds, he made them all creep into them from the top, without opening them at the side. This cannot have been quite easy for René and Achille with their " bad " legs, but they accomplished it nevertheless. After two days, Polydore courteously inquired how much longer they would have to drink our terrible English medicine with their breakfasts. This was the strong tea we had given them. Coffee was substituted for it, and smiles wreathed every face. Even Jan said a word or two in Flemish which sounded like approval.

The only thing in our establishment which surprised even Polydore was the mowing machine on the lawn. That amazed them all, and they were never tired of watching it. They walked round the garden with us, at least Polydore did, while the others followed at his heels, while Polydore admired the *roses d'Egypte* and the *gueules de lion* * still flowering in the autumn beds. They were all politeness itself, but I think they might have become rather bored with English country life if it had not been for Private Dawkins of the West Lowshires. Dawkins was also just out of hospital and was recruiting at his mother's cottage in the village, and he walked up, erect and soldier-like in his khaki, to call on his allies. A difference of language presented no difficulties. Immediate and agreeable intercourse was established and presently Dawkins and Polydore set out together, of course followed by the others ; the English soldier looking very slim in his khaki puttees compared with the low, broad, sturdy, blue-trousered figures of his companions in arms.

Dawkins took his comrades to call on every cottage in the village, and introduced them to the entire circle of his acquaintance, including his mother. Mrs. Dawkins, I found afterwards, was much impressed by Polydore's ignorance.

" The pore critter," she told me, " actually thought the clothes-line was a telephone. But lor, mum, I soon made him understand. I brought out a kitchen rubber and a peg, and made him fasten it on the wire, just to teach him. He's sharp enough, is Polly Dor, and such a silly name for a man."

As he grew to know us better, Polydore told us many tales of the fighting in Belgium, the others sitting round, and joining in like a chorus. With a perfectly impassive face he recounted how on one occasion when the dykes

* Mignonette and Snapdragon.

were opened, the Germans, after losing all their guns, had been forced to seek refuge in the trees, where he and René had assisted in capturing whole batches of them, sitting in strings in the branches like enormous barn-door fowls.

But he and his comrades recounted other incidents too ghastly to be written here. He had *seen*—Nestor Maria had *seen*—Achille had *seen*—the dusky, impassive faces darkened suddenly. Hands were clenched, grey eyes blazed. We had to draw them back to less grievous topics and make Polydore describe to us once more the contemptible fire of the German infantry. We were shown exactly how the Germans fired from the hip, with no effect at all. And then Polydore waved René forward and made him stand in front of us, expanding his chest, while he laid his hand on the second button of René's tattered blue coat, and explained to us that when a Belgian soldier fires at the enemy he always hits him exactly there, on the chest—*always*.

Our Belgian soldiers did not stay many weeks with us. They thrived exceedingly, and presently their country called them. Dawkins was sent for the same day. And the last I saw of Polydore was leaning out of a third-class railway carriage window with Dawkins, waving his peaked cap to us, with the others in a little bunch behind him. We had made searching inquiries before they left, and found that Jan's mother was safe at Alexandra Palace, where she had arrived clutching five coffee-pots as her entire luggage.

So good-bye Polydore and Nestor Maria and Achille and René and Jan. And may the world go well with you !

Mary Ch. Brontëlly.

By SIR VALENTINE CHIROL

IT is a privilege to join in any tribute to King Albert and his people. King Albert is the only sovereign whose royal title is not a territorial one. He is styled King, not of Belgium but of the Belgians ; as if it had been pre-ordained that though a ruthless conqueror might rob him for a time of his kingdom, none should ever rob him of his kingship. Never perhaps more proudly than to-day, when his Government has been compelled to seek refuge on the hospitable soil of France and he himself, at the head of his indomitable army, is fighting close to the French frontier for the last inch of Belgian territory, has King Albert vindicated his right to a splendid title: King of the Belgians, heroic head of an heroic people.

Valentine Chirol

UNCONQUERABLE

By ARTHUR RACKHAM, R.W.S.

By PROFESSOR PAUL VINOGRADOFF

THE RECORD OF BELGIUM

IN addressing the King of an heroic nation it is natural to recall to mind some striking memories of its past in which its temper and character have been revealed in former ages. It seems clear to us, outsiders, that the life of the Belgian people has been in many respects an exceptional manifestation of energy and courage. As far as we can look back into dim antiquity, we find the country occupied by Celtic tribes which, in the opinion of a great expert, Cæsar, were conspicuous for their political aptitude and prowess in war. The Roman Conquest of this region proved to be more than a military accident—it impressed a great part of the population with the indelible stamp of Romance culture and contributed powerfully to form the Walloon racial group.

The Franks brought in a fresh Teutonic element : it survives in the Flemings and, as in the case of the Saxons and Danes of England, it widened the outlook and the range of action of the nation without forcing the country into the narrow groove of purely Germanic development.

In the economic Renaissance of Europe during the later Middle Ages Flanders took the lead with the astonishing outburst of industry in Ghent, Ypres, and other cities—and the progressive movement was reflected not only in the output of their wares but also in the sturdy spirit of the redoutable burgher arrays. In the Renaissance of learning and arts Belgium has taken its place with the Van Eycks and Memling far ahead of many populous kingdoms : Bruges shares with Florence and Nuremberg the glory of emulating Athens in the wealth of its civic culture.

In the centuries of statecraft and absolutism the valleys of the Scheldt and of the Meuse became the battle-ground of European sovereigns, but the transition to a better age is marked again by a momentous act of the Belgian people—by the rising against the benevolent despotism of Austria.

The settlement of 1830 was more than a casual fabrication of cunning diplomats : it has brought together elements diverse in race but united by creed, by cultural aspirations and by a spirit of stubborn independence.

King Albert is fortunate to stand at the head of such a people and the Belgians can well be proud of a King who embodies in a full measure the best virtues of the nation.

In ages to come travellers will look with pious emotion on the sites of Liége, Louvain, Antwerp, the shores of the Yser, and if at the close of this terrible war a prize were to be adjudicated to the most valiant nation, as the Greeks did in their war of independence against the Persian King, the prize would surely fall by unanimous consent to Belgium. If there is justice in the world and a meaning in history, Belgium will arise out of the ashes, like Phœnix, in renewed vigour and splendour.

P. Vinogradoff

By SIDNEY WEBB

HUMANITY has found, after many a wound and countless ineffectual struggles, that Law is the Mother of Liberty. Now Belgium has been tortured by ruthless power. May it be so far not in vain that all the peoples of the earth may learn that only in the building up of a really effective International Law can national liberty be secured.

Sidney Webb

By BENJAMIN KIDD

NO tribute which civilisation is able to make can meet the debt which the human spirit owes to the Belgian people and to King Albert for ever.
When the tempter asked the Belgian people to be his accomplice against France and offered Belgium a price for her soul, King Albert, backed by his unanimous people, instantly took the terrible decision and gave firmly the answer by which our common humanity has been ennobled.
It is an immortal story of Right rendered invincible through the crucifixion of a People.

Benjamin Kidd

By SIR THOMAS BARCLAY

THE violation of Belgium's neutrality is a collective crime, including every crime that dishonours the individual : murder, robbery, arson, perjury, false pretences, broken faith, etc.
It is murder, not war, to wage bloodshed on those against whom there is no grievance. It is robbery to take from the innocent as from the guilty, and arson to burn down their homes. It is worse than perjury without provocation to break a solemn promise and violate the trust of others.
The magnitude of Germany's crime has not yet been realised by the German national conscience, but, sooner or later, it will be realised and then all honest and truth-loving Germans, at present victims of deliberate mis-representation, will feel the humiliation of having forfeited the respect and confidence of mankind. They will see in all its blackness a crime which will go down to posterity as one of the foulest deeds of all time—a treacherous breach of faith coupled with a ruthless cruelty unsurpassed in history. No casuistry will redeem the German people from the consciousness of having provoked and deserved the curse of an unoffending people and the unqualified reprobation of the whole civilised world.

Thomas Barclay

66

THE MARCH OF THE WOMEN.

Ethel Smyth, Mus.Doc.

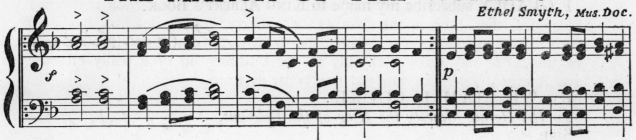

TO the King of the Belgians and his heroic people who, believing in right rather than in might, fought against overwhelming odds in defence of their honour and freedom—even as women in England are fighting to win theirs—undying gratitude, and everlasting glory!

Ethel Smyth

By **EMMELINE PANKHURST**

THE women of Great Britain will never forget what Belgium has done for all that women hold most dear.

In the days to come mothers will tell their children how a small but great-souled nation fought to the death against overwhelming odds and sacrificed all things to save the world from an intolerable tyranny.

The story of the Belgian people's defence of Freedom will inspire countless generations yet unborn.

E. Pankhurst

By CARDINAL GIBBONS
I GLADLY subscribe my name to KING ALBERT'S BOOK.

Ja. Card. Gibbons.

By WILLIAM J. LOCKE
To His Heroic Majesty the King of the Belgians,
SIRE,

One Fifth of November more worthy to live in the shuddering memory of man than the anniversary which we English celebrate—one Fifth of November, three hundred and thirty-eight years ago, the wintry dawn broke upon Antwerp burned and butchered by a soldiery " who," as the great American historian says, " seemed to have cast off even the vizard of humanity. Hell," he adds, " seemed emptied of its fiends." To-day a soldiery as ruthless and as bestial has entered the gates of Antwerp after spreading a desolation through your fair land such as Alva and his followers, supreme products of a race then braggart too of its " culture," had neither the wit to devise nor the ferocity to execute. More than three hundred years ago your country fought for everything that man holds dear, everything that man holds sacred. Against fearful odds she fought the greatest fight for Liberty that the world till then had seen. In that stupendous struggle, " women, old men, and children had all been combatants, and all therefore incurred the vengeance of the conquerors." To-day, Sire, your foes, molested by naught but the chivalrous resistance of your armies, have wreaked a vengeance thrice more damnable. Three hundred years ago your country, with unparalleled heroism, triumphed over the powers of darkness and established herself in Europe as one of the centres of inspiration in all that matters to the soul of mankind. She now, once more, has fought even a more glorious battle for Liberty than in those far-off days. She has struck an immortal chord that vibrates and shall vibrate through the united heart of the Anglo-Saxon, Latin, and Slav races—races who, in that sublimated expression of Life to which we give the name of Art, a term embracing all manifestations of spiritual discovery from a song to a cathedral, have abhorred Teutonic ideals. And as in those far-off days, your noble country, secure in her own integrity, and, now, inspired by the wondering admiration of the civilised world, once more shall triumph and once more shall play a prouder part than ever among the nations of the earth.

For yourself, Sire, what more fitting tribute can a humble writer lay at your feet than the words of the Anglo-Saxon historian regarding your predecessor and exemplar, the great saviour of your country three hundred years ago : " He went through life bearing the load of a people's sorrows upon his shoulders, with a smiling face. He was the guiding star of a great nation."

WJ Locke

68

With sincerest admiration.
Howard Chandler Christy. 1914.

ON THE FIELD
of HONOUR

By H. CHANDLER CHRISTY

By MARIE CORELLI

FOR BELGIUM ! *An Invocation*

" What shall we do for our Sister in the day when she shall be spoken of ?
If she be **a** wall, we will build upon her a palace of silver."

Song of Solomon

Maker of Heaven and Earth,
 Thou, who hast given birth
To moving millions of pre-destined spheres,
 Thou, whose resistless might
 Resolves the Wrong to Right
Missing no moment of the measured years,—
 Behold, we come to Thee !
We lift our swords, unsheath'd, towards Thy throne—
 Look down on us, and see
Our Sister-Nation, ruined and undone !
Martyred for nobleness, for truth and trust ;
Help us, O God, to raise her from the dust !

 Be Thou our witness, Lord !
 We swear with one accord
Swift retribution on her treacherous foe !
 Her bitter wrong is ours,
 And heaven's full-armèd powers
Shall hurl her murderer to his overthrow !
 Upon her broken wall
A silver palace of sweet peace shall rise
 At that high Festival
When Victory's signal flashes through the skies—
But—until then !—welcome the fiercest fray !
We fight for Freedom ! God, give us " The Day " !

Marie Corelli

By THE ARCHBISHOP OF YORK

THE King and people of Belgium were the first to meet the shock of this terrible war into which Europe has been plunged. They were the first to give proof of the spirit of heroic self-sacrifice by which alone it can be carried through. It was their honour to lay down their national life for their friends. It must be our honour to restore that national life to them, secured from menace, enriched and ennobled by the splendid sacrifice which it has made.

Cosmo Ebor

By THE REV. DR. JOHN CLIFFORD
THE BELGIAN PEOPLE AND THEIR KING

AGAIN and again as I have read the story of the unparalleled exploits of the Belgians and their King, the words of the prophet Isaiah have come to me: " A man shall be as a hiding-place from the wind and a covert from the tempest ; as rivers of water in a dry place and as the shadow of a great rock in a weary land." The outstanding hero of this stupendous war is King Albert. He has been a refuge for his people in this day of trouble and tragedy. Never has he hesitated from first to last. There has been no vacillation. His complete self-abnegation has been matched by the magnificence of his valour. He has stood his ground all the way through, and is still the strong, steadfast soul in whom his suffering people trust. He has led with courage and wisdom and self-sacrifice. He is the great hero of a nation of heroes, the brave leader of a brave and gallant people. By the clearest right, he goes to his place by the side of Leonidas and William the Silent, King Alfred and Oliver Cromwell, and all the other real kings of men. His noble and beautiful character, chivalrous spirit and whole-souled work will enrich the human race for ever. To him, and his people, we offer the most glowing admiration and the sincerest gratitude, for un-forgettable service rendered to all the generations of men, by undaunted resistance given to an unscrupulous and barbaric invader.

John Clifford.

By THE CHIEF RABBI

ONLY that nation can be called cultured which adds to the spiritual assets of humanity ; which by its living and, if need be, by its dying, vindicates the eternal values of life—conscience, honour, liberty. Judged by this test, two of the littlest of peoples, Judæa in ancient times and Belgium to-day, and not their mighty and ruthless oppressors, are among the chief defenders of culture, champions of the sacred heritage of man.

Israel, that has endured all things, suffered all things, and survived all things, believes with a perfect faith that Belgium, fighting for the Spirit, is as indestructible as the Spirit.

J. H. Hertz

70

JE m'associe de toute mon âme à l'hommage d'admiration et de respectueuse sympathie qu'on a eu l'heureuse pensée d'offrir à Sa Majesté le Roi Albert, à son armée et à son peuple.

Oui, honneur au Roi des Belges. Toutes nos sympathies vont à ce souverain magnanime, qui personnifie à l'heure actuelle aux yeux du monde entier le Droit opprimé, que la colère d'un puissant adversaire n'a point intimidé, et qui, malgré les revers de la fortune, persiste inébranlable dans la défense de l'indépendance de son pays.

Dès qu'il se sut menacé, sa résolution fut prise. Aux propositions tour à tour insinuantes et hautaines de laisser libre passage aux envahisseurs qui s'apprêtaient à se ruer sur une nation amie de la Belgique et à la surprendre par une attaque brusquée avant qu'elle eût le temps de concentrer ses troupes, il osa répondre par le refus formel que lui dictait sa conscience. Pour lui la neutralité de la Belgique n'était pas un vain mot, ni le traité qui la stipulait " un simple bout de papier " dont on ne tient compte qu'autant qu'on y a intérêt. Sans se laisser influencer par les menaces du solliciteur, ni par la crainte des conséquences immédiates de sa réponse, il n'écouta que la voix de la justice et de l'honneur. Sa résolution prise, il se mit en mesure de la soutenir avec une admirable énergie : " S'il faut résister à l'invasion, s'écrie-t-il, le devoir nous trouvera armés et décidés aux plus grands sacrifices. Un seul devoir s'impose à nos volontés : une résistance opiniâtre . . . l'étranger trouvera tous les Belges groupés autour de leur souverain, qui ne trahira jamais son serment constitutionnel.

Voilà un fier langage auquel le monde entier a justement applaudi.

Honneur à l'armée de la Belgique ! Ce fut un cri d'étonnement et d'admiration lorsqu'on apprit que subitement jetée en guerre contre la nation la plus fortement armée de l'Europe, elle tenait en échec les légions de son puissant ennemi à Liége et à Namur, brisait son élan, faisait échouer son plan d'attaque en l'empêchant de prendre l'avance sur laquelle il avait comptée. Obligée cependant de céder devant le nombre, elle se replia sur Anvers, et quand elle dut évacuer ce dernier boulevard de sa résistance, ce ne fut pas pour rendre les armes ; elle vint prendre place entre l'armée de la France et celle de l'Angleterre pour partager avec elles les périls de la guerre en attendant l'heure de partager l'honneur de la victoire finale.

L'armée Belge a écrit dans l'histoire du monde une des pages les plus glorieuses.

Honneur au peuple Belge! Il s'est montré digne de la confiance que son Roi avait en son patriotisme. Il a noblement ratifié l'attitude de son souverain en acceptant généreusement les sacrifices de la guerre. Levée de tous les hommes valides, siège et bombardement de ses forteresses, dévastation de ses villes et de ses campagnes, destruction de ses monuments et de ses chefs-d'œuvre, sévices de l'ennemi furieux de sa résistance, revers prévus, mais douloureux quand même, de ses armes, il a tout supporté avec une noble résignation et sans perdre courage. Liége, Namur, Tournai,

Gand, Bruges, Anvers, toutes ses villes si prospères, si pacifiques, Bruxelles, sa capitale, sont tombées l'une après l'autre sous les coups de l'ennemi dix fois supérieur en nombre, sans que son invincible constance soit ébranlée.

Il offre maintenant au monde le spectacle poignant qu'on n'avait pas vu depuis les invasions des Barbares, d'un peuple chassé de ses foyers, et réduit à l'émigration pour échapper à un joug qu'il ne veut pas subir.

Plein de confiance en sa cause et en son Dieu, il attend que la victoire revienne sous ses étendards qui sont ceux mêmes de la justice et de la liberté. La guerre actuelle a montré au monde que dans ce petit pays de Belgique habite un grand peuple.

Au Roi des Belges, à son armée, à son peuple, nous offrons respectueusement l'hommage de notre admiration et de notre reconnaissance.

Qu'il soit permis au Cardinal-Archevêque de Reims d'adresser aussi un salut fraternel au vénérable et illustre Archevêque de Malines, S.E. le Cardinal Mercier. Tous deux au retour du Conclave, nous avons trouvé fermée la porte de nos diocèses envahis. Nous n'y sommes rentrés que pour pleurer sur les ruines, et nous aurions pu, sur nos diocèses ravagés et sur nos cathédrales incendiées de Malines et de Reims, chanter les lamentations du Prophète sur les décimbres fumants de Jérusalem et de son Temple. Associés dans la douleur, nous le sommes aussi dans la prière pour implorer la protection du Ciel en faveur de nos deux peuples, qui, de tout temps frères dans la foi catholique, le seront désormais dans le souvenir des souffrances partagées et par les liens d'une amitié infrangible.

J. Card. Luçon, Arch. de Reims

TRANSLATION (abridged)

I associate myself whole-heartedly with the happily conceived tribute of admiration and respectful sympathy you propose to offer to King Albert, his army, and his people.

Yes, all honour to the King of the Belgians! All our hearts go out to this noble prince, who now personifies to the whole world oppressed Right, who, undaunted by the rage of a mighty adversary, and uncrushed by reverses, stands like a rock to defend the independence of his country.

*   *   *   *   *

All honour to the Belgian army! There was a universal cry of astonishment and admiration when it was known that, confronted suddenly with the most formidable army in Europe, it was holding the legions of its mighty foe in check at Liége and at Namur, breaking his onslaught, frustrating his plan of attack, and preventing him from taking the initiative on which he had reckoned. Forced at last to give way before numbers, it fell back upon Antwerp, and when it had to evacuate this last bulwark, it was not to lay down its arms; it came to take its place between the armies of France and England, and share with them the perils of war, while awaiting the hour when it should share with them the honours of the final victory. . . .

All honour to the Belgian people! They have shown

themselves worthy of the King's confidence in their patriotism. They nobly ratified their prince's attitude by a generous acceptance of the sacrifices of war. The call to arms of every able-bodied man, the siege and bombardment of their fortresses, the devastation of their towns and lands, the destruction of their monuments and works of art, the severities of an enemy infuriated by their resistance, reverses not less painful because they had been foreseen, they bore all with noble courage and resignation. Liége, Namur, Tournai, Ghent, Bruges, Antwerp, all their peaceful and prosperous cities, and Brussels, their capital, have fallen one after the other under the attacks of an enemy that outnumbered them tenfold, and still their unconquerable spirit is unshaken.

They now offer the poignant spectacle, unknown since the days of barbarian invasion, of a people driven from their homes, and obliged to emigrate to escape a domination they refuse to accept.

Confident in their God and their cause, they await the return of victory to their standards, the banners of justice and of liberty. This war has shown Europe that little Belgium is the land of a great people.

To the King of the Belgians, to his army, and to his people, we respectfully offer our tribute of admiration and gratitude.

*   *   *   *   *

LOUVAIN CATHEDRAL
By W. L. Bruckman

By W. L. COURTNEY
BY THE NORTH SEA

Death and Sorrow and Sleep :
Here where the slow waves creep,
This is the chant I hear,
The chant of the measureless deep.

What was Sorrow to me
Then, when the young life free
Thirsted for joys of earth,
Far from the desolate sea ?

What was Sleep but a rest,
Giving to youth the best
Dreams from the ivory gate,
Visions of God manifest ?

What was Death but a tale
Told to faces grown pale,
Worn and wasted with years—
A meaningless thing to the hale ?

Death and Sorrow and Sleep :
Now their sad message I keep,
Tossed on the wet wind's breath,
The chant of the measureless deep.

By SIR THOMAS BROCK
AID FOR THE FALLEN

I OFFER my picture as a small tribute to the splendid courage and fortitude
shown by the Belgian people in upholding the honour and integrity of their
country, offering as they do an example to the whole world.

It is our first duty to relieve their sufferings as far as possible, and when their
territory is once more free from the invaders to help them to restore their
devastated cities.

73

By J. L. GARVIN

WE in England would rather be blotted out of the book of nations than that Belgium should not be lifted up from ruin and gloriously restored. To that cause we have pledged our all, and until our pledge is redeemed in such sort that the justice of an overruling God shall be made manifest through us, never can we know soul's comfort in our own land spared by war nor cease our efforts to succour the bitter need of a desolate people and to hearten that little indomitable army of freedom and honour under its noble and beloved young King. No words of ours can be worthy of them and we can never do enough. The resistance of Belgium will live as one of the great legends of the world, and I firmly believe that its spiritual significance can only deepen with centuries. Nothing that we think of as heroic, tragic, inspiring in the past, or as confirming our faith that the best shall conquer the worst, exceeds what Flemings and Walloons over there have dared, suffered, and done in the twentieth century. They have made the name of their country an immortal word like Marathon—" the trumpet of a prophecy " that the reign of public law and peace shall yet be stablished upon the inviolable faith of treaties and that the sanctity of a scrap of paper shall be mightier than Krupp guns.

By A. G. GARDINER

WHATEVER the course of the war, whatever the fate of Europe, it is in King Albert that the future will see the most human, the most knightly figure of this Titanic struggle.

Belgium has died for freedom, for our freedom, for the freedom of the world. Let us see that she rises again triumphant from her tears and ashes. And if righteousness endures beneath the sun she will rise.

By J. A. SPENDER

SYMPATHY with Belgium must be mingled with envy—envy of the noble courage and matchless national spirit which, in the hour of her affliction, make her great among the peoples of the world. She has fought the Thermopylæ of the allied cause and it remains for her brothers-in-arms to see that her sacrifice is rewarded and her country restored. Our homage to the brave King who has dared all for the honour and liberty of the people committed to his charge.

74

ALL SAINTS' DAY, 1914

I have been wandering through the English fields, and under the English woods in a last lingering blaze of summer, before the winter comes. All day the sun has been clear in heaven ; all last night the moon shone without a cloud. The oaks are still—the majority of them—defiantly green as though they challenged a tyrant ; and where the woods lie close and thick in the basins of the hills, they show sharp patterns of deep green and flaming gold, patterns of Nature's finest weaving. Amethyst and gold, the beeches ; amethyst, blue, and gold, the distances ; and here and there a yew, violently black, or a hedgerow elm, its rounded leaf masses topped with yellow, or—on the common—furze-bushes, alive with blossom. The children are in the park picking up acorns and walnuts ; a green woodpecker is paying his autumn visit to the lawn before my window, pecking and stabbing for dear life ; the friendly robins sing round the house ; slowly, slowly, the sun sinks into the quiet mists that rise towards it ; and the glorious day will soon be done.

Thus goes All Saints' Day in this valley of the Chilterns. And, meanwhile, how goes it 150 miles away, where Belgians, Frenchmen, and Englishmen are fighting in the blood-stained trenches of West Flanders ? No blood here, no hint of it !—save where the sun strikes the deep carpet of fallen beech leaves, and the bright colour startles our sad thoughts. But there, men are pouring out their blood like water ; and all that, in this quiet English scene, we dare picture to ourselves of horror, of devilish pain and destruction, comes nowhere near the truth. Frenchmen and Englishmen, closely inter-linked, from west to east, from the sea to the Vosges, fronting the hideous onslaught of men, in whom a world uprisen sees a branded race—traitors to civilisation and to humanity ! And far to the north-west, in land hardly distinguishable from the sea, which has been won from the sea by infinite labour, there are thin lines of men in the Belgian trenches, " holding the pass " against the barbarian, as truly as any Greek did at Thermopylæ. Yet here are no blue mountains looking on. Only flat grey land, and featureless grey sea, and that grey advancing flood, where the Belgians have called in the sea to fight with them, and have given him in payment their hard-won fields, their dykes, and villages, to keep in trust for a nation of heroes, till the battle is won. " They told us to hold the trenches for 24 hours ; we held them ; then they said, ' Hold them 48 hours more,' and we have done it." So ran one of the most soul-stirring messages of war ever written. They *have* done it ! And now the English and French have come up, and the little army which has saved the left wing and protected Calais may fall back a while to count its dead. One in three, they say—*one in three !* Shall we not write over the fallen Belgians what was written over the Spartan dead at Platæa :

" These men having set a crown of immortal glory on their own land, were folded in the dark cloud of death. Yet being dead, they have not died,

75

seeing their fame in battle hath raised them up for ever from Forgetting and the Grave."

What can we do, we Englishwomen at home in our sheltered island, for this heroic little nation that has held the pass ? Day and night the fleeing army of women and children, of old men and boys passes northward to Holland, and westward over the sea to England. The other night, in a London social settlement, which has been largely given over to the refugees, a woman I know watched the incoming stream—peasants in their *sabots*, small *bourgeois*, carrying with them a few last possessions, children weary to death and wailing for food. But English hands were proud to wait on them, and English brains to plan for them. Here were a father and mother and seven children from Louvain—who had been tramping and hiding in the Flemish fields for days and nights. The mother was on the point of maternity. There was no accommodation for her in the settlement, where the large hall and the gymnasium have been turned into wards for men and women respectively, of the peasant class, and the separate rooms looking out on the garden have been mostly assigned to the elderly men and women of the educated professional type. Much perplexity, accordingly, as to the poor expectant mother, in the mind of the kind Scotch lady who is the house-keeper of the settlement ! But, suddenly, she remembers an address in Kensington ; she flies to the telephone ; she calls up a house in Queen's Gate, and its mistress. " Did you say the other day you would take in Belgian women for their confinement ? " " Certainly ! Have you got such a case ? " The note of joyful eagerness in the voice was unmistakable through the tube. Details are given. " All right. I will bring my motor round directly." And in an hour or so from her arrival, the dazed and wearied woman, with another Belgian woman and her little boy of three to keep her company, are speeding in a luxurious motor to the house in Queen's Gate. A warm room, a comfortable bed, nurse, clothing, food—everything is ready ! In a few days the poor soul's trouble is over, and the pretty babe lies peacefully beside its resting mother. For three days ! Then the soul of the peasant woman who waits on others, and is never waited on, rebelled. " I am always up, madame, in three days." " This time, take five ! You were so worn out ! " Most unwillingly, the tired body rests a few more days ; and then the whole family goes to a cottage ready for them, in an English village, the children go to school, the whole village become their protectors and friends, the Flemings learn a few words of English, the English a few words of Flemish, kindness and gesture do the rest, till, occasionally, an interpreter comes round and promotes a more satisfactory intercourse.

But among the incoming throng on this October night there are figures of another type. A mother and three daughters—the widow and children of a Belgian officer—soft-spoken, refined women, flying in terror from Antwerp, with a few scanty parcels of luggage, plus a grey parrot !—who is no sooner set down in the rooms allotted to them, than he vents his opinion on the discomforts of the journey in some vigorous cursing of " Guillaume " !

76

And for the fallen

By Sir Thomas Brock, R.A.

The settlement shelters them all for a week or two and then they become the honoured guests of an English country house, belonging to one of the most distinguished of English soldiers, and his wife, one of the gentlest of English ladies.

If tender sympathy can soothe the private and public grief of such exiles, theirs should indeed be soothed ; and mercifully, three out of this party of four are young, and to the young it is natural to smile, when the faces round them are all kindness, and a tragic flight has become an adventure, which would be only delightful—but for that low coast-line, and that grey sea, those ruined towns, those wounded men, that are in the minds of us all ! Thus all over England, and all over hospitable Holland, the fugitives spread, hands of welcome and pity are stretched out, and the great exile goes on—interminably. But the hours are passing, and the hours of darkness are slowly, slowly, handing on the torch to the hours of hope and dawn. Steadily the Huns retreat ; steadily the defenders of freedom and civilisation press their way forward over the ruined and bloodstained land. Surely, with the spring, the Belgian life-wave will turn homeward again ! It will flow back into the waste places and the scourged heroic land will bloom again with young life, and peaceful labour, and home joy. The dead, the dead will not be there !—save in our hearts that mourn. But they rest in the Lord, and their works shall follow them. A little nation has become for all time a song and a story, to refresh and kindle the " holy spirit of man "—so that when these evil days are over, and we count up the score, we shall not put what has happened in Belgium, during these autumn months, among the tragedies of history, but rather among the imperishable triumphs of the soul.

Mary A. Ward

By SIR CHARLES WYNDHAM
From Shelley's " Hellas "

> *Let the tyrants rule the desert they have made ;*
> *Let the free possess the Paradise they claim ;*
> *Be the fortune of our fierce oppressors weighed*
> *With our ruin, our resistance, and our name !*
>
> *Our dead shall be the seed of their decay,*
> *Our survivors be the shadow of their pride,*
> *Our adversity a dream to pass away,*
> *Their dishonour a remembrance to abide !*

Ch Wyndham

By LORD NORTHCLIFFE

THE Christmas message we all wish to send across the North Sea is this : that we British will fight to the end and work to the end for the King of Belgium and the Belgian people, because we believe that for all time in the world quiet homes and noble lives and surer peace will spring from the seed of their sacrifice.

The noble king of a true democracy has fought with his people against military tyranny and the lust of power, as rarely king or nation has fought before. Even in the midst of suffering and loss too great for words Belgium may feel that the fruits will surpass the sacrifice and all the world one day share in the Belgian victory.

Northcliffe

By SIR EDWARD J. POYNTER, BART., P.R.A.

NOT only for myself but for the body of which I am president I have no hesitation in affirming that all my colleagues of the Royal Academy are with me in the horror we feel at the treatment which the unoffending population of Belgium has received at the hands of the barbarous hordes of Prussians who have devastated that beautiful and peaceful country— outrages of the most savage kind inflicted under pretences invented for the occasion by that race which has proved itself so prolific of lies and spies.

But above all this do we admire the magnificent bravery with which the Belgians have withstood the onslaught of overwhelming numbers : for it is to their splendid courage, under their heroic King, in bearing the first brunt of the treacherous Prussian attack that the world owes it that the vast German scheme of conquest has hitherto failed.

Edward J Poynter

By LORD REDESDALE

To the King of the Belgians,

 SIRE,

Fighting on behalf of the whole world—a Hero at the head of an heroic people—Your Majesty has made the cruellest sacrifices. The world will not forget.

Sire, you have lost much—you have won Immortality.

 I have the honour to be,

   Sire,

    Your Majesty's

     Most obedient humble servant,

Redesdale

By LORD BURNHAM

THE position at this moment is without precedent in our history. A noble and gallant little nation has imperilled its very existence, and brought upon itself immeasurable calamities, by resistance to the aggression of a powerful, arrogant, and heartless foe. It has done this with a courage and devotion that have won universal admiration.

The independence and integrity of Belgium are vital interests to Britain. What she has done and suffered constitute, therefore, a claim on the British people that is irresistible.

With no assigned pretext of justification, the hordes of Germany have invaded and wasted her territory, and by acts of war, and by deeds that are murder not warfare, have done to death thousands of her people and driven hundreds of thousands into exile.

Countless homes desolated, families broken and scattered, children orphaned, the trade and means of existence of the most thickly peopled and most industrious country of continental Europe paralysed, chaos and ruin where there had been peace and happiness—these are some of the elements of the tragic fate that has overwhelmed this brave, unoffending nation. Never in our time has a people been so cruelly treated.

The splendour of the efforts and the magnitude of the self-sacrifice of this gallant people, no less than the dauntless heroism of the King and his army in resisting the invasion of their country, defying terrors and undergoing outrages that are unknown in civilised warfare, appeal to us equally with their appalling and indescribable sorrows.

The world's admiration has been moved, and the world's compassion aroused by unsurpassed bravery and unparalleled suffering.

May this volume generate a world-wide feeling that not enough can possibly be done to honour the courage and assuage the grief of this noble-hearted and afflicted people.

No one can feel more poignantly than I do this pressing necessity. But we must not be content to think only of a terrible past—irradiated though it be with magnificent patriotism and valour. We must look to the future. As far as human sympathy and help can do it, we must bring to Belgium, great in virtue of her martyrdom, consolation and atonement for the wrongs which she has endured.

Burnham

By WILL CROOKS

THE Story of the Ages does not give us anything so soul-inspiring as the fighting martyrdom of Belgium, its King and its people in 1914. Its failure to keep its homeland from bloody hands for awhile will prove its mighty triumph for the whole world. Its sacrifice will thrill generations yet to be, who will call Belgium blessed both in their memory and their prayers.

Will Crooks

By EMILE VERHAEREN

A sa Majesté Albert Ier, Roi des Belges,

SIRE,

C'est peut-être, depuis les belles journées de Liége, la première vraie joie que l'on me permet d'éprouver en me priant de vous rendre hommage. Vous êtes, à cette heure, le seul roi du monde que ses sujets à l'unanimité, sans exception aucune, aiment et admirent de toute la force de leur âme. Ce sort unique est le vôtre, Sire. Aucun conducteur d'hommes ne l'eut au même point que vous, sur la terre.

Malgré l'immensité du deuil qui vous entoure, il me semble que vous avez le droit de vous en réjouir. D'autant que votre compagne, Sa Majesté la Reine, participe à votre rarissime privilège.

Sire, votre nom sera désormais très grand. Vous vous êtes à tel point confondu avec votre peuple que vous en demeurez le symbole. Son courage, sa ténacité, sa douleur tue, sa fierté, sa grandeur future, son immortalité résident en vous. Notre âme profonde est la vôtre. Vous êtes nous tous en étant vous seul. Et vous le resterez.

Plus tard, lorsque vous rentrerez dans votre Belgique reconquise et infiniment glorieuse, vous n'aurez qu'à parler, Sire, pour que les querelles baissent de ton et que les antagonismes s'évanouissent. Si bien qu'après avoir été celui qui maintient et défend vous serez celui qui rapproche et reconcilie.

Sire, croyez à mon respect fervent.

Emile Verhaeren

TRANSLATION *by Florence Simmonds*

Sire,

This request to pay my respectful homage to you has given me the first real pleasure I have been permitted to feel since the good days of Liége. At this moment you are the one king in the world whose subjects, without exception, unite in loving and admiring him with all the strength of their souls. This unique fate is yours, Sire. No leader of men on earth has had it in the same degree as you.

In spite of the immensity of the sorrow surrounding you, I think you have a right to rejoice, and the more so as your consort, Her Majesty the Queen, shares this rare privilege with you.

Sire, your name will be great throughout the ages to come. You are in such perfect sympathy with your people that you will always be their symbol. Their courage, their tenacity, their stifled grief, their pride, their future greatness, their immortality all live in you. Our hearts are yours to their very depths. Being yourself, you are all of us. And this you will remain.

Later on, when you return to your recaptured and glorious Belgium, you will only have to say the word, Sire, and all disputes will lose their bitterness and all antagonisms fade away. After being our strength and defender, you will become our peacemaker and reconciler.

With deepest respect,

By SIR JOHN BLAND-SUTTON

" *I sin in envying his nobility.*"
Could I be anything I wished,
" *I would wish me only he.*"

John Bland Sutton

80

By SIR ADOLPHUS WILLIAM WARD
Master of Peterhouse

IT so happens that, more than three-quarters of a century ago, my father was personally much connected with the leaders of the movement that resulted in the recognition of Belgian independence and in the guarantee of Belgian neutrality by the European Great Powers. He remembered very well how, not long after the day had been won and King Albert's illustrious grandfather, King Leopold I, had mounted the throne on which he achieved so much for the prosperity of his own monarchy and for the peace of Europe at large, the King dismissed him after an audience with the words : " You know I am not without difficulties here ; but I take England as my model, and try to get on in a constitutional way." In this spirit the Kings of the Belgians have ruled for three generations over a people that loves liberty, without throwing to the winds respect for authority in Church and State.

But between the Belgians and ourselves there is something besides international obligations and political sympathy. These are the glorious traditions of a history which in the course of many centuries has established between England and the Belgic lands a connection closer than that between her and any other part of continental Europe. The measure in which the inhabitants of this island are kith and kin with the neighbours of the Saxons and Frisians is a question that has long attracted students, but it is most assuredly a question of measure only. What is more to the purpose, the main industry of the great Flemish communes became in the later Middle Ages the chief customer of English pastoral productivity, and, besides leading to much immigration to these shores, became the basis of a cordial political alliance. Times changed with the decline of the mercantile and the downfall of the political greatness of the good towns ; but the commercial relations between Great Britain and the Spanish (Austrian) Netherlands remained of vital interest to both countries, and formed an essential element in the system of alliances and conditions of treaties from the sixteenth to the eighteenth century.

The debt owing to Belgian art and Belgian letters—to the labours of Belgian historians, I may venture to add, in particular—is one which this country shares with the world at large. But I cannot close without recalling how to the history of religion—an influence often united with that of trade and with that of politics, but working in more profound and mysterious fashion —and to the history of education, which is inseparable from it, Belgium has contributed in many ways, but above all in that of deepening these movements of soul and mind. The beginnings of Christian mystical thought and of the fraternities from which both Renaissance and Regeneration drew some of their truest spiritual force are in no small part traceable to the saintly influence of Ruysbroek, whose birthplace was not far from the modern Belgian capital. And the foremost representative of this learning and this teaching was a professor of the earliest and most venerable of those

Belgian universities to which our hearts are going out to-day—the friend of Erasmus in the chair of St. Peter. It may seem almost idle in these days of bloodshed and destruction to look back for half a thousand years. But with the stillness as well as with the profound earnestness of the noblest part of Belgian spiritual life from the fourteenth to the sixteenth century may well be compared the sustained efforts for peace between the nations which long seemed one of the most hopeful signs in the public life of the latter half of the nineteenth century and in the early years of our own ; and in these efforts Belgian statesmen and publicists have notably taken what may be called a leading part.

For the sake of the long historical connection between the two peoples ; for the sake of the deep compassion and the high admiration to which the Belgians have become entitled by what they have suffered and what they have done in the dark days of the present, and for the sake of the peace which they and we have at heart—we have welcomed among us the subjects of our King's kinsman and ally, and we pray for their restoration, in God's good time, to their own fair and gracious land.

A. W. Ward

By THE RIGHT. REV. BISHOP OF LONDON, D.D., LL.D.
THE real difficulty of writing about Belgium is to find language adequate to express in the first place the scandalous injustice of her treatment. Whatever any other State may have done, or not done, Belgium had done absolutely nothing to deserve this treatment ; she had maintained her neutrality with perfect impartiality, and her treatment will be considered one of the crimes of history.

But, if language is inadequate to describe the injustice of her treatment, who can describe the pathos of that fleeing multitude, homeless, ruined, and in terror of their lives? The heart of the world goes out to them in pity. But, with pity is mingled the deepest admiration. Led by their splendid King, they have given an example of sublime courage and unflinching valour which has ennobled the world. They have shown that the soul of a people can be unconquerable while its whole territory is ravaged and its towns and villages are in flames. It must be the prayer of every lover of justice in the world that the Great God in Heaven may avenge the wrongs and reward the courage of the Belgian people.

82

By PROFESSOR GILBERT MURRAY

I SAW yesterday a regiment of British cavalry returning from manœuvres, every man of them wearing the colours of a foreign nation. That is not a common sight. Sometimes the soldiers of a conquered people have been forced to wear foreign colours, but they would not wear them with pride as these men did. Sometimes the soldiers of a weak and oppressed people have been proud to wear the colours of some great and conquering Power which was its ally. But these men were wearing the colours of a small and unfortunate nation, a nation in exile, whose lands are ravaged, its towns destroyed, and its territory in the occupation of the enemy. It is not for any material or worldly reason that British soldiers are proud to wear Belgian colours ; it is because Belgium in a time of terrific trial has done what we all should be most proud to have done, and has become an emblem to all the world of freedom and heroic courage.

The sufferings of Belgium would be enough in themselves, and more than enough, to constitute a claim on all the help that we can give. Every one admits the claim. In the town where I write it is not only well-to-do people who are offering every kind of help and hospitality. Shops from time to time refuse to take money when they hear that the goods they have supplied are for the Belgians. Artisans and tradesmen come and offer to work in their spare hours without payment. In the last few days the town workmen in one very poor neighbourhood have offered food and lodging rent free for a year ; the agricultural labourers in small villages have clubbed their pennies together and rented and furnished cottages. The same spirit is to be found all over England.

Now it is not mere sympathy, not mere pity for misfortune, that has stirred our whole nation like this. There is that in it, of course ; but still more there is admiration and gratitude. And we are grateful not only because Belgium stood, as a matter of fact, between us and the first fury of the German onslaught, but because Belgium has raised our ideal of human life and taught us to expect greater things of the world.

We did not know that our comfortable liberal-minded western civilisation had in it this heart of heroism. We had read of the heroes and martyrs of history, and we felt with a misgiving that they were perhaps out of date. Life was no doubt easier now and less cruel ; but it seemed looser in quality and woven of cheaper material. We have been shaken out of that false resignation. We have discovered that the days of cruelty are by no means past ; and, just when the shock of that discovery came, Belgium rose and showed us that the days of heroism are not past either. She stands as an example to all nations who doubt whether national life is a thing worth suffering for, to all individuals who doubt their own value as free souls or their capacity for facing danger or martyrdom. Consciously or unconsciously there has come to each man's heart a secret message, raising his confidence in himself and bracing all his faculties : " The Belgians have done these things: why should not I ? "

CARILLON

(POUR GRAND ORCHESTRE) POUR ACCOMPAGNER

"CHANTONS, BELGES, CHANTONS!"

POÈME

D'EMILE CAMMAERTS

MUSIQUE PAR

EDWARD ELGAR, O.M.,

ASSOCIÉ DE L' ACADÉMIE ROYALE DE BELGIQUE.

Chantons, Belges, chantons,
   Même si les blessures saignent, même si la voix se brise,
Plus haut que la tourmente, plus fort que les canons,
   Chantons l'orgueil de nos défaites,
Par ce beau soleil d'automne,
   Et la joie de rester honnêtes
Quand la lâcheté nous serait si bonne.

son du clai - ron, Sur les rui - nes d'Aer - schot, de Di - nant, de Ter - monde,

Dan - sons,   Bel - ges, dan - sons,

En chantant notre gloire.
Même si les yeux brûlent,
si la tête s'égare,

pppp

Formons la ronde !

8va

pp   f a tempo.   ff sf giocoso.   sf   sf   sf

Ped.   sf

sf   sf   sf   sf   sf

sf   sf

3   3   3   3   3

allargando.

88

89

Avec des branches de hêtre, de hêtre flamboyant,
Au son du tambour,
Nous couvrirons les tombes de nos enfants.

Nous choisirons un jour,
Comme celui-ci,
Où les peupliers tremblent doucement
Dans le vent,
Et où l'odeur des feuilles mortes
Embaume les bois,
Comme aujourd'hui,
Afin qu'ils emportent
Là-bas
Le parfum du pays.

Nous prierons la terre qu'ils ont tant aimée De les bercer dans ses grands bras, De les ré-

-chauffer sur sa vaste poitrine Et de les faire rêver de nouveaux combats: De la

prise de Brux - elles, de Ma - lines, De Namur, de Li - ège, de Lou - vain,
Et de leur entrée triomphale, là-bas, A Berlin !

Chantons, Belges, chantons,
Même si les blessures saignent et si la voix se brise,
Plus haut que la tourmente, plus fort que les canons,
Même si les blessures saignent, même si le cœur se brise,
Chantons l'espoir et la haine implacable,
Par ce beau soleil d'automne,
Et la fierté de rester charitables
Quand la Vengeance nous serait si bonne !

91

By SIR GILBERT PARKER

IT is given to some men and some peoples now and again in the world's history to represent mankind at its truest, its highest and best ; to offer upon altars of liberty the blood of sacrifice for all men in all the world ; and to pledge for humanity once again devotion to eternal things. This is what the Belgian King and the Belgian people have done. A monstrous, destroying legion of terror and tyranny moved upon them out of the night, offered them gain and gold if they would forswear their bond, and give freedom to the legions of an Emperor to whom the ink of honour and the pledged paper were no obstacles to the march of ambition. Belgium, its King and people, preferred death to dishonour. Their way was the ancient way—to lose the whole and gain their own souls. This they did, and while Time tells its story the torch that Belgium lighted will burn, and the hand of the King that held it aloft will be honoured among men.

> "*Oh, happy are all free peoples too strong to be dispossessed,*
> *But blessed are they among nations that dare to be strong for the rest.*"

By SIR SIDNEY LEE

THE King of the Belgians and his brave army have set an example which lends humanity a new glory. Their heroic resistance to the wholly un-merited wrongs which brute strength has forced upon them has shed fresh radiance on the history of the civilised world. In spite of the cruel suffering which the ruthless enemy has sown broadcast through the land, in spite of all the waste and desolation which German soldiers have inflicted without pity or remorse, Belgium, its ruler and its people, may find hope and consolation in the knowledge that the justice of their cause is recognised wherever truth and right prevail, and that the honour of all honourable men is pledged to secure for them due reparation of their unconscionable wrongs.

By PROFESSOR WILLIAM FLINDERS PETRIE
F.R.S., F.B.A., D.C.L., LL.D., Ph.D.

TO the Belgian Nation and its Noble Leader, I present the most sincere
Homage to its Bravery,
Respect for its unflinching Fortitude,
Gratitude for its saving of England and France,
Wishes for its speedy resettlement,
Hopes that by its sufferings it may be perfected in true greatness.

By SIR HERBERT TREE

THE ULTIMATUM : *or, Every Man Has His Price.*

CHARACTERS : *The Ruler of a Great People ; a Chiropodist ; Princes, Grand Dukes, Ministers of State, Priest, Professor, and Sycophants.*

SCENE : *The* RULER'S *marble bathroom in the Palace.*

> [*At the rise of curtain, the* RULER OF A GREAT PEOPLE *is discovered seated in his dressing-gown ; the* CHIROPODIST *plies his trade.*]

CHIROPODIST : What remarkable corns your Majesty has !

RULER : Yes, they are ancestral—all my predecessors were noted for them.

CHIROPODIST : I have heard, your Majesty, that in the seventeenth century many of the Court wore tight shoes in order to cultivate the Royal infirmity—[*correcting himself*]—prerogative !

RULER : I daresay. Take care—you hurt me. [CHIROPODIST *takes from his tray some drops from a little bottle labelled " Poison " and applies them with a brush to the royal foot, and resumes his pedicure.*] You may continue to address us.

CHIROPODIST [*after a pause, choosing his topic*] : The weather, your Majesty, is very—very regrettable.

RULER [*with the divine-right manner*] : Yes, we are much displeased with the weather !

CHIROPODIST : Yet the peasants have prayed for fine weather for the occasion of your Majesty's name-day.

RULER : The prayers of peasants are not always heard. To-day is Friday, is it not ? I have a superstition against signing important documents on Friday. To-night it is the Ultimatum. [*Bored.*] Oh, this war ! What is the feeling among the people ? You have leave to speak the truth.

CHIROPODIST : Your Majesty is too gracious. The people, your Majesty, do not wish for war.

RULER : The Minister of War assures me they do.

CHIROPODIST : The people, your Majesty, will regard the decision of their King as the will of God. [*Bowing over the royal foot.*]

RULER : You are a clever fellow. You might go far.

CHIROPODIST [*with momentary expansion*] : My hump has stood in my light, your Majesty.

RULER : There is a saying of my great ancestor, " It is lucky to have a hunch-back near you."

CHIROPODIST : Yes, your Majesty, the common proverb says : " A hump is a misery to him who hath it, but it fills him of the straight back with contentment."

RULER : We all have our compensations.

CHIROPODIST : Yes, your Majesty, my mother always had a premonition that before I died a great honour would be conferred on me.

RULER : I shouldn't wonder. By the by, I should like to keep you near me to-night. Your hump may bring me luck. I have to make a momentous decision. Now listen to me. I trust you—you have availed yourself of my permission to be truthful. I do not trust all my servants. Will you look to the wine to-night ? [*The* CHIROPODIST *cringes assent*.] The royal Dukes and my Ministers are to dine at my table. Be near me to-night, my little hunch-back.

> [*The* CHIROPODIST *kisses the royal toes in deep obeisance. The* RULER OF A GREAT PEOPLE *exits to his dressing-room. The* CHIROPODIST *rises*.]

CHIROPODIST : It has come—*the* day, *their* day, *my* day ! God of my fathers, keep me from madness. Mother, hold my hand from out of your grave ! You said it should be ! My hunger can be stilled—I can almost straighten my back with pride. [*He crosses himself beneath the image of the Virgin*.] Help me in my hour. There are two roads—which shall I take ? I have learned to flatter—it is my profession—I have walked across the plank—I am there—my ambition, my little ambition can be requited. I have blackmailed the world—I am in its palace. The open road is in front of me at last. I can move step by step, as others have done, nearer the throne—and then, who knows ? But there is another road—the road where humanity toils or trudges—the road my father and mother trod when I was a little child. It was the revolution—my mother was torn from my father's arms—before his eyes she was degraded by the soldiery—then they shot him for an anarchist. This hump of mine—a soldier struck me with his gun—my shoulder shattered. In our exile every night my mother would stroke my back while she prayed that God would straighten me. She starved that she might sprinkle my hump with holy water. And here I am what I am. This is my moment—shall I fall to ease, to comfort, and convenience ? I whose father shrieked for freedom as he fell. This war—I can prevent it. I see it coming on—I am not blind as those that make war—war for the vanity of a King, who made God in his own image. War for greed of commerce. Hundreds, thousands, millions of lives will be lost to satisfy the lust of five men ! Can five hundred years of happiness compensate for one year's spoil of a monarch's sport ? An Emperor of the Shambles declares war to make a madman's holiday. I can hear the yells of the poor deluded men in the trenches—they call it glory ! I can see their stark bodies mangled and twisted in the frozen mud—they call it glory ! I can smell the stench of their decay wafting disease through the land in the spring that is coming—they call it glory ! I can read the outpourings of their hireling professors. I hear Christ's priests chanting their blessings on the holocausts—they call it glory ! The moans of millions of mothers go up to God, unheeded by man. My mind is a mirage of ruined cathedrals, of devastated homes, of spectres of famished peoples—all these I see—they

94

call it glory! My little hand can stay all this. [*He takes from his box the little bottle labelled " Poison."*] Here is my ally—a few drops of this in his liqueur to-night, and it is done. [*He tastes the poison.*] Revenge is sweet! I shall be the undying benefactor of mankind. After all, he is only one man, like myself. He who cuts the corns of a monarch knows the equality of man. Murder—yes. To kill one man is to be a murderer—to kill ten thousand is to be a hero! Strange is the logic of the world! What is he then who murders one to save millions? [*He takes up his paraphernalia and exits.*]

> [*The scene changes to the private dining-room of the great* RULER. *Seated round the table are* PRINCES, CABINET MINISTERS, *a* PROFESSOR, *and a* PRIEST. *It is the end of dinner. There are signs of debauchery. The* RULER, *steeped in wine, gazes before him with pale eyes. Papers are in front of him and an ink-stand, into which he dips his pen irresolutely. The clock strikes twelve.*]

WAR MINISTER : At twelve the decision was to be given—it has already struck.

A PRINCE : Octavian, sign.

> [*The* RULER *hesitates and takes a liqueur from the hands of the now resplendent* CHIROPODIST.]

PRIME MINISTER : It is time to sign, your Majesty.

RULER : I am thinking.

PRIME MINISTER : A King should never think, your Majesty, when he knows his power. It is two minutes past the hour—history is rushing by. You are two minutes less powerful than you were at midnight.

WAR MINISTER : Might is right.

RULER : Is Might always right? [*Turning to elderly* PRIEST.] Father, you have often told me that the true divine right of kings is peace. What did you say in your sermon during the Peace Conference? If the sacred head of the State were to pronounce himself to the world as the leader of Peace—if he will declare himself—if he will proclaim that the highest prerogative of kings—that their true Divine right is universal peace—if in his greatness he will carry this ideal into effect, then he will go down the centuries not only as King of his land, not only as Emperor of the globe, but as the temporal saviour of mankind. Those were your words, father—— Surely God is good.

PRIEST : Yes, your Majesty, very good. But now we are talking war. The needs of your people sanctify the sacrifice of your ideals.

RULER : I am wondering, at what point a King is justified for the sake of his country in sacrificing his ideals. [*He takes another liqueur.*]

PRIEST : His conscience must decide.

PROFESSOR : Ideals are only official ideals when they have concrete foundations. Ideals must be backed by cannon, or left alone. With all submission to your Majesty, man is but a brute—we all devour each

95

other if we can. Our rivals are sunk in the sloth of what is called humanitarianism. The new religion of so-called thinkers and feelers threatens to become a force which may so miseducate the masses, that the workmen of the world may sweep away our own Culture of intellectual materialism by a universal strike for peace. This new movement, whose praise is being sung by poets and seers, must be throttled before its growth shall have become a menace to our fatherland. Already the people are singing the hymns of the new religion of humanity in secret places. Socialism is rife in our land. Now is the moment to crush it for a hundred years and so preserve the ancient dynasty of which your Majesty is God's chosen head, and secure the supremacy of our race.

> [*Great cheers ring out from the Square from many thousand voices. Here and there angry imprecations too are heard. The cheers come nearer and nearer and the jingle-jingle of approaching cavalry is heard below.*]

RULER : Are they cheering me ?

CHORUS OF MINISTERS AND PRINCES [*surrounding the* RULER] : They are cheering the war. They are cheering the Prince—he waves his hand to them.

RULER : Ingrates—is my popularity then waning ?

PRIME MINISTER [*his watch in hand*] : You are twelve minutes and fifteen seconds less popular than you were at midnight, your Majesty.

RULER [*twisting the quill pen in his hand*] : That is the voice of the people !

PRIEST : Vox populi, Vox Dei !

WAR MINISTER : It is the voice of the Army !

> [*The royal* DUKES *and* MINISTERS, PRIEST, *and* PROFESSOR *surround the* RULER, *cajoling, flattering, and brow-beating him in turn. A military band blares out the National Hymn in which a hundred thousand voices join.* RULER *takes the pen once more ; nerving himself to the great effort, he beckons to the* CHIROPODIST, *who makes to serve the liqueur.*]

CHIROPODIST : Now is my moment ! [*Taking from his pocket the little bottle labelled " Poison," he is about to pour it into the glass when a royal* DUKE *approaches him with something glittering in his hand.*]

ROYAL DUKE [*to* CHIROPODIST) : In recognition of your valuable services His Majesty desires me to confer upon you the order of the Golden Lamb, of the second class. [*Pins decoration on his breast.*]

CHIROPODIST [*overcome, mechanically as in a dream, he clasps the bauble in his hand, then hesitates, gasping*] : O Mother, Mother !

RULER : It is war !

CHIROPODIST : Let it rip ! [*He spills the poison on the floor.*]

> [*The* RULER OF A GREAT PEOPLE *signs the Ultimatum. The* CHIROPODIST *shrugs his hump.*]
> THE CURTAIN FALLS.

A LITTLE BELGIAN REFUGEE
By Charles Dana Gibson

By GENERAL BOOTH

SIRE,

Have this consolation in the supreme agony of your dynasty and of your people, that you have enthused with new life and force the great principle that men ought not only to love their country, but their kind.

We of the Salvation Army pray God that His great Salvation may strengthen you ever to honour Him in Mercy and Righteousness.

W. Bramwell Booth.

By PREBENDARY WILSON CARLILE

DAVID has fought Goliath. The victory is not yet, but it is coming. The God of Battles will avenge His shattered houses, the burned and ruined homes, the trampled harvest fields, the slaughtered, outraged, tormented, exiled people, for their cry has reached Him in His Holy Place. Though the time be long, we shall most surely see a new Belgium arise from the ashes of war, purified, made more noble and strong, uplifted by the fiery trial. And although so many of her soldiers, and others of her bravest and best, must sleep until the Archangel shall sound réveillé, yet their blood has not been shed in vain, for their spirit lives for evermore. God give strength to Belgium's King, people, and Allies to fight on in this righteous cause until complete victory crowns the struggle, made holy by the blood and tears of so great a multitude.

Wilson Carlile

By ALMA E. BELMONT

IN expressing my sympathy with the Belgian nation, I am compelled to say there can be no being from any realm calling itself human but feels its very life-blood pulsate with grief and its heart overflow with love for the great manhood of this stricken nation. Words seem poor and lame. This display of courage, this will to carry Right against Might, this defence of country and home, calls for action, imitation.

What is any nation, what are any people doing, who stand idly aside, and by their inertia and fear of injury to themselves, permit murder, pillage, and wilful destruction of a land of peace, of honest industry, of a God-fearing race? What are we doing in Washington? Where is our boasted civilisation? Where is Christianity? Is not our brother being annihilated? Why is not our hand stretched out to shield him? How much longer will the strong and mighty stand aside and see the brave and free trampled under foot by a monster power intoxicated with arrogance? If the United States believes in democracy; if she stands for States' rights; if she believes in the defence of national honour and political liberty, the crime committed against Belgium demands such action from our great Republic that this murderous carnage shall stop.

98

By FLORENCE L. BARCLAY

IN HOC VINCE

To His Majesty the King of the Belgians

SIRE,

AS my contribution to the tribute of universal sympathy and admiration now presented to Your Majesty, I have been asked to write a short story, bearing upon the great events of the past months.

In humbly accepting this privilege, I cannot but be conscious that this is not a time for fiction ; therefore the story which I now have the honour of offering to Your Majesty is fact—true in its main details—given as it reached me, in the sublime simplicity of a soldier's letter from the front.

* * * * *

During the masterly retreat of the allied forces after the battle of Mons, a young British officer was ordered to round up stragglers in a small town, which had just been evacuated by our troops.

There was no time to lose. The enemy, in overwhelming force, was sweeping down upon the defenceless place. Shells were falling on all sides. The distant rumble of a relentless approach drew, every moment nearer.

The young officer, marching his little company rapidly along the deserted streets, crossed a cobbled square, and came upon a municipal building, temporarily converted into a hospital.

He stepped within.

" Any men here, able to march ? " he began—then paused abruptly and looked around him.

There was no question of stragglers, here.

Scores of wounded and of dying lay helpless upon the floor, each where he had been hurriedly placed.

A little party of British Red Cross nurses moved among them, doing their utmost to tend, relieve, and comfort.

While the tall youth in khaki stood silent in the doorway, a shell shrilled over the building, crashed into a house close by, and burst with a deafening noise. A moment of tense silence. Then a Tommy laughed.

" It'll save the doctors trouble, if a few of them things come in here," he said. " Do our amputating for nothing, they will ! "

The Sister in charge of the little band of English nurses chanced to be kneeling near the door, supporting the head of a dying lad. He pushed away the cup she was holding to his lips and gazed into her face, sudden terror in his eyes.

" They won't shoot on the Red Cross, will they, nurse ? " he whispered. " Ain't we safe under the flag ? "

Her quiet smile was reassuring. " Perfectly safe, my lad. Don't you worry. Drink this, and lie still."

Then, looking up, she saw the young officer standing in the doorway.

He raised his hand in salute.

" I suppose there is nothing I can do," he said. " I am rounding up stragglers

99

and marching them out. But nobody here could do any marching. Shall I take a message through for you ? I'll send back help, if possible."

Kneeling there, with the dying boy's head upon her arm, she looked steadily at him, and it struck him that he had never before met eyes so full of a calm and steadfast courage.

" We are all right," she said, slipping a folded jacket beneath the head she was supporting ; " quite all right—doing famously ! "

But the next moment she was beside him in the doorway, and had caught him by the arm.

" Don't go ! " she whispered. " For God's sake, don't go ! I need help ; and you must help me."

" Do you want to get out of this ? " asked the young officer, speaking hurriedly, and very low.

The Englishwoman looked at him.

" Oh, I say, I beg your pardon ! Of course I know you wouldn't leave them. Tell me how I can help. What can I do ? "

" Listen," she said. " There is not a moment to lose. Did you notice the roof of this building, as you crossed the square ? There's a flagstaff and cord, all complete ; but no flag. Do you understand ? No Red Cross flag. And the Germans are beginning to shell the town. You must find me a Red Cross flag, and hoist it, before you go."

The young officer stood beside her, uncertain, perplexed ; dismay in his honest eyes.

" I'm awfully sorry," he said. " But I have no Red Cross flag ; and, for the life of me, I don't know where to get one."

" Then you must make one," she urged. " We have over a hundred wounded men under this roof." She shook him by the sleeve. " Can't you contrive something ? Can't you think of something ? Can't you *make* me a Red Cross flag ? "

The boy stood for a moment in stern thought. All the man in him awoke, eager to meet this woman's desperate need.

His eye travelled slowly round the bare, unfurnished hall. At length it rested on the floor.

Suddenly he started. She saw him hesitate. Then his face grew firm and purposeful.

" Give me half a sheet," he said, " and some bandages."

He helped her to tear the sheet in two.

At sound of the sharp rending, many eyes turned their way.

He spread the sheet upon the floor, and held out his hand for the bandages.

" Give me some pins," he said, huskily ; ' plenty of them. Then leave the rest to me. This is my job."

All at once she knew what he was going to do ; and she, who had times without number faced unspeakable sights without flinching, turned away while, stooping, he dipped the bandages in the blood which lay in pools upon the floor.

100

When she looked again, he was on his knees, carefully pinning the crimson strips across the white sheet.

Her hand flew to her throat, striving to control an irrepressible sob.

He had not recognised her, in her nurse's uniform, but at first sight she had known him, and now vividly recalled the scene of their former meeting—a sunny cricket-field in England; he, in spotless flannels, the hero of the hour, winning a match for his school eleven. She had sat beside his mother and watched her pride in the gay, handsome boy. All eyes had been bent upon him, as he hit out straight and true, made the winning stroke, and carried his bat for top score in the match.

And now . . . As he knelt in his stained khaki, dying eyes watched, in the quiet calm of a strange detachment, the making of that Red Cross flag. Wounded men rolled over, raised themselves on their elbows, and smiled in grim approval.

After that one choking sob she also smiled bravely back at them.

Her flag was ready.

He rose to his feet. "Now then! Show me the way to the roof, please. No—I can carry it. No need for you to touch it, Sister. This is my show."

She stood beside him on the roof.

As he drew the cord taut and fastened it, the breeze caught and unfurled the heavy folds of the sheet, and, slowly opening out, the Red Cross flew, clear and unmistakable, in the sunshine.

She laid her hand once more upon the khaki sleeve.

"God bless you," she said, a tremor of emotion in her quiet voice. "And, when you write home, don't forget to tell your mother of this thing which you have done."

Half an hour later, as he marched his men, under cover of a wood, over the crest of the hill, the young officer stepped out for a moment into a clearing and looked back upon the little town.

German shells were falling to right and left; but above the hospital flew the Red Cross flag, brave in the breeze, bright in the gold of the sunset; and the wounded lay beneath, sheltered by the crimson of their own life-blood.

Florence L. Barclay

By THE RT. HON. THOMAS BURT

HEARTILY do I associate myself with you in expressions of appreciation of the Belgian people and their heroic King.

Thos Burt

By J. C. CHRISTENSEN

BELGIENS Skæbne vækker den stórste Medfólelse i vort Folk. Hvis den belgiske Konge og hans Folk ikke faar Oprejsning for alt, hvad de nu maa lide, da synes vi, at Retfærdigheden trædes ned, og at Talen om den evropæiske Kultur maa forstumme. Vore Fólelser opróres saa meget mere, som vi selv er et lille Folk, der altid maa appellere til Retfærdighedsfólelsen og Hójsindet hos andre.

TRANSLATION by C. A. Bang
The fate of Belgium awakes in our nation the greatest sympathy. If the Belgian King and his people do not get redress for all they are now suffering, then it seems to us that justice is trampled down and that all talk about the European Kultur must become mute. Our feelings are roused so much the more as we ourselves are also a small nation, who must always appeal to the righteousness and highmindedness of others.

By THE Rt. Hon. SYED AMEER ALI

I DESIRE to express my deepest sympathy for the undeserved sufferings of the Belgian nation. I cannot help feeling that Belgium, which had wronged no one and simply stood on her own rights, has been cruelly treated by a powerful nation to whom she might naturally have looked for protection and help. One searches in vain for any justification for the ruthlessness with which the armies of Germany, who claimed to stand in the forefront of the civilised world, have conducted themselves in unhappy Belgium. The country devastated, ancient seats of learning rendered desolate, the people driven from their homes for refuge in distant lands make the heart throb with infinite sorrow and pain.
The sorrow I feel for her is shared by the whole world—no less by Moslems than by Christians.

Ameer Ali

By ARTHUR C. BENSON

ABOVE all we must keep in the forefront of our minds the immense debt we owe to Belgium for her staunch fidelity and for the supreme heroism of her army. Never has a small and peaceable nation risen more nobly to a great occasion. We must ease the strain upon Belgium by every means in our power, welcome and comfort her refugees, house them, feed them, take them to our hearts ; and we must also resolve that when the time comes we must undergo any sacrifice to repay them for their splendid public spirit and their generous sacrifices. We cannot heal their griefs or remove their sufferings ; but we can do all that human kindness and liberality can do to atone for the sickening wrongs which have been done them, and show our gratitude for the loyalty which has indeed been faithful unto death. God bless and reward Belgium !

A C Benson

102

THE BROKEN ROSE

To King Albert

Shy, youthful, silent—and misunderstood
In the white glare of Kinghood thou didst stand.
The sceptre in thy hand
Seemed but a flower the Fates had tossed to thee,
And thou wert called, perchance half-scornfully,
Albert the Good.

To-day thou standest on a blackened grave,
Thy broken sword still lifted to the skies.
Thy pure and fearless eyes
Gaze into Death's grim visage unappalled
And by the storm-swept nations thou art called
Albert the Brave.

Tossed on a blood-red sea of rage and hate
The frenzied world rolls forward to its doom.
But high above the gloom
Flashes the fulgent beacon of thy fame,
The nations thou hast saved exalt thy name—
Albert the Great !

*   *   *   *   *

Albert the good, the brave, the great, thy land
Lies at thy feet, a crushed and morient rose
Trampled and desecrated by thy foes.
One day a greater Belgium will be born,
But what of this dead Belgium wracked and torn?
What of this rose flung out upon the sand? . . .

Behold ! Afar where sky and waters meet
A white-robed Figure walketh on the sea.
(Peace goes before Him and her face is sweet.)
As once He trod the waves of Galilee
He comes again—the tumult sinks to rest,
The stormy waters shine beneath His feet.

He sees the dead rose lying in the sand,
He lifts the dead rose in His holy hand
And lays it at His breast.

O broken rose of Belgium, thou art blest !

Amie Nivault Chartres

By GERTRUDE ATHERTON

WE have experienced so many emotions in America in the course of this terrible war that it would be difficult, had not Germany violated the neutrality of Belgium, to assert definitely what has been our dominant sensation. But, as it is, I think I can safely speak for my countrymen, and state that nothing has so horrified us and aroused our indignation and sympathies as the cruel fate of this valiant little country.

Above all, no chapter of the war, as yet presented to us, has so excited our admiration as well as our profound respect. We are the only country, owing to our geographical position as well as to our facilities, that has been able to look at all sides of the European imbroglio from the beginning ; and propaganda has made no impression whatever upon us. We have had the opportunity to make up our own minds, and, wholly out of order as this would appear in certain quarters, we believe ourselves to be quite equal to this feat without exterior assistance. We know, among many other things, that the magnificent resistance at Liége upset all the long-matured plans of the German War Office, and that had Belgium proved either weak or ignoble, the history of the war would be very different reading to-day.

I venture to say that every town in the United States, big and little, has its Belgian relief society, even if it does not spread beyond the dimensions of the weekly sewing circle ; and that the most consistent democrat in the country takes off his hat to King Albert of Belgium. The Americans are always alert to recognise a MAN, and are capable of being quite indifferent to the niche presented to him by destiny. What he does in that niche is the point. If the result of this upheaval is a great European Republic (I refer of course to the Continent) I feel positive that if the people of the United States of America were allowed to vote, the popular candidate would be King Albert of Belgium.

Gertrude Atherton

THE GLOOMY THICK WOOD
By Kay Nielsen

By ROBERT HICHENS
THE END OF LITTLE BELGIUM

WHEN war began and the German army appeared before the forts of Liége, the world said, " This will be the end of little Belgium." There was deep pity in all hearts, but with it was mingled a certain sense of the impotence of the tiny nation confronted by the brutal might of Germany.

I heard two men in a London street discussing the question of the opening war and the tragic situation of the Belgians. One of them, with a twist of his shoulders, said,, " What on earth can they do ? " The other man replied, " The right thing, and that's what they're going to do."

The little nation had decided. The guns of Liége opened fire. " The martyrdom of Belgium," as it has been called, began. Men, women, and even children were slain. Villages and cities were burned. Thousands were wounded ; tens of thousands were rendered homeless.

And people said, " Unhappy Belgium ! "

Where has that exclamation not been uttered ? Even in Germany it has come from the lips of Germans, and from time to time the ruler of Germany sent to the ruler of Belgium suggestions of peace. " Haven't you had enough of doing the right thing ? " The answer was " No." And more human beings were slain, and more villages were burned, and more families were driven out homeless and starving to live how and where they could.

But people said no more, " Unhappy Belgium ! "

Strangely, as the tragedy deepened and darkened, the world almost ceased from pitying. " Wonderful Belgium ! " we said. And the days and the nights went by, and the roar of battle drew nearer to our coasts. And still the Belgians went on obstinately doing the right thing. Antwerp fell.

The Belgian army avoided capture and retreated. All that " was left of it " was said to have passed into France, and the English papers announced that it would " rest " for awhile to recover spirit and strength after its terrible trials and exertions.

Not many hours later the world knew that it was still in Belgium, attacking the German army with fierce tenacity, and giving splendid help to the Allies. Its King was with it, and its Queen was not far off.

Since then people speak of " Glorious Belgium ! "

The pilgrimage has been accomplished and the peaks have been gained. How then can we pity Belgium ?

I went among the crowds of refugees at Folkestone, and sat in the midst of sick Belgian soldiers. I talked to old and young, to non-combatants and fighting men, and I gathered from my experiences a dominant impression, which was not an impression of despair. Misery of the body there was. But the far deeper, the far more terrible misery of the soul was so seldom apparent that it could not be said with truth, " This is a nation in despair. This is a ruined nation."

The simple fact is that through all this tragedy Belgium has been upheld by the splendid knowledge that " little Belgium " is no more. When the first shot was fired from the forts of Liége a little nation died, but a nation that is great was born.

By JEAN RICHEPIN
AU PEUPLE BELGE ET A SON ROI

EN place de la fausse grande nation, qui prétendait asservir toutes les autres et les modeler à l'image de ses cuistres mâtinés de tortionnaires, c'est toi, vaillant, loyal, généreux et sublime petit pays, dont il faut ériger l'image en exemple à tous les pays. Peuple dont l'histoire est une incessante leçon de labeur, d'indépendance et d'héroïsme ; peuple dont la terre est la plus peuplée du monde ; peuple où fleurissent à la fois toutes les cultures, matérielles et morales, l'industrie, le commerce, les arts, les lettres ; peuple des belles cathédrales, des splendides hôtels de ville, des musées incomparables ; peuple comptant parmi ses fils le poète et philosophe Maeterlinck qui vient de vouer l'âme allemande à l'extermination, et le noble bourgmestre Max qui tint tête à Von der Goltz, et enfin le magnanime Roi Albert, qui dort dans la tranchée après y avoir fait le coup de feu avec ses soldats, le Roi Albert, parfaite incarnation de l'âme belge ; ô peuple des bons travailleurs, des grands artistes, des braves guerriers, peuple de vrais hommes, c'est toi qui portes, à cette heure de l'histoire, dans tes poings de martyr et de héros, le *palladium* de l'Humanité.

TRANSLATION

To the Belgian People and to their King,
In place of that false great nation, which aspired to subjugate all others and mould them in the image of its own ideal—a combination of pedant and inquisitor—it is thine image, O valiant, loyal, generous, and sublime little land, which should be set up as an example to all other countries. People whose history is a perpetual lesson of labour, independence, and heroism ; people whose country is the most densely populated in the world ; people among whom every kind of culture, material and moral, flourishes : industry, commerce, art, and letters ; people of beautiful cathedrals, of splendid town-halls, of incomparable museums ; people counting among your sons the poet and philosopher Maeterlinck, who has condemned the German spirit to extermination ; the noble Burgomaster Max, who held out against Von der Goltz ; and lastly, the magnanimous King Albert, who sleeps in the trenches after fighting in them with his soldiers, King Albert, the perfect incarnation of the Belgian soul. O people of good workers, of great artists, of brave warriors, people of true men, it is you who at this hour of history bear the palladium of Humanity in your martyred and heroic hands.

By ROMAIN ROLLAND

LA Belgique vient d'écrire un chant d'épopée, dont les échos retentiront dans les siècles. Comme les trois cents Spartiates la petite armée belge tenant tête, trois mois, au colosse germanique—Leman—Léonidas—les Thermopyles de Liége—Louvain, comme Troie, brûlée—la *geste* du Roi Albert entouré de ses preux—quelle ampleur légendaire ont déjà ces figures que l'histoire n'a pas encore fini de dessiner ! L'héroïsme de ce peuple qui s'est, sans une plainte, sacrifié tout entier pour sauver son honneur, a éclaté comme un coup de tonnerre en un temps où l'esprit de l'Allemagne victorieuse faisait régner sur le monde la conception d'un réalisme politique, lourdement appuyé sur la force et l'intérêt. Ça a été une libération de l'idéalisme opprimé de l'Occident. Et que le signal ait été donné par cette petite nation a semblé un miracle.

Les hommes appellent miracle l'apparition subite d'une réalité cachée. C'est le brusque danger qui fait le mieux connaître les invidus et les peuples. Combien de découvertes cette guerre nous a fait faire parmi ceux qui nous entourent, et même parmi ceux qui nous touchent de plus près ! Que de cœurs de héros et que de bêtes féroces ! L'âme profonde se révèle—ce n'est pas une âme nouvelle.

En cette heure redoutable, la Belgique a vu soudain surgir le génie caché de sa race. La valeur qu'elle a montrée, dans ces trois derniers mois, frappe d'admiration ; elle ne doit pas surprendre qui a senti, dans l'histoire, couler à travers le temps la sève abondante de ce peuple—petit par le nombre et l'espace—l'un des plus grands d'Europe par sa vitalité de fleuve débordant. L'héroïsme des Belges d'aujourd'hui est le même que celui des Flamands de Courtrai. Les hommes de cette terre n'ont jamais craint d'affronter leurs puissants voisins, rois de France ou d'Espagne—tout à tour héros et victimes, Artevelde et Egmont. Ce sol qu'a détrempé le sang de millions de combattants est le plus fécond d'Europe en moissons de l'esprit. C'est de lui qu'est sorti l'art de la peinture moderne, que l'école des Van Eyck rayonna sur le monde, au temps de la Renaissance. C'est de lui qu'est sorti l'art de la musique moderne, de cette polyphonie qui ruissela sur la France, l'Allemagne et l'Italie, pendant près de deux siècles. C'est de lui qu'est sortie cette superbe floraison poétique d'aujourd'hui ; et les deux écrivains qui représentent à présent avec le plus d'éclat les lettres françaises dans l'univers, Maeterlinck et Verhaeren, sont fils de la Belgique. C'est le peuple qui a le plus souffert et le plus vaillamment, le plus gaiement supporté, le peuple martyr de Philippe II et du Kaiser Wilhelm ; et c'est le peuple de Rubens, le peuple des Kermesses et de Till Ulenspiegel.

Qui connaît l'étonnante épopée, qu'a reprise et chantée Charles de Coster, *les Aventures héroiques, joyeuses et glorieuses d'Ulenspiegel et de Lamme Goedjak*, ces deux gaillards de Flandre, dignes de marcher de pair avec l'immortel Don Quichotte et son Sancho Pança—qui a vu à l'œuvre cet indomptable esprit, rude et facétieux, révolté de nature, qui fronde toutes les puissances, qui traverse toutes les épreuves, et qui en sort toujours, guilleret et riant—celui-là connaît aussi les destinées du peuple qui enfanta Ulenspiegel, et il regarde sans crainte, même aux heures les plus sombres, l'aurore prochaine des jours de richesse et de liesse.

La Belgique peut être envahie. Le peuple belge ne sera jamais ni conquis ni soumis. Le peuple belge ne peut mourir.

A la fin du récit de Till Ulenspiegel, alors qu'on le croit mort et qu'on va l'enterrer, il se réveille :

" Est-ce qu'on enterre, dit-il, Ulenspiegel l'esprit, Nele le cœur de la mère Flandre ? Dormir, soit ; mais mourir, non ! Viens, Nele ! "
Et il partit avec elle, en chantant sa sixième chanson. Mais nul ne sait où il chanta sa dernière.

Romain Rolland

TRANSLATION by Florence Simmonds

Belgium has just written an Epic, the echoes of which will resound throughout the ages. Like the three hundred Spartans, the little Belgian army holding at bay for three months the gigantic hosts of Germany ; Leman—Leonidas ; the Thermopylæ of Liége ; Louvain, burnt like Troy ; the deeds of King Albert surrounded by his valiant men ; what legendary grandeur already encircles these figures, whose tale history has not yet completed ! The heroism of this people who, without a murmur, sacrificed everything for honour, burst like a thunderclap upon us at a time when the spirit of victorious Germany was offering to the world a conception of political realism, resting stolidly on force and self-interest. It was the liberation of the oppressed idealism of the West. And it seemed a miracle that the signal should have been given by this little nation.

Men call the sudden appearance of a hidden reality a miracle. The shock of danger brings out the true character of individuals and nations. What revelations this war has made in those around us, aye, even among those nearest and dearest to us ! What heroic hearts and what savage beasts ! The inner soul reveals itself. It is no new soul.

In this crucial hour Belgium has seen the hidden genius of her race suddenly emerge. The courage that she has shown during the last three months evokes admiration ; it should not surprise any one who, in the pages of history, has felt the vigorous sap of her people flowing through the ages. Small in space and numbers, she is one of the greatest nations in Europe in her abounding vitality. The heroism of the Belgians of to-day is the same as that of the Flemings of Courtrai. The men of that province never feared to oppose their powerful neighbours, the Kings of France or Spain—now heroes and now victims, Arteveldes or Egmonts. Their soil, watered by the blood of millions of warriors, is the most fertile in Europe in the harvests of the soul. From it sprang

the art of modern painting, which the school of the Van Eycks spread throughout the world at the time of the Renaissance, and the art of modern music, of that polyphony which thrilled through France, Germany, and Italy for nearly two centuries. It has given us the great poetic efflorescence of our times ; and the two writers who most brilliantly represent French literature in the world, Maeterlinck and Verhaeren, are sons of Belgium. They are the people who have suffered most and have borne their sufferings most bravely and cheerfully ; the Martyr-Nation of Philip II and of Kaiser Wilhelm ; and they are the people of Rubens, the people of Kermesses and of Till Ulenspiegel.

He who knows that amazing epic re-told and sung by Charles de Coster : The heroic, joyous, and glorious adventures of Ulenspiegel and Lamme Goedjak, those two Flemish worthies who might take their places side by side with the immortal Don Quixote and his Sancho Panza—he who has seen that dauntless spirit at work, rough and facetious, rebellious in grain, always in opposition to established powers, accepting all hardships and emerging from them gay and smiling—believes in the future destinies of the nation that gave birth to Ulenspiegel, and even in the darkest hours will fearlessly await the approaching dawn of great and happy days.

Belgium may be invaded. The Belgian people will never be conquered nor crushed. The Belgian people cannot die.

At the end of the story of Till Ulenspiegel, when they think he is dead, and are going to bury him, he wakes up :

" Are they going to bury Ulenspiegel the soul, Nele, the heart of Mother Flanders ? Sleep, perhaps ; but die, no ! Come, Nele," said he. And he departed with her, singing his sixth song. But no one knows where he sang his last.

By AUSTIN DOBSON
TO BELGIUM

For Right not Might you fought.   The foe,
Checked in his wild World-overthrow,
*   Ravaged, with his remorseless band,*
*   Your ancient fanes and peaceful land,*
Thinking to crush you at a blow !

You are not crushed—as well we know
If you are trodden, 'tis to grow ;
*   Nor shall they fail at last who stand*
*   For Right, not Might !*

GOD speed you, Belgium !   Time will show
How large a debt to You we owe ;
*   To You, through all reverses grand—*
Men stretch to-day a grateful hand :
GOD speed you still—in weal and woe—
*   For Right, not Might !*

Austin Dobson

By EDWARD CARPENTER
TO THE LAND AND PEOPLE OF BELGIUM

AFTER all, dear Land and People of Belgium, do not be dismayed by all this that has come upon you, but have good courage and hope for the future. Mad violence and monstrous warfare may truly have damaged and crippled your body ; but they have not destroyed, and I do not think that they will destroy, your soul.   Perhaps indeed your Spirit will rise all the clearer and more commanding out of this great fire of suffering.

If being small and without material power you have by your devoted solidarity and democratic courage drawn the admiration and respect of all the peoples of the earth, you have already in so doing inspired us with an idea which perhaps neither the science of Germany nor the wealth of England nor the genius of France nor the vast resources of Russia could alone have won for us—the belief that the power which ultimately rules the world proceeds from the generosity of a nation's heart rather than from the force of its armament.

It may be that this belief, born of your act of devotion and heroism, will one day become the salvation of Europe, and bring to its distracted peoples —instead of endless violence and jealousies—the gift of true culture and fraternity.

BY THE LAKE

Poem by Ethel Clifford.

SONG
To be sung by Madame Clara Butt

Music by Liza Lehmann.

My son my little son we two will rest Beside the water red in sunset light. And watch the evening fade, the lake grow grey. Un-til the moon's en-chant-ment fills the night. Who knows what sombre fate stands near us now, What rich-robed destiny no eye can scan. What scented-sandalled Love —? Ah! son of mine, Play not with love when you are grown a man. Feign nothing & love greatly when you love And having chosen, till the end be true. So shall one woman out of all the world Keep faith in

By MISS BRADDON

WHAT can I say of Albert, the King ? What can I think of him, except what we are all saying in these dreadful hours, except what we are all thinking, with thoughts too deep for tears ? To whom can we compare him ? He has no parallel in the story of the nations, no parallel in Romance or Legend. He stands alone on a hideous page of the world's history, and will so stand till the last hour of recorded time, sublime and adorable, with the halo of saints and martyrs round his head.

M. E. Braddon.

By WILLIAM DEAN HOWELLS

THE proposed tribute is part of the debt of honour and reverence which is due from the whole world to that most nobly heroic people and the Prince who has shown himself worthy of them. The tragedy of their great little land is of a pathos matchless in the history of the past ; and in the future when, as we all hope, the military spirit of Germany shall be brought low, I believe the Germans themselves will share our horror of the ruin they have wrought among its homes and shrines.

W. D. Howells.

By SIR H. RIDER HAGGARD

THE desolation of Belgium is perhaps the most appalling world-crime since the wrecking of the Netherlands by Alva. That iniquity was followed by the decay of Spain while, in the end, Holland recovered and grew great in freedom. It may well be that the eternal laws of Justice shall work in such fashion that a like judgment will fall upon the proud head of Germany and that a like triumph awaits her victim.

H. Rider Haggard

By WILLIAM ARCHER

THE BIG AND THE GREAT

> *When they to History's judgment-seat shall come,*
> *Which will shine glorious in the eyes of men,*
> *Huge Germany or heroic BELGIUM ?*
> *Which will be hailed Great, Wilhelm or ALBERT, then ?*

William Archer

By ROBERT W. CHAMBERS

By Cable

GOD bless Belgium and the Allies ! They fight for decency and civilisation.

112

DIES IRÆ
By MAXFIELD PARRISH

By WILLIAM DE MORGAN
A VISIT TO LOUVAIN

FIFTY years ago ! And I who write this had never been out of England, though I was a quarter of a century old !

I decided to go, on an impulse. In those days the *Baron Osy* went from London Bridge to Antwerp. Antwerp was on the Continent and would do —so I went on board the *Baron Osy*. I remember lying on deck all night looking up at the sky. For it was meteor night in August, and phenomena were doing themselves credit, astronomically.

I fell asleep and woke in the dawn, to find the banks of the Scheldt sliding past us, and the river outstripping the banks. Then, Antwerp. I went to an inn on the quay. The keeper thereof was an Englishman who had invented a saxhorn. He had a low opinion of the Continent, but gave me very good boiled beef.

Next day I proceeded to sample Flanders. I can't say which town I tasted first. But I remember being in Bruges, Ghent, Oudenarde, Malines, Louvain, and Ypres. I have now the most vivid remembrance of Bruges, Oudenarde, and Louvain.

Especially the last. For the hotel where I stayed was close by the old Town Hall, and the carillon sounded the hours and quarters all through the night. Every hour it played through

> *Voici le sabre, le sabre, le sabre,*
> *Voici le sabre, le sabre de mon père,*

and, at each quarter, took an instalment ; at the rate of a sabre for the first quarter, two for the half-hour, and the whole line for the three-quarters. The night was hot, and I could not stand the windows shut—so I got very little sleep.

Next day I schemed *causerie*, based on this, with my delightful hostess below. It was an opportunity to practise my French.

" Je ne poovay par dormir parceque du song des cloches. Ils songt assez pour éveiller les morts."

" Plaît-il ? Dites-le-moi encore une fois. Ze bell weck you up ? Ees that ride ? "

I felt my forces demoralised, and merely answered : " We ! "

Marie—she was Marie—turned to a clean old fossil, like a Van Eyck portrait, and said : " Eh—grand'mère, écoutez-ça ! M'sieu n'a pas pu dormir. Il entend toujours les cloches du carillon." To which the old lady, after hearing it a second time, louder, said : " Eh, mon Dieu ! "

I adventured yet a little more into French speech, saying : " Il me prendrait beaucoup de temps à m'accoutumer . . . " and stuck. But Marie helped me out, saying : " A vous y accoutumer ? Oui vraiment ! Mais ici on entend la carillon dès sa naissance—jusqu'à la mort. Je suis née dans la maison, moi ; grand'mère aussi. S'il n'y avait plus carillon, il n'y aurait

113

plus sommeil, ni pour elle, ni pour moi." At least I think that is what came through those white teeth, or very near it, fifty years ago.

And Marie may be turned of seventy if . . . Well!—if German Culture has spared her. But neither she nor any other Louvainoise will ever sleep the better now for the music of the bells, nor any guest of hers be kept awake an hour. For the old hostelry, I take it, is a heap of ashes, and the sound of the carillon is ended for ever.

Wm de Morgan

By PROFESSOR W. J. ASHLEY

BEFORE this fateful year the cities of Belgium had already done great things for humanity. The man who could pass across the market-place from the statue of Van Artevelde, the artisans' hero of the Middle Ages, to the home of *Vooruit*, that noble working-class undertaking of to-day, without a touch of emotion, must have been of sluggish imagination. No one, again, who knew how Ypres, in the age of the Renaissance, taught the whole western world to reform its treatment of the poor, could look without profound respect at the commemorative fresco in its Cloth Hall. Originality of social insight is still alive in the land ; for it was from Ghent that the modern State learned in recent years to think out practicable measures of insurance against unemployment.

It was with thoughts like these—fresh, also, from the reading of Quételet, the organiser and inspirer of social statistics—that I went for my holiday in Belgium, a week before the war. I could not but reflect that it is not to the great States alone, with their vast scientific and administrative apparatus, that the student of social conditions must look for example and guidance. And with me I took one of the volumes of Pirenne, an historical scholar of whom any country might well be proud, and read how Belgium had grown into unity under the House of Burgundy, and how, through the harsh experience of centuries, had been developed the soul of a nation. I was idly wondering whether indeed this was so, and whether Belgium would ever have an opportunity to assert and display its essential independence, when the mobilisation came. Let me confess—I do it with humility—I could not at first take it seriously. I knew there had for some time been a military party in Germany which talked of marching into France through Belgium ; but I was confident German statesmanship would keep this party in check. Germany could never be so unwise, I thought, as to put itself in the wrong with the world by infringing Belgian neutrality. But I was blinded by partiality. The little country was only too well justified in arming itself against the giant. And with tragic rapidity, also, events showed how entirely right Pirenne had been : that out of different races, Romance and Teutonic, combining the characteristics of opposing peoples, had been created a strong and self-reliant individuality among the nations, determined to be master in its own house, ready to risk everything to be itself.

114

By HENRI LAVEDAN

KING ALBERT

LE Roi Albert est la plus grande figure du temps présent. Il possède l'Immortalité sans avoir eu besoin de mourir et en y étant toujours prêt.

Devenu commémoratif en un jour de sainte révolte, il a conquis, de son vivant, la suprématie de la statue. Le marbre et le bronze, animés, sont en lui, et l'ombre du laurier ne quitte pas son front.

Son nom, quand on le prononce, le place aussitôt debout sur un socle ou l'exhausse au sommet d'une colonne.

Il domine. On le voit de partout, de tous les horizons, parmi les embrasements de la guerre, et au-dessus.

Pur et beau comme une idée, fort et doux comme une foi, calme et ardent comme une volonté, grave comme une réligion, digne comme un devoir, muet comme un chef, sachant se taire, surtout dans le bruit, et puis parler pour dire les seuls mots décisifs qui sont les commandements du Droit et la consigne de l'Honneur, personnage Shakespearien d'histoire et de légende, de rêve et de réalité, de flamme et de mélancholie, d'épopée et de poésie, prince errant et confiant, cavalier de la sublime Croisade qui va, le long des dunes de l'éxil, sans même chercher à deviner où Dieu le conduit par la bride . . . roi-chevalier, roi-paladin, roi simple-soldat qui n'a plus que son peuple épars et son armée en lambeaux, roi sans royaume enfin. . . . Albert sans-terre, Albert de Belgique et de France est à cette heure cependant le plus fameux, le plus aimé, le plus puissant des rois, car c'est sur nos esprits et sur nos cœurs transportés de reconnaissance qu'il *règne*, d'une façon absolue, et qu'il étend son magique pouvoir. Voilà son empire, spirituel et moral, indestructible et sans limites, celui que l'on ne peut pas lui enlever et qui lui restera, même après qu'avec notre aide il aura regagné et agrandi —l'autre, son terrestre royaume.

Qu'a-t-il à faire d'ailleurs, pour le moment, de trône et de palais ? Partout où il passe, il est *chez lui*, reçu, salué par l'amour et le respect des nations civilisées, fières de l'accueillir. Tous ceux dont il a embrassé le premier la cause commune, se regardent comme les fidèles sujets de la Majesté, deux fois sacrée.

Il a pour sceptre son épée sans tache, il est le Héros dont la tête nue et libre dans la bataille dépasse soudain la couronne pour appartenir à l'étoile !

Vive à jamais Albert Ier, notre sauveur, monarque admirable et douloureux, tout resplendissant d'idéal !

Henri Lavedan

TRANSLATION

King Albert is the greatest figure of the time. He has achieved immortality without dying, and by being always ready to die.

Commemorating as he does a day of holy revolt, he has won the supremacy of the statue while still living. Marble and bronze have awakened to life in him, and the shadow of the laurel wreath is always on his brow.

The very mention of his name evokes him standing on a pedestal, or exalted to the summit of a column.

He dominates the scene. We see him everywhere, from all horizons, amidst and above the smoke and flame of war.

Pure and beautiful as an idea, strong and gentle as faith, steadfast and ardent as will, grave as religion, dignified as duty, taciturn as a chieftain, knowing how to keep *silence*, especially in tumult, and then how to speak *the decisive words* which are the commands of Right and the countersign of Honour ; Shakespearean figure of history and legend, dream and reality, fire and melancholy, epic and poem— wandering and trustful Prince, horseman of a sublime crusade, advancing on the dunes of exile, asking not whither God is leading him by the bridle—knight-king, paladin-king, plain soldier-king, who possesses nothing but his shattered army, and his flying people —this King without a kingdom, Albert Lackland, Albert of Belgium and of France, is at present the most famous, the best beloved, the most mighty of kings, for he reigns, an absolute monarch, and holds magic sway over our grateful hearts. This is his empire, spiritual and moral, indestructible and limitless, a domain that cannot be taken from him, and that he will hold even after he has regained *and* extended his terrestrial kingdom with our help.

What need has he at the moment of throne or palace ? Wherever he passes, he is at home, received and saluted by the love and respect of civilised nations, proud to greet him as their guest. All those whose common cause he was the first to defend, look upon themselves as the faithful subjects of his twice sacred Majesty.

His sceptre is his untarnished sword ; he is the Hero whose free, bare head in battle towers above the crown and touches the stars.

Long live King Albert I, our saviour, admirable and suffering King, magnificent in his idealism !

By SARAH BERNHARDT

VIVE le Roi Albert ! Héros pur ! Martyr de la foi jurée ! Il s'est avancé, suivi de son tout petit peuple—si grand ! au devant de la horde innombrable des Barbares.

Refusant tous les dons, rejetant toutes les promesses, impassible à toutes les menaces ; des jours et des nuits il a tenu en échec les forbans allemands. Jamais la France ne pourra oublier sa dette de reconnaissance. Mais l'heure du triomphe approche ; et la Victoire qui tient dans ses mains glorieuses la balance de la Justice donnera au Roi Albert et à son vaillant peuple une large part de territoire allemand.

Et les peuples germains soumis aux belges apprendront enfin ce que sont l'honneur et l'humanité.

TRANSLATION
Long live King Albert ! Spotless hero ! Martyr to his plighted faith ! He went forth, followed by all his little people—the little people that is so great !—to meet the innumerable hosts of the Barbarians.
Refusing all gifts, rejecting all promises, dauntless in the face of threats, for days and nights he held the German freebooters in check. Never will France forget her debt of gratitude ! But the hour of triumph approaches ; and Victory, who holds the scales of Justice in her glorious hands, will give King Albert and his valiant people a large share of German territory.
Thus Germans under the rule of Belgium will at last learn something of honour and humanity.

By SIR F. C. BURNAND

I AM deeply grateful for this opportunity of expressing my heartfelt sympathy with King Albert, his brave soldiers, and his undaunted people, in this time of fearful trial.

By ADMIRAL SIR JOHN JELLICOE
A Message from the Grand Fleet

H.M.S. Iron Duke,
October 29, 1914

I HAVE much pleasure in sending a message from the Grand Fleet. It is this:

That even as Belgium has shown her heroism in deeds, while her sufferings are too bitter to express in words, so those of the Grand Fleet trust to show their sympathy in deeds, knowing that silence becomes them best at all times.

Jellicoe

By SIR EDWARD RUSSELL

SMALL countries have great ideals. Yet the grandeur of the Belgian ideal has been a surprise to the world. It has arrested universal attention. It has inspired universal admiration.

The Belgians always enjoyed the respect of other peoples. But no nation can absolutely avert the influences upon it, or avoid the diversions of its course, which come of associations imposed by dominant personalities, and by compelling events. So it happened that Belgium, though secure in its constitutional liberties and zealous in the exercise of them, encountered moral and political difficulties; had to face awkward exigencies of administration and policy; and did not create for her future expectations of heroism or of higher excellence than commercial enterprise and probity.

Then, without warning, came the temptation, cynical and alluring, of the Berlin Satan. Belgium rang true. She repelled the tempter. She scorned the bait. She elected martyrdom—martyrdom not merely for political theory, not at all for any projects or aims of material well-being—martyrdom for national honour and for international right. Thus, at the touch of a tragic exigency wickedly created, sprang into being a magnificent conscience void of offence before God and man, and an enthusiasm for heroic life and struggle and sacrifice, which glorified every Belgian with the noblest glory; from the harassed King, more than sharing the troubles of his subjects, to the poorest peasant, driven by the villainy of unscrupulous and oppressive hostility to the loss of his all and to the anxious miseries of impoverished and forlorn exile.

A wonderful expansion of traditional sympathy and appreciation has been experienced by the British nation in presence of this noble spectacle. Touching memories distinguish with a new and rare quality of homage the accession of faith in Belgium which Belgian conduct—finer than any possible professions—has produced in our people.

Leopold the First, husband of a darling English princess, grandfather of Albert, King of the Belgians, who is worthy of him, was the Nestor of Europe, the counsellor of Queen Victoria. There were few problems his sagacity could not solve—solve with honour, with dignity. But he never had to confront a problem such as has been solved by his grandson and like-minded statesmen and subjects. The solution has been simple honesty and valour, rising from the level of mere State prudence into the empyrean of highest enthusiasm and virtue.

When Belgium was threatened once before, Mr. Gladstone, wielding as he then did almost absolutely the might of Britain, stood by her side as an honoured and honourably protected small State. But that seemed essentially an act of British power and rectitude—the conscious fulfilment of a grand pledge of redemption.

Now, the sentiment of the situation is different—an interesting contrast—harmonious but in another scheme and key of harmony. Britain indeed has been as true as her great statesman declared she would be to the little kingdom ; but the kingdom, diminutive in size, has shown itself colossal in strenuous honour and public virtue.

Belgium passes into history a splendid paragon of ideal and agonised heroism—heroism for world-wide right as well as a heroism of patriotism—a heroism devoted to the purgation of power from the curse and blight of sinister aggression, of sanguinary rapine, of domineering usurpation.

Edward Russell

By WALTER CRANE

To BELGIUM

We measure not in numbers or in land
The greatness of a people, but the test
Is in the hour of peril, when they breast
Hard strokes of fate, and dauntlessly withstand
A strong and ruthless foe, whose armoured hand,
Foresworn, is stretched to smite and seize their best,
Spoiling a bleeding country, sore distrest,
Laid waste by ravagers with flaming brand.

Through blood and tears, from noble cities razed,
Shines Belgium's name unvanquished, brave and clear,
Resplendent writ in Honour's runes of gold,
Who stood for Faith and Freedom unamazed,
Defending Right, without reproach or fear,
As kindred with the hero-race of old.

By ALFRED CAPUS

ON prend une idée très juste de la valeur et de la noblesse d'Albert Ier, Roi des Belges, si on le compare à Guillaume II. Le plus effroyable carnage des temps modernes, la bataille de l'Yser, nous en fournit l'occasion.

L'Empereur d'Allemagne, c'est le tragédien sinistre—*qualis artifex pereo*, a dit un de ses pairs—qui de son estrade a jeté à ses soldats l'ordre de mourir jusqu'au dernier, afin d'assurer le succès du dernier drame sorti de son imagination, *La Prise de Calais*.

Le Kaiser ne recule devant aucun massacre pour n'être pas sifflé par son peuple. Mais nous avons l'ardente conviction que tout ce sanglant cabotinage finira dans la malédiction et les huées.

Quel contraste avec l'autre rive de l'Yser ! Ici, pas de maître donnant à ses sujets des ordres de mort. C'est un Roi à la tête de son armée, un chef de race.

L'histoire les confrontera tous les deux : le puissant Kaiser qui conduit quatre millions de soldats à la curée, et le jeune Roi vaincu à qui il ne reste plus sur le sol de son pays que la place de dresser sa tente.

Mais déjà l'un et l'autre on peut les mesurer, tant les événements les éclairent d'une tragique lueur. Le premier a fait piétiner par ses chevaux une fière et pacifique nation. Dans sa rage de n'avoir pu la dompter, il en arrive aux plus monstrueux efforts et il espère encore une fois faire trembler le monde avec ses derniers gestes de fureur.

Rien que de simple, au contraire, d'aise, d'humain, chez le jeune Roi de Belgique. Admirable et claire figure qui a surgi tout à coup dans cette crise pathétique de la civilisation pour incarner l'idée de patrie, la Justice et le Droit ! Et on dirait que le destin s'est plu à la modéler en grace et en noblesse afin de l'opposer aux traits rudes et au rictus des barbares.

TRANSLATION

A very true idea of the worth and nobility of Albert I, King of the Belgians, may be gathered by comparing him to William II. The most frightful carnage of modern times, the Battle of the Yser, gives us the opportunity.

*The Emperor of Germany is the sinister tragedian—*qualis artifex pereo, *as one of his peers said—who from his throne gave the order to his soldiers to die, even to the last man, to ensure the success of the latest drama emanating from his fertile imagination : The Taking of Calais.*

The Kaiser flinches before no massacre to avoid the derision of his people. But it is our firm conviction that all this bloody stage-strutting will end in curses and hisses.

What a contrast is to be found on the other bank of the Yser ! No master here giving his subjects orders to die ! Here we have a King at the head of his army, a racial chieftain.

History will confront these two : the mighty Kaiser leading his four million soldiers to slaughter, and the young conquered King, who has nothing left of his country save the spot on which his tent is pitched.

But their measure may be already taken, so clearly have events shed their tragic light on them. The first has trampled underfoot a proud and peaceful nation. In his rage at not being able to subdue it he has resorted to the most monstrous expedients and he still hopes to make the world tremble at his final deeds of fury.

In the young Belgian King, on the other hand, we find perfect simplicity, cheerfulness, and humanity . . . his admirable and luminous figure has emerged suddenly in this pathetic crisis of civilisation as the incarnation of Patriotism, of Justice, and of Equity ! And it may well be thought that Destiny delighted to model him with grace and nobility as a contrast to the rude features and sardonic grimaces of the Barbarians.

A STUDY

By SEYMOUR LUCAS, R.A.

By THE Rt. Hon. AUGUSTINE BIRRELL

WHEN first asked to write something for this book it seemed a pitiful task to sit down and string together a few phrases about a crime, so heinous, so horrifying, and perpetrated under our eyes, as this attempted murder of peaceful and prosperous Belgium. We saw the crime committed and mean to avenge it or disappear. To shed ink over such an episode is hardly apposite—not pens but pikes is the motto of to-day. And yet who would not do anything he could to assuage so great a grief and to compassionate so excruciating a sorrow ?

The other day in Ireland whilst arranging for the temporary occupation of Belgian refugees of a commodious, sturdily built, and happily half-empty country house with a spacious mediæval-looking refectory, large and airy dormitories and a private chapel, in a word, a workhouse, I noticed, standing by and hearkening to our talk, an aged but still bright-eyed pauper leaning over his pitch-fork. Recognising in him the legitimist of the establishment, the Bourbon of the workhouse, I expressed to him the hope that he would extend a kindly welcome to these poor exiles for a few days, whilst other arrangements were being made for their accommodation. The old man replied with eagerness, and with that splendid command of the English language which belongs almost exclusively to the Irish poor, that he was only waiting to rise to the level of a great opportunity. It would therefore seem as if there were a part for all of us—and if it be but a small part, we yet must do it, whilst deploring its littleness.

Belgium had hardly entered into the fullness of her inheritance when this great trouble befell her. In trade and commerce, in industrial life she had indeed already made for herself a great name. She had a Black Country almost fit to compare with our own. Her iron and flax had made her feared in Birmingham and necessary to Belfast, and wherever cheap contracts, honourably performed, are held in reverence, there the name of Belgium stood high in men's regard. A thrifty, practical people, fully abreast with all the troublesome problems of peace we knew them to be, but in other affairs appertaining more to the realm of taste and spirit, Belgium was also fast forging ahead, vying with France and altogether eclipsing Germany. Poets, artists, novelists, philosophers, and theologians, as well as scholars and mathematicians, were carving for Belgium a foremost place among the nations.

One cannot but wonder what will be the effect of this catastrophe upon the genius of Flanders. Blood and tears are powerful ingredients in the manufacture of manhood, and it may well be that in due time those who come after this blood-stained age will be able to see in the masterpieces of the new Flemish art and literature some traces of the heroic resolve and fierce determination to bear cruel misfortune we have witnessed with so much admiration.

121

By JUAN RAMON JIMENEZ

A Su Alteza Real la Princesa María

POR el telégrafo sin hilos, te mando, tierna Princesa, como regalo de Pascua, mi inmenso corazon de hombre bueno. Dígnate recibirlo en tus breves manecitas celestes.

¡Si te pudiera servir de algo! ¿De qué te serviría? ¿De bala, para hacer huir de tus jardines a los terribles rubios rapados de Prusia? ¡Pues carga con él, ¡con mucha pólvora!, un espantable obus del . . . 52!

¿De globo, para espiar el descuido de los campamentos enemigos, ó las secretas marchas contra tu palacio fino? ¡Pues embarca en él tu esperanza, y vete sobre el propio Berlín, que yo soplaré desde aquí, obstinadamente, a do carrillos!

¿De insospechado submarino? Pues échalo al agua honda, y que sea el asombro de las enormes ballenas de hierro que tremolan el negro, el blanco y el rojo por el picado y luctuoso Báltico.

¡Pero no! Todo esto es malo, y poco grato a una Princesa de Bélgica y a un poeta de España. Que me corazón te sirva de semilla de amor. Siémbralo en el campo de este otoño, arado por los cañones; y que, a la más temprana primavera, brote de su sangre el árbol puro de la paz.

Juan Ramón Jimenez

TRANSLATION by Prof. Fitzmaurice-Kelly
To Her Royal Highness the Princess Marie,
Gentle Princess, as a Christmas gift I send thee by wireless telegraphy the whole large heart of a kindly man. Deign to take it in thy small angel-hands.
Could I but be of use to thee! What could I be for thee? A bullet, to drive from thy gardens the fearsome, blonde Prussian plunderers? Well, load with it—not sparing powder!—a terrible 52 howitzer!
An air-ball, to spy out some oversight in the enemy's lines, or his festive march on thy charming palace? Well, place all thy hopes aboard, and be wafted on it to Berlin itself, for I shall blow it resolutely from here, with both cheeks puffed out!
An unsuspected submarine? Well, cast it in deep waters, and may it be the dread of the huge iron whales from which the black, white, and red flutter on the raging, mournful Baltic!
But no! All this is evil, displeasing to a Belgian Princess and to a Spanish poet. Let my heart be for thee the seed of love. Sow it in the cannon-ploughed autumn fields, and in the earliest springtime may there rise from its blood the virginal tree of peace!

By JACK LONDON

By Cable

BELGIUM is rare, Belgium is unique. Among men arises on rare occasion a great man, a man of cosmic import; among nations on rare occasion arises a great nation, a nation of cosmic import. Such a nation is Belgium. Such is the place Belgium attained in a day by one mad, magnificent, heroic leap into the azure. As long as the world rolls and men live, that long will Belgium be remembered. All the human world owes, and will owe Belgium a debt of gratitude, such as was never earned by any nation in the History of Nations. It is a magnificent debt, a proud debt that all the nations of men will sacredly acknowledge.

By SIR OWEN SEAMAN

BETWEEN MIDNIGHT AND MORNING

You that have faith to look with fearless eyes
Beyond the tragedy of a world at strife,
And trust that out of night and death shall rise
The dawn of ampler life ;

Rejoice, whatever anguish rend your heart,
That God has given you, for a priceless dower,
To live in these great times and have your part
In Freedom's crowning hour.

That you may tell your sons who see the light
High in the heavens, their heritage to take :—
" I saw the powers of darkness put to flight !
I saw the morning break ! "

Owen Seaman

By ALFRED SUTRO

I HAVE translated many books of Maeterlinck's—I have wandered, with him, among the canals of Bruges and the fragrant gardens of Ghent. I have seen the places where he dreamed of Pelléas and Mélisande, and the hives of the bees he loved. Through him I learned to know Belgium—to-day all the world knows. Her cities are laid waste now, and her people scattered—but her people will return and rebuild the cities, and the enemy will be dust. The day will come when the War will be far distant, a thing of the past, remote, forgotten—but never, while men endure, or heroism counts, will it be forgotten what the Belgians did for Liberty's sake, and for the sake of Albert their King.

Alfred Sutro

From a poem by Bishop Walsham How

By LUIGI BARZINI (*To represent the "Corriere della Sera," Milan*)

IL Belgio é caduto, ma ha conquistato il cuore del Mondo.

La Causa belga é cosi nobile e cosi pura, che essa assume nella coscienza degli uomini una maestà trionfale che nessuna sconfitta diminuisce. Il Belgio atterrato, calpestato, disfatto dal gigantesco nemico, rappresenta pur sempre qualche cosa d'invincibile : il Diritto. Difendendo fino alla morte la sua libertà, il Belgio ha difeso il più sacro patrimonio di tutti i popoli civili ; si è battuto per un principio che è fondamento di vita in ogni nazione moderna ; ha dato il suo sangue non per un interesse suo ma per un ideale che è anche nostro. La sconfitta lo innalza e lo glorifica come il Martirio santifica e sublima la vittima et la sua fede.

Il Belgio ha messo l'Indipendenza al di sopra dell' Esistenza. Non ha contato i nemici, non ha calcolato la probabilita : ha visto soltanto la giustizia e la santità della sua causa. Ha compiuto questa cosa sublime : combattere senza speranza. Ma, a mano a mano che sotto al galoppo degli Ulani dei territori belgi si staccavano dal corpo vivo della Nazione, e che, sempre più avanti, a ferro e a fuoco, da città a città, avanzava inesorabile la pesante marea teutonica, a mano a mano che il Belgio impiccoliva, noi lo vedevamo più grande.

Avanti al mondo ammirato sorgeva un Belgio nuovo. Dove noi non avevamo visto che un piccolo paese pacifico, inerme, calcolatore, industrioso, trascurabile entità nei conflitti delle nazioni, abbiamo sentito improvisamente palpitare lo spirito di una grande razza. Abbiamo avuto la rivelazione inaspettata di un popolo che, condotto dal suo Re valoroso, riusciva ad assumere delle proporzioni dominanti per il suo eroismo, per la sua lealtà, per la sua generosita, pur perdendo lembo a lembo il dominio sulla sua terra insanguinata. Ai nostri occhi il Belgio ingigantiva sulle rovine stesse del Belgio.

La grandezza di un popolo è nella sua anima.

Noi consideriamo il destino del Belgio con una commozione in fondo alla quale vibra un senso di solidarietà. Milioni e milioni di uomini di ogni nazione e di ogni stirpe si sono sentiti ferire dai colpi inferti spietatamente al popolo belgo e alla gloria secolare della sua cultura, e dividono con lui dolori, passioni e speranze. Si è formato come un sentimento di cittadinanza belga in ogni persona di cuore. E da tutti i Continenti va verso il Belgio un onda immensa di affetto e di augurio come verso una patria ideale devastata e dolente.

TRANSLATION

Belgium has fallen, but she has conquered the heart of the whole world.

The Belgian Cause is so pure and so noble that to the conscience of mankind it has assumed a victorious majesty which no defeat can minimise. Belgium, overthrown, trampled upon and destroyed by her gigantic enemy, still represents a thing invincible : Right. Defending her liberty to the death, Belgium has defended the sacred patrimony of all civilised peoples ; she has fought for a principle which is the basis of life in every modern nation ; she has given her blood, not for her individual interests, but for an ideal which is also ours. Defeat ennobles and glorifies her, as martyrdom sanctifies and exalts the victim and his faith.

Belgium has set Independence above Existence. She

did not count her foes, nor calculate her chances ; she saw only the justice and sanctity of her cause. She understood that sublime thing : to fight without hope. But as one by one, Belgian territories are severed from the living body of the nation beneath the gallop of Prussian Uhlans ; as the heavy German flood rolls on inexorably, carrying fire and sword from city to city ; as Belgium dwindles from day to day, we behold her greater and ever greater.

A new Belgium burst upon the sight of an admiring world. Where we had seen only a little peaceful country, calculating, industrious and unarmed, a negligible quantity in the strife of nations, we heard the mighty stirring of the spirit of a great race. We witnessed the unexpected revelation of a people who, led by their valiant King, assumed commanding proportions by virtue of their heroism, their loyalty, and their generosity, the while their bloodstained territory was torn from them strip by strip. We saw a colossal Belgium rising from the ruins of Belgium. The greatness of a people is in its soul.

We watch the fate of Belgium with an emotion underlaid by a strong sense of solidarity. Millions of men of every nation and of every race have felt themselves wounded by the impious blows dealt at the Belgian people and at the ancient glories of their culture ; these millions share their anguish, their passion and their hopes. A sense of Belgian citizenship has grown up in every feeling heart. And from all continents an immense wave of affection and good will sets towards Belgium as to an ideal land, stricken and devastated.

By THE Rt. Hon. SIR GEORGE REID

THE Parliament and Government of Australia, nobly representing the feelings and wishes of the people of the Commonwealth, have given a magnificent proof of the unbounded admiration and sympathy they feel for the people of Belgium, having authorised a grant of two and a half millions of francs in aid of the movement to lessen the sufferings of that heroic people. The following Resolution was passed by the Australian Senate and House of Representatives :

> *That in the opinion of this House a sum of £100,000 from the Consolidated Revenue Fund should be made payable as a grant-in-aid to Belgium in grateful acknowledgment of the heroic services the citizens of that country have rendered mankind in defence of their national right to live in peace in their own country and that His Excellency the Governor-General be invited to transmit this Resolution to the Secretary of State for the Colonies.*

The Right Honourable Andrew Fisher, M.P., Prime Minister and Treasurer, directed me, as High Commissioner, to hand over the above amount to the Imperial Government, which I did, and the following acknowledgment was addressed to me by the head of the Imperial Government :

> *My dear Sir George,—I have to acknowledge with much gratitude the cheque for £100,000 which you have been good enough to hand to me.*
> *I esteem it a great honour to be the medium for transmitting to our gallant Belgian allies, to alleviate the calamities which the war has brought upon their people, this munificent expression of the good-will and fellow feeling of the Commonwealth of Australia. Yours very sincerely,*
>
> *H. H. Asquith.*

I have never performed a more agreeable duty. They may cease to be allies, and regain their neutrality again, but the Belgians will remain in our loving regard a kindred people whose full rights and national existence the whole British Empire will always defend.

George Reid

126

By THE BISHOP OF LUND

MIDT i trängseln af det ontsäglige elände, som det förfärlige kriget vållar, skönjes dock något, som verkar upplyftande. Från alla länder, som äro invecklade i kriget, komma vitnesbörd om huru folken där enas, som funnes hos dem ej skilda klasser eller partier i en offervillighet, som ej räknar med hvad som offras för ett älskadt fosterlands räddning och ära.

Alltså minst kan den, som står på långt afstånd från krigsskådeplatserna, ana, huru mycket lidande, kriget redan har åstadkommit och kommer att i framtiden medföra, då de många smärtans hvardagar, den, ena efter den andra, måste genomlefvas under erfarenhet af hvad man har förlorat. Medlidande ur hjärtats djup måste man känna med alla de i kriget deltagande folken, men väl mest med Belgiens, som, efter hvad man kan förstå, lidit mest.

Och innerligt önskar man framgång åt hvarje bemödande, som afser att i någon mån aftorka tårarna.

Gottfrid Billing.

TRANSLATION by Edmund Gosse, LL.D.

Amidst the press of incalculable sorrows, of which this terrible war is the cause, there is yet one element which uplifts the spirit as we contemplate it. From every country which is involved in the war, there is evidence that that nation is united, that no schism of class or party exists, but that all citizens are one in accepting every sacrifice which may be required for the safety and honour of the Fatherland.

Little can he who stands afar off from the scene of fighting realise how much suffering has already been caused and must continue to be caused by this struggle. To comprehend the agony one must live, day by recurrent day, under the very experience of anxiety and loss. But sympathy we give, from the depths of our heart, sympathy to all the nations who are taking their part in this war. Most of all to Belgium, which, so far as we can understand, has suffered most.

And inwardly we yearn to see advance every effort made to stanch the flow of the tears.

By RENÉ BAZIN

JE crois que le Roi Albert et la Belgique, en se sacrifiant, comme ils l'ont fait, pour le droit, ont sauvé l'Europe.

Je crois, pour agir avec cette décision, il fallait un roi, c'est-à-dire un chef responsable devant l'histoire, de famille ancienne et préparée.

Je crois qu'il fallait aussi un peuple chrétien, capable de comprendre, d'accepter et de porter l'épreuve.

Je crois que les Alliés devront d'abord restaurer le royaume de Belgique, et que l'exemple donné par le Roi et par le peuple sera glorifié dans tous les pays de civilisation, tant que le monde lira l'histoire.

TRANSLATION by Florence Simmonds

I believe that King Albert and Belgium, in sacrificing themselves, as they have done, for Right, have saved Europe.

I believe, that in order to act with such decision, it was essential to have a King, that is to say, a leader responsible to history, of an old and proven stock.

I believe, that for such action, a Christian nation was essential, a nation capable of understanding, of accepting and of enduring the ordeal.

I believe, that the first duty of the Allies will be to restore the kingdom of Belgium, and that the example shown by the King and his people will be exalted in all civilised countries as long as the world reads History.

127

By CAMILLE SAINT-SAËNS
A Personal Memory of King Albert

C'EST chez un autre ami de la France, chez un autre Albert Ier, chez son Altesse Sérénissime le Prince de Monaco, que j'eus l'honneur d'être présenté à Leurs Altesses Royales le Prince et la Princesse Albert de Belgique, futurs souverains. Grands amateurs de musique, ils me firent le plus gracieux accueil et témoignèrent le désir de m'entendre sur l'orgue de la Cathédrale de Monaco, excellent sans doute, mais de petite dimension, plus apte à l'accompagnement des voix qu'à l'exécution proprement dite. Je fis de mon mieux et l'indulgence des auditeurs fit le reste. Le Prince et la Princesse se promenaient sur la Côte-d'Azur dans une minuscule automobile à deux places, offrant le tableau charmant du ménage le plus uni dans le bonheur le plus parfait. La Princesse était toujours vêtue avec la plus grande simplicité, cette inimitable simplicité des grandes dames. Elle s'amusait beaucoup à prendre des clichés ; j'étais souvent le point de mire de son appareil et j'eus même le grand honneur, à sa demande, de former un groupe avec son noble époux.

Très grand, svelte, élégant, réservé, parlant d'une voix douce avec lenteur, le Roi des Belges déconcerte au premier abord comme une énigme : à qui ne le connaît pas, il semble avoir mis sur son visage, sur toute sa personne, un voile impénétrable. Or, il n'y a pas de voile, il n'y a pas d'énigme. C'est avec le même aspect de froideur et d'insensibilité qu'il se révèle, dans la conversation, causeur le plus affable, homme de premier ordre ayant tout étudié, tout approfondi, à qui rien n'est étranger. C'est à lui, n'en doutez pas, qu'est due la supériorité dont l'armée Belge a donné des preuves si éclatantes dans la lutte inégale et glorieuse contre l'Allemagne. Sans rien perdre de sa tranquillité, le jeune souverain connu jusqu'à présent comme un diplomate, un savant, un artiste, s'est révélé tout à coup, à l'étonnement et à l'admiration du monde, un héros.

Et cette gracieuse Reine, d'apparence si frêle, si délicate, quelle indomptable énergie elle a montré dans son triple rôle de souveraine, d'épouse et de mère ! Quelle grande figure fera dans l'histoire ce couple royal, qu'illumine la double auréole de la jeunesse et du martyre !

Saint-Saëns

TRANSLATION (abridged)

    *   *   *   *   *

Very tall, slender, elegant, and reserved, speaking slowly in a softly modulated voice, the King of the Belgians is somewhat disconcerting and enigmatical at first. To those who do not know him, he seemed to have drawn an impenetrable veil over his face and his whole person. Now, as a fact, there is no veil and no mystery. Under this superficial aspect of coldness and insensibility, he reveals himself in intimacy as the most affable of conversationalists, a man of the highest abilities, who has studied much, gone deeply into all manner of subjects, and knows something of everything. There can be no doubt that to him the Belgian army owes the efficiency of which it has given such brilliant proof in its unequal and glorious struggle against Germany. Without any loss of his habitual tranquillity, the young sovereign, known hitherto as a diplomatist, a scientist, and an artist, revealed himself suddenly, to the surprise and admiration of the world, as a hero !

And the graceful Queen, so fragile and delicate in appearance, what indomitable energy she has shown in her triple rôle of sovereign, wife, and mother ! What great figures this royal couple, glorified by the double aureole of youth and martyrdom, will be in the pages of history !

THE SYMPATHY OF THE CIVILIZED WORLD FOR BELGIUM

SYMPATHY

By J. Montgomery Flagg

By LORD READING, LORD CHIEF JUSTICE OF ENGLAND

HONOUR the Belgians and their King for their fame endureth for ever !

If there existed in the world a formal Court of Public Opinion it would long since have recorded its horror at the cynical contempt of solemn obligations displayed by Germany in the name of " Kultur."

The judgment of the Court would also have expressed its whole-hearted admiration for the courage and fortitude of Belgium under the most terrible shocks ever sustained by any nation. Germany's attack upon Belgium is a tragedy in the history of human progress ; it is a stab at the heart of civilisation. Fortunately Belgium has minimised the gravity of the blow to the human race by the moral grandeur she has attained under the leadership of her King.

Belgium was an unoffending " little nation." She had no quarrel with Germany, her people were industrious, law-abiding, and peace-loving, desiring only to be left alone ; they sought no extension of territory, they claimed no part in the conflict of Great Nations.

That her treaty rights should be respected and her neutrality observed by all the signatories without discrimination was the whole sum and substance of Belgian policy. The most microscopic German eye could not detect in it the least cause of complaint or the faintest trace of offence.

When it appeared that the flagrant breach of faith was to be committed Belgium stood in profound and sorrowful amazement. She had not yet learnt the German doctrine that little nations have no rights. Indeed, so recently as the year 1911, Germany had declared through Herr von Bethmann-Hollweg that it had no intention of violating the neutrality of Belgium. Again, two years later, Herr von Jagow stated that the neutrality of Belgium had been determined upon by international conventions and Germany was determined to respect those conventions. Even in the last week of July 1914 the German Minister to Belgium repeated the assurances of his predecessor to a similar effect. In fact, Germany insisted upon the neutrality of Belgium until it suited its purpose to violate it. The treaty hitherto regarded as a solemn and binding obligation then suddenly became " a scrap of paper." There was and could be no justification for this sudden change, the excuse was necessity in the interests of Germany. Now that so much has happened and Belgium is still the battle-ground, one cannot but think that Germany's interests, viewed apart from her moral reputation, would have been better served had she adhered to her pledges. Belgium, to her eternal glory be it said, refused to be cajoled or bullied into abandoning her sovereignty and independence. She withstood both blandishments and threats and resolutely declined to help Germany to crush France via Belgium. King Albert in this supreme hour of need turned appealingly to us, and our response was swift and direct—it was war against Germany. Belgium counted upon us, she has not counted in vain ; we remain true to our word. The righting of her wrongs has become our sacred duty.

129

Belgium then gave the world its great surprise. Her little army, unexpectedly called to battle, withstood for many days the most carefully prepared onslaught of as powerful and efficient a military machine as had ever been seen. Every day, indeed every hour and even every minute gained, was admittedly of the utmost consequence. The immediate rush into France was stopped for a time. Before they had " hacked " their way through Liége, the apostles of the latter-day civilisation had learnt that the soul of a nation is a very effective fighting force and that this elementary truth had been omitted from the precise methodical calculations of the German machine. They did not forget, because apparently they did not know, in these days of modern scientific development of warfare (the days of Zeppelins, armoured cars and Krupp siege guns) that a small army led and inspired by great and noble thoughts could hold up even the mighty army of Germany. The sacking and burning of Louvain, the destruction of Malines, Termonde, and the many thousand homes of Belgium, the devastation of the whole country, the killing of its inhabitants and the horrible atrocities recorded in the reports of the Belgian Commission, all in pursuance of the policy of " frightfulness," have not added laurels to the brow of Germany ; they will be found in the records where all men may read. Not content with defying the elementary basic principles of International Law by its breach of faith it has further shown its contempt for aught but might by ruthless outrages upon the laws and customs of civilised warfare. It is in this scorn of right and adoration of might that the tragedy of Germany is to be found. Even if it could have won the most triumphant victories its name would still be blackened for ever. But no defeats, however decisive, can take from the Belgian people the memory of their high-souled resistance. No suffering, however poignant, can deprive them of the spiritual elation of their defiance. So long as great deeds are sung and noble purposes are extolled, the heroism of the Belgians and their King will be held up to the wonder of the world.

By GUGLIELMO MARCONI

ALMOST does the war lose part of its horror and sorrow when the unexampled heroism, patience, and fortitude of the Belgians and their King rise in their effulgent light before the mind's eye. The material loss and damage sustained by this brave little nation may perhaps never be repaid, but of her people we might say with Longfellow,

> " *Noble souls through dust and heat*
> *Rise from disaster and defeat*
> *The stronger.*"

130

By GUGLIELMO FERRERO

TERRIBILE è la prova ; ma, dopo le dovute riparazioni, immensa sarà la gloria del Belgio, e grandissima la autorità del suo Re. Offrendosi, martire intrepido, alla rabbia teutonica, il Belgio ha risvegliata la coscienza morale del mondo, che, già troppo stordita dalla cupidigia, dalla sete dei piaceri, dall' orgoglio del sapere e della ricchezza, avrebbe altrimenti corso il pericolo di smarrirsi interamente tra le ferocie e i furori di questa guerra terribile. Il mondo ha capito, vedendo una forza ubriaca d'orgoglio straziare a quel modo un piccolo popolo innocente, che il lavoro, la ricchezza, il sapere, il coraggio, la potenza non bastano : occorre ai popoli, come ai singoli uomini, conoscere pure che cosa è onore, lealtà, giustizia, fede, veracità. Perciò dopo la sicura vittoria delle coalizione, dopo la reintegrazione solenne del popolo belga nella sua terra e nel suo diritto, incomincierà una nuova gloria dell' Europa, e una gloria più bella ; la cui prima pagina sarà stata scritta, con il suo sangue più prezioso, dal Belgio. Eviva il Belgio !

TRANSLATION

Dire is the ordeal, but when due reparation has been made, great will be the glory of Belgium, and great the authority of her King ! Belgium, an intrepid martyr, offering herself to the fury of the Teuton, has awakened the moral conscience of the world—that world which, dulled by cupidity, by thirst for pleasure, by the pride of wealth and knowledge, might otherwise have been reduced to chaos in the furies and ferocities of this terrible war. When the world saw a Great Power drunk with pride, thus torturing a small, in-offensive nation, it understood that work and wealth and knowledge and courage and power are not all-sufficient ; peoples as well as individuals need to know the worth of honour, loyalty, justice, faith, and truth. And therefore, after the certain victory of the coalition, after the solemn restoration of Belgian territory and Belgian rights, a new and fairer glory will begin for Europe ; its first page, written in its most precious blood, will tell the story of Belgium. Long live Belgium !

By SALOMON REINACH

SI la Belgique devait être un jour une province allemande, l'infamie du partage de la Pologne pâlirait dans l'histoire à côté de celle qui n'aurait de nom dans aucune langue. On a pu dire de la Pologne qu'elle expiait ses divisions, ses complaisances pour des voisins puissants et perfides ; que peut-on dire de la Belgique, sinon qu'elle a souffert pour le droit et pour l'honneur, qu'elle a fait de son corps un rempart contre la barbarie et le parjure, qu'elle s'est laissée martyriser et broyer plutôt que de se salir ?

On dira tout cela, comme on le dit à cette heure, mais à une Belgique consolée, vengée et infiniment grande. Ce petit pays de plaines ce sont les Thermopyles de l'Europe ! Et l'homme héroïque qui a l'honneur sans pareil de combattre en roi pour la plus juste des causes, pour la plus noble des patries, dites s'il n'est pas plus digne d'admiration que Léonidas !

TRANSLATION

Should Belgium ever become a province of Germany, the infamy of the partition of Poland would be eclipsed in history by one which no language could adequately stigmatise. It may be not unjustly said of Poland that she atoned for her dissensions, her complaisance to false and powerful neighbours ; what can be said of Belgium, save that she has suffered for Right and Honour, that she has given her body as a rampart against barbarism and perjury, that she has preferred martyrdom and ruin to a stain upon her honour ?

All this will be said again, as people are saying it to-day, but it will be said to a Belgium comforted, a Belgium avenged, and infinitely great. This little country of plains is the Thermopylæ of Europe ! And that heroic man who has the supreme honour of fighting, as a King, for the most just of causes, for the noblest of countries—is he not more admirable than Leonidas !

By RAMON D. PERÉS

QUEL beau rêve d'être l'auteur d'une grande épopée ! Quelle sublime réalité d'en être le héros ! C'est avec une immense pitié que j'ai suivi, les larmes aux yeux, les exploits de ce jeune et vaillant Roi, guidant ce petit peuple de Belgique que l'Histoire mettra à côté des plus admirables nations ; et je suis fier d'avoir pleuré, par la seule raison que comprendre la beauté et l'héroïsme c'est l'humble consolation de ceux qui n'ont pu être des héros ou créer des beautés parfaites, éclatantes.

La Belgique possédait des poètes profonds, touchants, au vol audacieux : elle peut se vanter aussi d'avoir l'audace du beau geste, à la saveur antique, qui offre la vie pour garder l'indépendance et la dignité. L'Espagne a un peu le droit d'admirer cette ombre en deuil qui passe, fière au milieu des ruines, et moi, le dernier des écrivains espagnols, je la salue avec ce grand frisson que fait naître, dans tout homme de cœur, ce qui est grandiose et noble autant que terrible.

Ramón D. Perés

TRANSLATION by Florence Simmonds

How splendid to dream of being the author of a great epic ! How sublime to be actually the hero of such a work ! With tears in my eyes, and an immense pity in my heart, I have followed the exploits of that young and valiant King, guiding the little country of Belgium, which History will rank among the most admirable of nations ; and I am proud of having wept, because to understand beauty and heroism is the humble consolation of those who cannot be heroes, or create perfect and glorious beauty.

Belgium possessed deep and moving poets, capable of daring flights ; she may also claim to have ventured upon a noble and daring action in the antique spirit, offering life itself to safeguard independence and dignity. Spain has some prescriptive right to admire this mourning shadow, passing proudly among the ruins, and I, the least of the Spanish writers, salute her with the thrill that every feeling heart must feel in the presence of what is grandiose and noble as well as terrible.

By M. H. SPIELMANN

THE indomitable people which in the past emerged unchanged and unchangeable from the foreign flood, Spanish, Austrian, and Napoleonic—loyal to its blood and staunch in the maintenance of its historical character—will make good triumphantly to the end. Its Art, the expression of its ideals and the pageant of its soul, has ever remained unspoiled and uncoloured by stranger domination.

Belgium's heroic leader personifies her spirit. Superb in the business of war, he has proved his conviction that the peaceful arts are not less truly the expression of its being. It is fitting, therefore, that acclaimed by the civilised world, idolised by his grateful and admiring country, and consecrated in the lustre of his heroism, he should be destined to become henceforth an immortal theme of his country's Art and Letters.

By M. ALEXANDRE F. RIBOT

LE monde entier s'incline avec respect devant le peuple Belge et devant son chef admirable le Roi Albert, qui donnent un si grand exemple à toutes les nations civilisées. Leur cause est celle du droit : elle ne peut succomber, parce qu'elle a pour elle la conscience universelle.

TRANSLATION
The whole world bows in respectful homage before the Belgian people and before their glorious leader, King Albert, who are showing such a great example to all civilised nations. Their cause is the cause of Right : it cannot fail, because the conscience of the world is one with it.

By PADEREWSKI

THERE is no country where the tragedy of Belgium created more sorrow and indignation than in Poland. Nowhere did the unshakable heroism of the Belgians and their glorious King inspire more sincere admiration, more profound reverence. And yet of these sentiments no tangible proof has been given ; no Polish voice has been heard. Though over one million and a quarter of her sons are under arms, Poland has no right to speak ; though before spoliation her territory was much larger than the whole of present Germany, she is now destitute, poor. The terrific storm which destroyed Belgium's most deserved prosperity is raging furiously over our country, and wherever it comes it leaves nothing—nothing but eyes to weep. There is no land where Belgium's fate has moved so many hearts, but we do not weep, we do not complain, we do not despair. King Albert's and his people's immortal example gives us courage and strength, as it always will comfort, strengthen, and encourage all countries and nations suffering and longing for Liberty.

By SIR FREDERICK POLLOCK, BART.

NEARLY two thousand four hundred years ago the Bœotian city of Platæa was one among the many lesser Greek republics. Her citizens earned immortal fame by taking part with the leading States of Athens and Sparta in the decisive battles, fought on their own territory, which delivered Greece from the fear of Persian conquest and saved the light of Greek freedom and civilisation from being extinguished. To this day the name of Platæa is held in honour throughout the world ; for many centuries that honour was unique. Belgium has now done and dared, for the freedom of modern Europe, as much as Platæa did of old ; she has unhappily suffered far more. As her valour has been equal and her suffering greater, her reward will be no less immortal. Belgium will be remembered with Platæa centuries after the military tyranny of the Hohenzollerns has vanished like an evil dream.

Frederick Pollock

By M. JUSSERAND

LES grands carnages internationaux se faisaient plus rares, les triomphes de la force brutale plus difficiles ; d'aucuns commençaient à les croire choses du passé ; des accords avaient été signés admettant que de peuple à peuple, comme d'homme à homme, pourrait régner la Justice.

Dans le passé, les férocités barbares ; dans l'avenir, la Justice.

A la Belgique, petite par le territoire, grande par le cœur, laborieuse, lettrée, stricte observatrice des traités, pays de travailleurs, de penseurs, d'artistes, aux villes célèbres par leur industrie et leur beauté, Liége où naquit Grétry, Louvain où professa Vésale, Anvers où Rubens mourut, l'alternative fut offerte. Prendrait-elle parti pour le passé ou pour l'avenir ; pour la Force Brutale ou la Justice ? La Force Brutale était debout, avec ses promesses et ses menaces : serait-ce la tranquillité, la prospérité—la soumission ; ou serait-ce les ravages, les exécutions sanglantes, les dévastations, peut-être la mort ?

A la Belgique frémissante, à la Belgique ensanglantée, à la Belgique mourante, mais qui ne mourra pas, trois fois, quatre fois, l'alternative fut présentée. Nulle souffrance, si atroce fût-elle, douleur de femmes et d'enfants, de pauvres gens sans foyer, sans pain, sans autels, ne put changer la détermination de la Belgique et de son Roi ; pour eux il n'y avait même pas d'alternative ; un devoir est un devoir et il faut le remplir, c'est tout. Une fois de plus, et sous nos yeux, David s'est dressé devant Goliath.

Le jour viendra où, avec le reste du monde, l'ennemi même s'inclinera devant tant de vertu, enviera une si pure gloire, qui est celle du Roi comme du plus humble de ses sujets ; Roi digne d'un tel peuple, peuple digne d'un tel Roi.

Jusserand

TRANSLATION by Florence Simmonds

Great international slaughter had become rare, and the triumph of brute force a difficult matter ; some began to look upon them as things of the past ; agreements had been signed, admitting that between nation and nation, as between man and man, Justice might reign.

In the past, there were barbarous ferocities ; in the future there would be justice.

The alternative was offered to Belgium, a country small in extent, but great of heart, industrious, lettered, a strict observer of treaties, a land of workers, thinkers, and artists, of towns famous for their activities and their beauty : Liége which gave us Grétry, Louvain where Vesalius taught, Antwerp where Rubens died. Would she range herself on the side of the Past or of the Present, the side of brutal Might or of Justice? Brutal Might was afoot, with his promises and threats : would she have tranquillity,

prosperity—and submission ; or rapine, bloody executions, devastation, perhaps death?

Thrice, four times was this alternative presented to quivering and bleeding Belgium, a Belgium dying, but not to die. No suffering, however atrocious, not even the agony of women and children and of poor folk without homes, without bread, and without altars, could shake the determination of Belgium and of her King ; for them the alternative did not even exist ; a duty is a duty, and must be performed, that is all. Once more, and this time before our eyes, David rose up against Goliath.

The day will come when with the rest of the world the enemy will pay homage to such virtue, and will envy the stainless glory of the King and of the humblest of his subjects, a King worthy of such a people, a people worthy of such a King.

By THE BARONESS ORCZY

SUNLIGHT AND SHADOWS

Being Extracts from the Diary of Nurse Bellamy of the Voluntary Aid Detachment at Ladrock

October 14th.

MY pet Belgian wounded is making very little progress. His heart doesn't seem to be in it. I don't think that he means to get well. He is so sure that he will never see his wife and little children again. He won't be comforted. I wish I could understand all that he says, but he is a Walloon and hardly knows any French.

October 15th.

To-day we have moved his bed close to the window, and turned it so that he can watch the children when they come out of school. They scramble on the railings and peep in at him, and he smiles at them, oh! so pathetic-ally : it nearly breaks my heart to see him.

October 16th.

I got on better with my poor wounded Walloon to-day. I know now that his wife and five little children were at Liége, and why he is so sure that he will never see them again. When I try to comfort him, he just looks at me with utter hopelessness in his eyes, and makes with his limp, emaciated hands pathetic gestures indicative of the horrors which he has seen— women murdered—children mutilated : " J'ai vu, madame ! " he says, " j'ai vu ! "

October 17th.

Great excitement at Ladrock to-day. Five hundred Belgian refugees arrived early this morning and we at the V.A.D. are hoping that there will be a few among them who speak a word or two of English and Flemish or Walloon, so as to act as interpreters between us and our wounded.

October 18th.

My poor wounded Walloon has been watching the children through the window all the morning, and I watched with him for a little while. One wee mite ran and brought some flowers which she held tightly squeezed in her very grimy little fist, and these she held out at arm's length to the sick man whom she could see through the window. The sight of the flowers and of the child seemed to cheer him. He smiled and I opened the window to take the flowers from the tiny tot. The autumn air was very sweet and balmy, and when I had thrown the window wide open, I stood aside so that my wounded man should get a good view of the street and a good whiff of fresh air. I watched him as he gazed out in his usual pathetic, hopeless way, when suddenly a change came over his face. Before I could stop him he had half-raised himself out of bed and stretched out his arms ; then he fell back with a loud cry upon his pillow.

The sister ran to my rescue and I left her to look after him for a moment, whilst I—moved by a strange intuition—leaned out of the window and looked out into the street. A melancholy little crowd of men, women, and children were wandering aimlessly along the pavement, turning wide, inquiring eyes on our quaint little provincial street, so typical of an English country town.

135

One woman, young and more than ordinarily wretched-looking, had four little children clinging to her skirts, and she carried a wee mite, wrapped in a ragged shawl in her arms.

It was instinct in me, of course, intuition, inspiration—whatever you like to call it. Certain it is that I threw every thought of order and regulations to the wind, left my post in the ward, ran out into the street, and to the poor woman's utter astonishment and bewilderment seized her by the hand, and dragged her incontinently into the V.A.D. hospital and into our downstairs ward. Nobody said a word, for the same inspiration or intuition had come to every one of us then : every one of us at least who happened to be watching our poor Walloon soldier at the moment. The woman gave one cry and ran straight to him, the children scrambling after her as best they could. But he made no sound, only stretched out his arms and she fell sobbing across the bed.

October 29th.

My pet Belgian wounded has just left the hospital to go to a convalescent home in the neighbourhood. His wife and children will remain in Ladrock during that time. He got well wonderfully quickly, and she is such a nice little woman. The children are darlings, and he is so proud of them.

Emmuska Orczy

By EDWARD H. SOTHERN
ELISABETH OF BELGIUM

Silent we look on her all pitiful
Who, stooping to the lowly Mary's mien,
Rises beyond the station of a queen ;
And, humble, wears a saintly aureole.
Laving the bleeding feet and making whole
The battle-broken ; and the plague-struck clean.
No diadem shall match the myrtle green
Which crippled hands shall proffer as their dole.
Poor shattered hearts and weary weeping eyes
Pulse to thy name and search the dark for thee.
The famished and storm-beaten scan the skies
And cry, as from a second Calvary,
" My God ! My God ! Hast thou forsaken me ? "
" Day breaks ! He is here." Thy steady voice replies.

Edward H. Sothern

136

By MAURICE DONNAY
"LES ELISABETH"

J'aime le carillon dans tes cités antiques,
O vieux pays gardien de tes mœurs domestiques,
Noble Flandre où le nord se réchauffe engourdi
Au soleil de Castille et s'accouple au midi.

VICTOR HUGO

CERTES, avant la grande guerre, nous aimions la Belgique, pour son histoire si souvent mêlée à la nôtre ; pour son peuple hospitalier et doux ; nous l'aimions parce qu'entre les nations armées, elle symbolisait les sécurités de la paix. O Belgique ! pays noir du charbon, blondes plages de sable, vertes prairies, eau dormante des canaux, et tant de vieilles villes aux merveilles d'architecture : belles cathédrales qui sont comme de la pierre solide ; hauts beffrois dont les cloches convoquaient à l'approche de l'ennemi les bourgeois qui pendant des siècles se sont unis de combattre pour leurs libertés ; vieilles halles, hôtels de ville, dont la façade, pierre et or, nous montre le style gothique dans sa richesse et son élégance tertiaires, silencieux béguinages. La Belgique ! elle est, comme l'Italie, une des patries sacrées de l'Art. Trois vers latins disent à peu près : Bruxelles s'enorgueillit de ses nobles hommes, Anvers de ses richesses, Gand de ses cordes au col (les bourgeois de Gand), Bruges de ses belles pucelles (*famosis puellis*), Louvain de ses docteurs et Malines de ses fols. Mais ces villes s'enorgueillissent aussi de Sainte Gertrude, de Saint Bavon, de Saint Rombaud et de leurs grand'places, et des anciennes maisons des corporations, et des grands vieux maîtres Hubert et Jean Van Eyck, Roger Van der Weyden, Jean Memling, Gerard David, Quinten Matsys, artistes admirables dont les œuvres immortelles sont une invitation à la sincérité patriote et passionnée. Immortelles ! peut-on écrire ce mot, quand les Barbares sont là ? Combien de monuments ne sont déjà plus que des ruines ? Malines, Louvain, vos gais carillons ne tinteront plus dans l'air léger. Guerre abominable où il faut pleurer les hommes et les pierres !

Oui, nous aimions la Belgique, avant la grande guerre ; mais, aujourd'hui, nous la chérissons, nous l'admirons. Artistique, commerçante, industrielle, pacifique, tout à coup elle devient guerrière, se lève pour défendre son droit, notre droit, le Droit ! Son territoire n'est pas vaste, mais elle n'entend pas que l'étranger le traverse sans coup férir ; son armée n'est pas nombreuse : elle l'oppose pourtant aux hordes innombrables. C'est la nation martyre qui accepte, s'il le faut, de mourir pour sa foi. Le lion de Brabant surgit : Liége protesta de tous ses canons. Liége tomba, puis Namur ; Bruxelles est occupé, enfin Anvers ! O douleur ! Mais les Belges résistent toujours. Cette résistance fait l'admiration des peuples, elle n'inspire que de la rage aux Allemands, incapables de respect, d'estime, de générosité, de ces sentiments qu'ont les hommes qui même dans les fureurs de la guerre, restent dignes du nom d'hommes. Les villes et les villages

137

sont pillés, incendiés, les femmes, les enfants, les vieillards massacrés, ou bien mutilés avec des raffinements que n'imaginerait pas un gorille, l'animal lubrique et féroce. D'ici sous les yeux des rapports, des témoignages : quand on les connaîtra, quand ils seront publiés, dans leurs détails, le monde entier, le monde civilisé, frémira d'horreur !

Cependant un roi jeune, charmant, et brave est dans les camps, dans les tranchées, à côté de ses soldats : une reine brave et vaillante est auprès de son chevalier.

*　　　*　　　*　　　*　　　*

Cet après-midi, dans un Paris d'automne voilé de brumes, un groupe de jeunes gens parcourt les rues. L'un d'eux porte le drapeau aux trois bandes verticales, rouge, jaune, noir, les couleurs de l'ancien comté de Brabant et de la Révolution qui triompha en 1789 du régime autrichien. A l'extrémité de la hampe un bouquet de roses blanches. Le peuple de Paris regarde avec un sourire et une émotion fraternels ces jeunes gens qui demain seront soldats, combattront pour la délivrance de leur pays.

Il y a un siècle, en 1813, les conscrits de France s'appelaient les " Marie-Louise." Conscrits et volontaires belges, du nom de votre reine, devenue belge par la couronne et par le cœur, ne pourrait-on pas vous appeler " Les Elisabeth ! "

Maurice Donnay

TRANSLATION (abridged) by Florence Simmonds
" THE ELISABETHS "

I love the chimes of thine antique cities,
O ancient land that guards its homely manners,
Noble Flanders, where the frozen North warms
itself in the sun of Castille, and mates with the South.

Even before the Great War, we all loved Belgium, whose history has so often mingled with our own ; we loved her gentle and hospitable people ; we loved her, because in the midst of nations in arms, she seemed to symbolise the safety of peace. O Belgium ! land of dark coalfields, of golden, sandy beaches, of green meadows, sleepy canals, and countless ancient towns full of architectural marvels : beautiful cathedrals, like masses of solid stone ; lofty belfries, whose bells rang out at the approach of the enemy to summon the burghers who for centuries had united to battle for their liberties ; old markets and town halls, whose façades of stone and gold show us the Gothic style in its tertiary grace and richness ; silent nunneries. Belgium, like Italy, is one of the sacred fatherlands of Art. There are three Latin verses which tell us something of this sort : Brussels is proud of her noble men, Antwerp of her wealth, Ghent of her " cords round the neck " (her burghers), Bruges of her fair maidens (famosis puellis), Louvain of her doctors, and Mechlin of her madmen. But these cities were also proud of Saint Gertrude, Saint Bavon, and Saint Rombaud, their stately squares, their ancient guildhalls, and their Old Masters, Hubert and Jan Van Eyck, Roger Van der Weyden, Memling, Gerard David, and Quinten Matsys, admirable artists whose immortal works are an invocation of real and passionate patriotism. I say immortal works, but is this a word to use when the Barbarians are in possession? How many monuments are now but heaps of ruins ! Mechlin and Louvain, your gay chimes will vibrate no more in the clear air ! Abominable war, which has made us weep alike for men and stones !

*　*　*　*　*

This afternoon, a group of young men were marching through the misty streets of autumnal Paris. One of them bore a flag with three vertical stripes of red, yellow, and black, the colours of the ancient County of Brabant and of the Revolution of 1789 which overthrew the Austrian régime. At the top of the standard was tied a bunch of white roses. The people of Paris looked with a smile and with brotherly emotion at these youths, who to-morrow will be soldiers fighting for the liberation of their country.

A century ago, in 1813, the French conscripts called themselves the " Marie-Louises." Belgian conscripts and volunteers might you not be aptly christened " The Elisabeths," after your Queen, who has become a Belgian by her crown and heart?

HYMN
[HOMAGE TO BELGIUM, 1914.]

Edward German.

By VISCOUNT ALVERSTONE

I HAVE for many years enjoyed the friendship of Belgians distinguished in science, jurisprudence, literature, and educated culture. My heart has been deeply grieved at the cruel fate which has befallen their nation ; the result of what is, in my opinion, the most wicked action of which any civilised nation has ever been guilty.

Germany can never remove this stain on her honour.

To every subject of the Belgian Crown, and to their gallant King, I humbly offer my true and heartfelt sympathy.

Alverstone

By SIR HIRAM S. MAXIM

IN the midst of the wickedest and most disastrous war that the world has ever known, we cannot fail to realise that civilisation demands the complete elimination of that system of government whereby it is possible for one selfish man, merely for the gratification of his own vanity and ambition, to cause such an infinite amount of suffering and destruction.

All honour and glory to the gallant Belgian nation and her brave and noble King !

Words fail to express the great sympathy that must be felt everywhere for the terrible sufferings that have been inflicted on this valiant little country in her noble struggle to maintain her honour and independence.

> " *Thou shalt live, thou shalt prosper*
> *Through thy united unity.*
> *With heart and voice in chorus we unite :*
> *For King, for Law and Liberty.*"

Hiram S. Maxim

By H. A. L. FISHER

SO long as a respect for right survives upon this planet it will be remembered that the King of a tiny nation once vindicated the public law of Europe against the brutal aggression of a mighty Power, knowing well that it would be for his heroic subjects to sustain the first furies of the attack and to endure the certain cruelties of a temporary conquest. It will be remembered that the capture of forts and cities, the defeat of armies, the murder of women and children, the burning of a cathedral and a library famous throughout the civilised world, neither weakened his resolution nor broke the spirit of his people, and that he and his fought on tenaciously to the end, saving the honour and liberties of Europe by their act of desperate and inspired valour.

H. A. L. Fisher

140

CHARLEROI
By Joseph Pennell

By MAY SINCLAIR

FIELD AMBULANCE IN RETREAT

Via Dolorosa, Via Sacra

I

A straight flagged road, laid on the rough earth,
A causeway of stone from beautiful city to city,
Between the tall trees, the slender, delicate trees,
Through the flat green land, by plots of flowers, by black canals thick with heat.

II

The road-makers made it well
Of fine stone, strong for the feet of the oxen and of the great Flemish horses,
And for the high waggons piled with corn from the harvest.
But the labourers are few ;
They and their quiet oxen stand aside and wait
By the long road loud with the passing of the guns, the rush of armoured cars
    and the tramp of an army on the march forward to battle ;
And, where the piled corn-waggons went, our dripping Ambulance carries home
Its red and white harvest from the fields.

III

The straight flagged road breaks into dust, into a thin white cloud,
About the feet of a regiment driven back league by league,
Rifles at trail, and standards wrapped in black funeral cloths. Unhasting,
    proud in retreat,
They smile as the Red Cross Ambulance rushes by.
(You know nothing of beauty and of desolation who have not seen
That smile of an army in retreat.)
They go : and our shining, beckoning danger goes with them,
And our joy in the harvests that we gathered in at nightfall in the fields ;
And like an unloved hand laid on a beating heart
Our safety weighs us down.
Safety hard and strange ; stranger and yet more hard,
As, league after dying league, the beautiful, desolate Land
Falls back from the intolerable speed of an Ambulance in retreat
On the sacred, dolorous Way.

May Sinclair

141

By WINSTON CHURCHILL

ONCE translated into action, the ideas of Von Treitschke and of Bernhardi have been repudiated by the civilised world. These ideas are peculiarly repugnant to Americans. Militarism, and monarchy which has in it any touch of absolutism, have always incurred on this side of the Atlantic suspicion and dislike ; a growing, enlightened portion of our population perceive an added menace to the world's peace and true prosperity in that militant, nationalised commercialism which has been so deftly woven by the Germans into the monarchical principle, in the hope of prolonging the life of that principle. This nationalised commercialism, moreover, is a logical consequence of the economic doctrine of enlightened self-interest, the adaptability of which to modern conditions is being seriously challenged. In this mongrel code of modern Germany not only is Nietzsche misrepresented—but even Christ. It is a code in which the finest spirits of Germany find no place ; nor does it contain any hint of that new economics of human needs for which the world owes so large a debt to Germany herself.

For the German people the people of America, like the people of Great Britain, have a sincere affection. The obsession of such a nation is difficult to understand. We can only hope that the time is not far distant when Germany will awake to her better self.

The British Empire is fighting as truly for the German people as for her own. Under the circumstances, our pity and sympathy for the Belgian people, and our indignation at what we must deem the ruthless destruction of that nation to satisfy German militarist, commercial, and monarchical ambition are overwhelming.

I can conceive of no greater rebuke to this ambition than that manifested by the contributions which to-day are being poured out by the world at large to care for those Belgians who have so ruthlessly and so needlessly been deprived of their homes and possessions. No aid was ever given more willingly. We give it, indeed, as a just debt to a gallant people to whom the world owes, and will ever owe, more than it can pay—to a people who have sacrificed their all in the cause of progress and liberty.

The name of their heroic sovereign, King Albert, will henceforth be written with those of the great liberators of the world.

Winston Churchill

By MARGARET DELAND

Liberty-loving America is stirred by the profoundest sympathy for the families of the gallant Belgians who are giving their lives that Liberty may live ; she has only admiration for the King who, in the face of overwhelming odds, is leading his people where honour calls. She can never forget her debt of gratitude to the martyr-nation whose King and people are giving all that they possess that the Spirit of Freedom may not wholly perish from their land.

Margaret Deland

142

By G. K. CHESTERTON
THE LARGEST WINDOW IN THE WORLD

IT is a terrible thing to have trod on battlefields before they were fought. It gives a man a cold and ghostly shiver, as of being the babe unborn. But I was a boy, and almost a babe, when I was first in Belgium; and I can only write down the reality that impressed me then. Beyond some streets burning with brass-ware which seemed perpetually on sale, almost out of sight of the great Belfry, there is (or was) a sort of museum of the great Memlinc. Among the pictures was one which even as a boy I could not forget: and very few poets or prophets can even imagine how much a boy can forget. It was a picture in which the window seemed hardly wider than the crack of a door. Yet through that crack the human eye could almost, in the strong Scripture rhetoric, take the wings of the morning and abide in the uttermost parts of the sea.

And I remember a voice near me speaking, in an accent that was neither French nor Flemish nor my own . . .

" You see how narrow the windows were in those days."

I did. I also began to see, for the first time, how narrow the minds are in these days. I looked at the little window again; and I thought it the largest window in the world. Simply because the aperture was narrow, I knew the landscape was wide. If modern artists had swept it in a larger style, I should have noticed it no more than some hundred miles of wall-paper. Then note not only the pride of the small nation, but the pride of the rich peasantry. Look from the slit of a turret in Cumberland or Calabria and there is a chance that your eye may strike something slightly depressing. But any strip of Belgium will be a string of jewels. Note, thirdly, that the thinness of the outlook is largely due to the thickness of the walls. There is no trace of what vulgar people call " a vista " : the house does not open up indefinitely to the world outside. The man of Memlinc sees the world from his window. But it is still the final fact that the window was his window and the world is not his world. I should have thought it, then, quite inconceivable that any one would assail that turret. But I should have thought it equally inconceivable that any one should fail to defend it. A man living in such a house might almost shut the front door to protect the beauty of the window.

I have never been in Belgium since; I have never met any who could possibly be in connection with any revolutionary or anti-national idea. Yet for me Belgium has continued to mean that small field of vision, making certain so vast a field of prosperity. That keyhole is still the largest window in the world.

Since then I have not seen the country, except in frightful photographs. I have gradually begun to understand what was meant by my alien friend when he spoke of the needless narrowness of the mediæval window. To judge by the photographs, he has broadened architectural effects very much; he has blown window into window and enlarged the premises; he has left long lines of street in which it is impossible to say whether he has combined the windows that exist, or spared the windows that never existed. He cannot make anything except a window ; for a window is simply a hole. When he has blown everything to atoms, when no stack or stone stands about us for many miles, he will say, with an insane simplicity : " I have made the largest window in the world."

G. K. Chesterton.

By SIR E. RAY LANKESTER

I ESTEEM it a high privilege to be allowed to express to His Majesty King Albert and to the heroic people of Belgium my heart-felt admiration for their incomparable valour. With a courage and self-sacrifice unparalleled in history they held back, only a few weeks ago, the treacherous attack on their country by the German hordes—a deed by which the designs of the ruthless Enemy of Europe against Britain and our beloved ally France were effectually checked and frustrated. The barbarous cruelties in which the defeated Germans have vented their rage on Belgium have filled every Briton with the desire to assuage her anguish and to exact from William of Prussia the full price of his unspeakable brutality.

All humanity glories in the revelation to it, at this crisis, of another man, a man who is worthy to be King, a King who has fought side by side with his people, ready to give his life rather than lose his honour, to die rather than accept the shameful bribes of the German bully.

My knowledge of Belgium and my friendship with her people date from the time when fifty years ago, intent on geological studies, I visited the excavations in progress for the new fortifications of Antwerp and was the guest in the old University buildings of Louvain of the great naturalist Professor P. J. Van Beneden. His son, a youth of my own age, became my life-long and intimate friend. In later years, when Edouard Van Beneden had become professor at the University of Liége and attained world-wide celebrity by his discoveries in biological science, I stayed with him in that flourishing city and he, in turn, was my guest in Oxford and in London. I have had many friends among Belgian naturalists, some connected with the wonderful museum in Brussels, others who sought collaboration with me in my own laboratory—and I have the honour of being a foreign Associate of the Royal Academy of Sciences of Belgium. Thus, I do not write here with an admiration and affection newly called into being but as an old and favoured comrade, who is familiar with the glories of ancient Flanders and the splendid achievements of her sons in science and in art. I venture to render my homage to King Albert and his people as one who knows and loves the unconquerable spirit, the unswerving fidelity, of the free and independent Belgian folk.

E. Ray Lankester

144

By DON ANTONIO LÓPEZ MUÑOZ

EJEMPLO REDENTOR

PARA escribir una página en honor de Bélgica, para llorar por sus hijos muertos, por sus fábricas deshechas, por sus campos arrasados, por sus monumentos destruidos, por sus hogares sin familia y sus familias sin hogar, por la augusta paz de su trabajo perdida, por sus horizontes de esperanza cerrados a la luz, por la aterradora soledad de sus almas sin refugio, sin término en sus dolores, sin el bendito patrimonio de sus tradiciones afectivas, único sostén en las humanas luchas, basta ser hombre. Sí, basta ser hombre ; y es en todo caso doble estímulo ser hijo de España, la patria del Quijote que encarna la exaltación del ideal y vibra con ecos de amor en todos los ámbitos del mundo, para rendir homenaje a un pueblo que por el ideal sacrifica la vida, dando un ejemplo que hará sentirse a la Humanidad redimida y orgullosa.

Rey Alberto, desdichado tú, que aun ofreciendo el pecho en las avanzadas, no has podido impedir que tu nación sea degollada en lucha desigual ; pero dichoso tú, que con la espada en la diestra eres la imagen viva del heroismo tallada en carne por la inspiración genial de tu pueblo, como serás mañana la muerta imagen inmortal tallada en piedra y en bronce por la admiración de los siglos. Y dichoso también, porque al tiempo mismo que tú fuiste caudillo en la brecha, la Reina ha sido en el hospital y en el campo el ángel de la piedad ; símbolo tú de la fortaleza en el combate, símbolo ella de la ternura y de la paz del alma que constituía la característica del culto y laborioso pueblo belga ; dándose así testimonio de cómo el trabajo civilizador, lejos de amenguar la virilidad del temperamento, lo dispone al arranque en toda ocasión gloriosa.

Bélgica, nación de héroes y de mártires, has caido al golpe de la fuerza ; pero sobre la fuerza que hunde has puesto la dignidad que glorifica ; has caido ; pero no has muerto ; y aunque no revivieras sobre tu tierra adorada, revivirás eterna en el amor de todos los corazones. La conciencia humana será tú hogar y tu templo.

TRANSLATION by Prof. Fitzmaurice-Kelly

To be a man is enough to write a page in honour of Belgium : to lament her slaughtered ones, her ruined industries, her devastated meadows, her demolished monuments, her homes untenanted, her homeless children, the august peace of all her efforts vanished, the horizon of hope cut off from light, the appalling solitude of her unsheltered population whose woes are illimitable, and who are bereft even of the sacred inheritance of fond traditions—the one mainstay in human contests. Yes, to be a man is enough. And, in any case, for every son of Spain, the land of Don Quixote, incarnating the exaltation of the ideal and thrilling with echoes of love throughout the world, there is a double obligation to pay homage to a race that surrenders life for its ideal, and sets an example which will make humanity feel proud and conscious of its redemption.

Unhappy thou, King Albert, who, though imperilling thy life in the vanguard, hast not availed to save thy nation from succumbing in an unequal conflict ! Yet happy thou who, sword in hand, art the living image of the heroism made bodily manifest by the dominant inspiration of thy people ! To-morrow thou shalt see its mute, immortal form sculptured in stone or bronze for the admiration of all ages ! Happy too, inasmuch as, at the very time when thou wast foremost in the breach, thy Queen was the angel of mercy in the hospital or field ! Thou the symbol of valour in the battle ! She the symbol of that tenderness and peace of spirit so characteristic of the

refined and hardworking Belgian people ! And thus proving that civilising labour, so far from diminishing manliness of soul, fosters its impetuous fire.
Belgium, nation of heroes and of martyrs, thou hast fallen beneath the blows of Might, but above that overwhelming force thou hast set a glorifying splendour!

Thou hast perished, but thou hast bequeathed us an example of how men die in the cause of justice ! Even if thou wert not to be born anew on thy consecrated soil, thou wilt live for ever in the love of all men's hearts. The conscience of humanity shall be thy dwelling and thy temple.

By SIR NORMAN LOCKYER

MEN of science have been accustomed to look upon German methods in education and applied science as worthy of imitation, and in my address as President of the British Association in 1903 I pointed out the serious danger we were running in allowing them to outstrip us in these directions. But we now know that their guiding spirit was not the advance of civilisation but the provision of means for the destruction of all who opposed the inordinate ambition of the ruling class for world power.

The story of the bravery which King Albert and his nation have shown in sacrificing everything rather than honour will be handed down from generation to generation, a monument to a great people.

The present is one of misery and suffering beyond all precedent, brought about by unexampled brutality in waging war by means of destruction, rapine, cruelty, and lies rather than by the best generalship and fighting power. But a time will soon come when Belgium will rise like a Phœnix from its ashes and she may console herself with the thought that even in the distant future it will be recognised that the history of the world has been ennobled by her deeds and her determination to defend her honour. Her efforts will be chronicled as a brilliant chapter in the annals of the human race.

Norman Lockyer

By SIR FREDERICK TREVES

> *With grave*
> *Aspect he rose, and in his rising seemed*
> *A pillar of state ; deep on his front engraven*
> *Deliberation sat, and public care ;*
> *And princely counsel in his face yet shone*
> *Majestic though in ruin.*—PARADISE LOST.

Frederick Treves

146

BERCEUSE HÉROÏQUE
BY
CLAUDE DEBUSSY

148

By ANTONIO MACIEIRA

E julgareis qual é mais excelente
Se ser do mundo rei, se de tal gente.

LUIZ DE CAMÕES, Luziadas, Canto I, estancia 10

A " BARBARIE multiplicada pela sciencia " ou seja a acção alemã, assim definida ha pouco e com rigor scientifico por *M. Boutroux*, tornou agonisante o grande povo de uma pequena nação. Essa *barbarie civilisada* faltou á fé dos tratados, trucidou, incendiou, matou, depois de tentar o suborno do povo laborioso que entregue ao seu progresso, sem ambições externas, não dando razão a odios nem odiando, jamais pretextara a feroz arremetida do *imperialisimo divinizado*.

Nem rigor de formulas, nem deveres de humanidade, nem simples piedade, nem intuitivo sentimento artistico ; ou seja : nem direito, nem ideias liberaes, nem lagrimas de inocentes, nem respeito pela beleza—nada poude detel-a !

N'essa tragedia formidavel que abriu ferida larga e funda em todas as almas piedosas, existe a mais admiravel lição que um povo pode dar em fulgurações de honra—lição que de ouvil-a a alma se arranca em convulsões de dôr, e que de pensal-a o espirito se alevanta na mais profunda e afectiva e grata das admirações.

Grande povo na paz como na guerra, a Belgica ! Nação de herois que embargaram essa avançada fulminante que tentou esmagar a vida da França —a vida de nós todos—e impedir o esforço protector da Inglaterra, digna colaboradora na defeza das nossas vidas ! Nação estremecida, relicário das maiores dôres sofridas sob o peso das maiores injustiças !

Sobre esse glorioso Paiz caem as sagradas bençãos dos que amam a liberdade querendo-a para todos, dos que adoram a belesa das ideias e da forma com a artistica paixão das almas simples.

A Belgica é a nação exemplar da dôr glorificada.

O imperialismo alemão não venceu a Belgica, porque a dôr dos povos não se vence ; a dôr dos povos fortalece-os.

Onde quer que esteja o valoroso Rei dos Belgas, está a Belgica ; onde quer que esteja essa figura de nobre Rainha que errou pelo territorio da sua Patria sempre bem perto de cada alma dos epicos lutadores que a defendiam, está a Belgica.

E se a Belgica existe na guerra moralmente mais querida, mais amada, mais respeitada, mais forte com o seu territorio devastado, os seus monumentos arrasados e o seu povo sem lar, na paz, que não tardará, ela ficará moral e materialmente o padrão das nações que sabem lutar por sua honra, em defeza propria e das grandes causas da humanidade.

Cidadão de uma Patria gloriosa que ama o seu territorio como a propria carne ; republicano de inteligencia e de sentimento, esta homenagem que presto comovidamente ao bravo e alto representante do Grande Povo, ao

150

rei Alberto, é aquela mesma, que, no fundo—embora com melhores palavras, e decerto, espero bem, em breve com actos—lhe prestaria e prestará a nacionalidade portugueza.

Antonio Macieiras

TRANSLATION *by Florence Simmonds*

And you will judge which is the better :
To be King of the world, or King of such a people.

LUIZ DE CAMOËNS, Lusiad, Canto I, l. 10.

" *Barbarism multiplied by science,*" *as M. Boutroux has defined German action with scientific precision, has brought the pains of death upon the great people of a little nation. This " civilised barbarism," repudiating a solemn treaty, has proceeded to kill, burn, and massacre, after a vain attempt to suborn an industrious people, wholly absorbed in progress, cherishing no external ambitions, giving no pretext for hatred, and hating no one—a people who had never given the least justification for the savage onslaught of deified Imperialism.*

Nothing sufficed to avert this—neither the duties of humanity, nor pure pity, nor artistic sentiment—in other words : equity, liberal aspirations, the tears of innocence, beauty itself !

From the dire tragedy that has so deeply wounded all souls capable of pity, we may learn the most admirable lesson of untarnished honour that any people could have given ; to listen to the lesson is to have one's heart torn by pain, to think of it is to feel one's spirit uplifted to the most intense, the most effective, and the most grateful of admirations.

Great is Belgium, both in peace and war ! Heroic nation, which has arrested the thunderbolt aimed at the life of France—our common life—and foiled the attempt to baffle the protecting effort of England, *worthy collaborator in the defence of that common life ! Nation groaning and travailing, the shrine of supreme suffering brought about by supreme injustice ! Blessed be this glorious country by those who love liberty, desiring it for all, by those who worship the beauty of ideas and of form with the art-inspired passion of simple souls !*

The Belgian nation is the prototype of Pain glorified. German Imperialism has not conquered Belgium, for triumphs cannot be achieved over a people's pain ; a nation grows stronger by suffering.

Wherever the brave King of the Belgians is, there is Belgium ; wherever we find that noble Queen who has wandered over the territory of her kingdom, always close to the souls of its heroic defenders, there is Belgium.

And if in war Belgium seems morally more beloved, more respected, and mightier, with her devastated fields, her ruined monuments, and her homeless people, in the peace that will come before long, she will remain the model for all nations who fight for their honour, for their own defence, and that of the great causes of humanity.

Citizen of a glorious land, who loves his country as his own flesh and blood ! Republican in heart and mind ! This homage I pay with deep emotion to the brave representative of a brave people is one with the homage which the Portuguese nation offers him in better terms—will offer him shortly, I hope, in terms of action !

By GEORGE H. PERLEY (*representing the Canadian Government in London*)

ALL honour to the boundless courage of the Belgians and their brave King ! They have given to the world the most splendid example of a small country fighting against enormous odds in defence of its soil and for the principles of freedom and liberty. We can never repay them for their tremendous sacrifices, but it is our duty to drive the enemy from Belgium as quickly as possible and to punish him for his ruthless slaughter and wanton destruction.

By WILLIAM CANTON

IT has now been for months, it will be for centuries, one of the glorious things of history, that in this world-war it was one little nation, which had no ambition to serve, which had much to lose, but which was intrepid and unbribable, that flung itself across the first rush of a great empire, and held it in check single-handed. It was overborne by the weight of brute millions ; its storied cities, its prosperous villages, its fruitful fields were looted, drenched with blood, ruined by fire ; yet it fought on alone, with unshaken faith ; it was never defeated. Its very reverses were material and moral triumphs ; the success of its amazing courage and tenacity is visible to-day in the gigantic battle-front of the Allies from the sea to the Vosges.

Every drop of blood that Belgium has shed has been a testimony to the heavenly Powers ; a vindication of the world's ideals of liberty, justice, mercy, honour, chivalry ; an appeal to the conscience of Christendom. Yes, and every outrage of the drunken and unclean hordes of Berlin has been a cry to Heaven for vengeance. Our material debt to Belgium is enormous ; our moral debt is beyond calculation. And these are not our debts only, but the debts of the world.

The heroisms of old days rise before me—Leonidas at Thermopylæ, our own Byrhtnoth holding Blackwater ford below Maldon, the Swiss peasants with their boulders and tree-trunks at Morgarten. They are dim shadows beside this little people, whose women and children are heroic. I see their King in the trenches, sharing the dangers and hardships of his comrades in arms, inspiring them with the cheerfulness of an indomitable soul. And I see another king, frantically fussing from front to front under the protection of the Red Cross, and sleeping at night, when he *can* sleep, in a huge iron cage encircled by a swarm of Uhlans and a guard of airmen.

His iron cage ! The words evoke another memory. Out of the far past I hear the voice of a greater Kaiser, scared by a dream of the night :

> *Behold, a watcher and an holy one came down from heaven ; he cried aloud, and said thus, Hew down the tree, and cut off his branches ; shake off his leaves, and scatter his fruit : let the beasts get away from under it, and the fowls from his branches :*
> *Nevertheless leave the stump of his roots in the earth, even with a band of iron and brass, in the tender grass of the field ; and let it be wet with the dew of Heaven, and let his portion be with the beasts in the grass of the earth : Let his heart be changed from man's, and let a beast's heart be given unto him ; and let seven times pass over him.*

The same watchers and holy ones still look out of the clouds. Surely no man, whatever his love of peace and horror of war, can consent to any end of this unprovoked and barbarous aggression but " a fight to the finish " ; and when the tribunal of the nations sits in judgment, to any plea of mistaken pity or of high policy, of diplomatic expediency, or of kinship to stay the hand of justice and retribution.

A GLASS OF WINE WITH CÆSAR BORGIA
By The Hon. John Collier

What shall be said of this sorrowful nation eating the bread of the exile? What need there be said? The " tears of these things " grip the heart of two hemispheres. These houseless men and women and children are in a bitterly literal sense our blood-brothers and blood-sisters and little ones. They are the kinsfolk of all right-minded and true-hearted people. All the material help they need will be given gladly and gratefully. But they need more—the uplifting of the heart by admiration, by honour, by the cheering strength of personal affection.

A new spring will come to the ravaged land; new cities and villages will replace the old. Lament not overmuch the great and beautiful art that has vanished—it lives everlasting in the heavens and in the memory of men. And the dead—weep for them, but with a proud joy that they died for all that makes life worth living.

O King, O people, the sound of a great bell is ringing over your land—a mightier bell even than " Roland "; it is the bell of eternal justice and right, crying that there is " Victory in the land."

William Benton

By MRS. W. K. CLIFFORD
To His Majesty King Albert

GREATLY daring I venture to address you, while I bow my head, as all the world does, Sir, to you and to your crucified country—crucified, as Christ was, to save others. You are bereft of the temporary deckings of your Kingship, and your people of all they possessed; and yet so much has come to you and them, though it is obscured now by the wreckage of many homes, the vanishing of many lives, by all the calamities that a cruel dishonourable enemy could bring.

For a splendid immortality is yours—even here in this mortal world—and none can take it from you. Your enemy came in shining armour that is for ever blackened with crime and stained with blood; but your armour none can hurt nor time disfigure: it is woven of Truth and Honour, of Courage and Endurance, and through the centuries it will shine to those who sit in darkness, to those who doubt or hesitate. You have made the whole world better because of all that you have put into it. And for thought of you, and your people, many will become great, and brave deeds will be done; and thousands whose courage would fail will take heart, feeling that they must be worthy of a world in which you lived, that as you kept faith so in turn will they; and whether their swords be strong or weak they will fight and endure, as you have done, without flinching. Do you realise it all, Sir, the divine example you have set us; does it help you a little, does it comfort you, to know that our hearts go out to you as we reverently bow our heads, to you and your Queen, to your soldiers and your dead?

Lucy Clifford

153

By HJALMAR BARNTING

MIN personliga hyllning åt Belgien betyder så litet. Därför vill jag berätta om mitt folk.

Sverge var förutbestämt att se med tyska ögon på världskrisen. Tyskarna äro våra stamfränder, dit går våra förbindelsers tätaste nät, från Tyskland har svensk odling starkast påverkats. Våra ledande klasser beundra tysk ordning och plikttrohet, de underordnades disciplin och landets väldiga materiella uppsving. Och vår arbetarrörelse växte som tysk planta, innan den slog helt rot och formades om efter den svenska jorden ; när Sverges arbetare år 1909 kämpade sin storstrejks väldiga försvarskamp, gåvo oss tyska bröder ett mäktigt stöd. Och naturligt lystrade Sverge till den första tyska förkunnelsen : tsardömet är fredstöraren, Europas fara—vi svenskar ha ju sett på nära håll Finlands besvurna självstyrelse förintas, medan de ryska militärförläggningarna där ökats och vårt eget land utsatts för närgånget ryskt spioneri.

Men så kom folkrättsbrottet mot Belgien. För oss, som själva vilja till det yttersta bevara vår neutralitet, kändes det som en stöt mot eget hjärta. Det vände hela stämningen hos vårt folks djupa leder, och det var som om t.o.m. i den mest tysksinnade delen av vår press stämmorna förlorade sin självsäkra klang. Och ju hårdare framfarten blev, ju mer genomtåget tog karaktär av en härjande erövrares invasion, desto starkare växte svenska hjärtans sympati för det lilla tappra folk, som höll ut för rätt och frihet oförskräckt, utan att räkna krossande övermakts tal.

Måhända vann tysk strategi, trots att den missräknat sig på motståndet, någon fördel av inbrottet över folkrättsskyddat land. Men det finns makter i världen, som på längden betyda mer än strategi.

Må kortsynt småklokhet räkna ut : Belgien borde ha stannat vid ett första motstånd, tillräckligt att markera dess neutralitet. Nej, mitt i förödelse och förtvivlan måste det svaras : nu först, när Belgiens unga nation visat att den tagit fädernas offermod helt i arv, nu först är dess frihet, dess säkra plats bland folkens brödrakedja oryggligt tryggad för tider som komma. Att Belgiens hela folk, ej minst dess socialistiska arbetarklass, satt in så oändligt mycket mer än lama ord-protester, det har gjort dess sak helig för alla män och kvinnor världen runt, vilka ännu akta rätt och frihet.

Därför : hell Belgien ! Och min varmaste önskan som svensk måste bli denna : skulle en dag, mot vad vi hoppas och till trots för den folkfred vi söka förbereda, vårt eget neutrala land hotas av våldet, må vi då veta att endräktigt följa Belgiens lysande föredöme, segerbetryggande mitt i skenbar undergång ! " Hällre dö än bli slav," säger ett friesiskt ord. Det är samma anda som i vår svenska biskop Thomas' sång från 15 : de seklet :

> *Frihet är det bästa ting,*
> *som sökas kan all världen kring,*
> *ty frihet följer ära.*

Hjalmar Branting

154

My personal homage to Belgium means so little. Therefore I will speak about my people.

Sweden was predestined to look upon the world-crisis with German eyes. The Germans are our kinsmen. To them goes the closest network of our communications, the strongest influence on Swedish culture has come from Germany. Our upper classes admire the German orderliness, sense of duty, the discipline of the subordinate classes among the people and the enormous material growth of the country. Our labour movement grew as a German plant before it took root in and was reshaped for the Swedish soil. And when the Swedish workers fought their great defensive battle in the general strike of 1909, their German brethren gave them a powerful support. Naturally enough Sweden was ready to listen to the first German proclamation : "Tsarism is the peace disturber, the danger of all Europe." We Swedes had had the opportunity to see how the confirmed self-government of Finland had been destroyed, we had seen how troop concentrations in that country had been increased, while our own had been subjected to a system of intrusive Russian espionage.

But then came the crime against International Law, the violation of Belgium's neutrality. For us, we who intend to defend to the very utmost our neutrality, it was like a thrust directed against our own heart. It changed altogether the feelings among the broad ranks of our nation. Even in the most Germanophile part of the newspaper press it seemed as if the voices had lost their note of self-confidence. The more ruthless the methods became, the more the "march through" assumed the character of a ravaging conqueror's invasion, the stronger grew the sympathies in Swedish hearts for the little brave nation that undaunted held on for right and liberty without counting the crushing superiority of numbers.

Perhaps German strategy, in spite of it having miscalculated the resistance, won some advantage through the invasion of an internationally protected country. But there are powers in the world which after all count more than strategy.

Short-sighted wiseacres may calculate that Belgium ought to have yielded after a first resistance sufficient to mark her neutrality. No, in the midst of destruction and despair, it must be said : Only now, when the young Belgian nation has shown how thoroughly she has taken over from her ancestors the heritage of courage and power of sacrifice, only now is her liberty, her place in the chain of brother-nations irrevocably secured for all time. That the whole Belgian nation, her socialistic working class not least, has staked so much more than feeble protests of words has made her cause sacred to all those men and women in the whole world, who still value justice and liberty.

Therefore : Hail to Belgium ! And my sincerest wish as a Swede must be this : if in spite of the hope we cherish and the peace between the nations we are trying to prepare, the day should arrive, when our own neutral country is threatened by violation, may we then unanimously follow the magnificent example of Belgium, securing victory in the midst of apparent ruin. "Rather die than become a slave," says a Frisian proverb. It is the same spirit as in the song from the fifteenth century by our Swedish Bishop Thomas :

> Liberty is the best of all things
> that can be sought in the whole world,
> Because with liberty comes honour.

By ERMETE NOVELLI

> *" Godi ! barbarie." Poiche se' sì grande*
> *Che per Mare e per terra batti l'ali*
> *E per l'Inferno il tuo nome si spande !*

UNA nube nera, densa, minacciosa, incombe sulla terra gittando sovr' essa rovinosa pioggia di sangue e grandine di fuoco ! . . . Guerra ! . . . Quanti morti . . . quanti lutti . . . quante lagrime d'insanabile dolore ! . . . Guerra . . . Guerra ! . . . In queste angosciose tenebre nelle quali brancoliamo attoniti e smarriti, un punto luminoso rimane, a speranza di un domani di Sole ; il sublime Martirio del Belgio, unico forse nella storia dei popoli ! Martirio che insegna ora e insegnerà ne' secoli futuri come un popolo conscio della forza dei proprii diritti possa cambiare uno sconfitto nella più grande gloriosa Vittoria ! . . .

Ermete Novelli

155

LAMENTATION

BY
P. E. LANGE-MÜLLER

158

By VINCENTE BLASCO IBÁÑEZ

EL REY CABALLERO

EN España llamamos asi a Alberto I de Bélgica.

Nuestra época ofrece dos clases de soberanos a la atencion publica.

Los hay que estudian sus gestos y palabras como si fuesen actores, adoptando posturas teatrales, haciendo mil cosas a la vez, queriendo en todos los instantes recibir el incienso de la admiración y asombrar a las gentes. Quemarían medio mundo si esto pudiese dar nuevo brillo a su gloria neroniana. En fuerza de locuras pueden llegar a infundir miedo, pero nunca amor ni verdadera admiración.

Alberto I no ha pensado jamás en deslumbrar a nadie, no conoce las actitudes escénicas, su deseo era vivir en una paz laboriosa rodeado de su pueblo de trabajadores, y en todos los momentos ha seguido una vida recta, tímida y larga a la vez, como las líneas de su cuerpo. Es un héroe sin desearlo ni buscarlo ; el héroe más grande y más simpático de todo el siglo XX. Es " el rey caballero."

El resorte de su heroismo no fué el amor a la gloria ni tampoco las ambiciones de conquista. Fué el deber, el cumplimiento de la palabra dada, el respeto de los propios derechos, todas las virtudes modestas y sólidas de las gentes de bien.

Plegándose a las exigencias del fuerte hubiese sido feliz. Es cierto que esta felicidad la habría pagado con la deshonra ; pero hay tantos deshonrados triunfantes ! . . . Alemania agradecida a su obediencia le habría sostenido siempre. Tranquilidad, abundancia, protección ; la vida sumisa y bien cebada del animal doméstico que reconoce un dueño. Pero a estas ventajas positivas que hubiesen tentado a los más, prefirió los viejos idealismos en los que aun creen algunos ; el honor, la libertad, el odio al atropello, la independencia de su patria.

*   *   *   *   *

Este general improvisado ha sabido hacer la guerra como no la harían muchos profesionales. Su tenacidad heroica al frente de un pueblo pequeño y valeroso, ha quebrantado desde el primer momento el monstruoso empuje alemán.

Gloriosa epopeya la de Bélgica y su rey caballero ! Muchos de sus conciudadanos murieron. El vive porque la Muerte no quiso su persona. Manejó como simple artillero los cañones de Amberes bajo una lluvia de metralla. Tomó el fusil de un soldado é hizo fuego en las tricheras de la infantería. Los belgas han perdido sus casas ; él casi ha perdido su reino.

No recordeis como modelos inimitables de caballería a aquellos reyes sin corona, de la Edad Media, vagabundos y desgraciados, que la poesía y el drama han hecho interesantes. Nuestra época de vulgar positivismo tiene figuras más románticas.

Alberto Sin-Tierra vale más que todos los monarcas *Sin-Tierra* de la historia. Estos perdieron la corona por hechos de familia y ambiciones de conquista.

159

El rey caballero se ve sin reino por la libertad, por el derecho, por no haber consentido los atropellos del fuerte.

Y con la noble tristeza del héroe repelido pero jamás derrotado, que sabe que la razón va con él, se mantiene en un rincón de Flandres, al frente de un puñado de bravos, para que vea el mundo como lucha un hombre pacífico convertido en guerrero por las exigencias del honor, come perece, si es preciso, el primer ciudadano de una monarquía democrática en defensa de su dignidad.

*   *   *   *   *

Un periodista lo vió a la caida de la tarde, asomado a una ventana del Hotel de Ville de Furnes, contemplando la puesta del sol, soñando tal vez.

Parecía triste. Contemplaba melancólicamente el astro moribundo.

Iba a llegar la noche y con ella la sombra, las horas de incertidumbre, las horas de desesperación.

Pero la noche no es eterna y después de ella viene otra vez el día, con un nuevo sol.

Vicente Blasco Ibáñez

TRANSLATION (abridged)

THE NOBLE KING

This is what we in Spain call Albert of Belgium.

Our period offers to public attention two different types of monarchs.

Some there are who rehearse their actions and words as if they were actors, adopting theatrical poses, trying to do a thousand different things at once, seeking at every moment to receive the incense of the admiration of the people and to astonish the popular mind. They would burn down half the world if that could add to their Nero-like glory and make them more renowned. The force of their madness may succeed in inspiring terror, but never in exciting affection or genuine admiration.

Albert never thought of dazzling any one ; he is not familiar with theatrical poses ; his wish was to live in peace and industrial prosperity, surrounded by his hard-working people, and at all times he has led a good and upright life, gentle and liberal at the same time, like his own physical traits. He has become a hero without wishing or seeking to become one ; the greatest and most attractive hero of the entire twentieth century. He is " the noble King."

*   *   *   *   *

This sovereign, so suddenly called to lead his army, in spite of his inexperience, was able to conduct the war as many old campaigners could not have done. His heroic tenacity at the head of a small but brave nation was able from the very first moment to drive back the terrible German onslaught and to break its might.

What a glorious epic is this episode of Belgium and her noble king ! Many of his subjects perished. He still lives because Death wished to spare him. Like a simple gunner, he served the guns of Antwerp under a hail of lead from the machine guns of the foe. Taking the rifle of a soldier, he fought among the ranks of his own infantry as their comrade.

The Belgian people have lost their homes, he has almost lost his kingdom.

Do we not recall those inimitable models of chivalry, the uncrowned kings of the Middle Ages, wandering and unfortunate, but renowned in poetry and drama ? Our period of ordinary material prose holds still more romantic heroes in its records.

Albert the Landless is worth more than all the Landless Monarchs of history. They lost their crowns through deeds of their own or of their families, desire of conquest and further power. The Noble King sees his kingdom lost for liberty, for justice, for brave resistance to the dictates of overbearing force.

And with the noble sadness of the hero who may be defeated but is never conquered, who knows that he has right on his side, he stays in a corner of Flanders, at the head of a handful of courageous souls, enabling the whole world to see how a man of peace fights when he has been forced to become a warrior through the necessities of honour, how, if it be needful, the first citizen of a democratic monarchy will know how to die in defence of his own nobility.

*   *   *   *   **

A journalist caught sight of him one afternoon as the twilight fell, leaning from a window in the City Hall in Furnes, watching the setting sun, dreaming perchance.

He appeared sad, and he watched the sinking God of Day with an aspect of deep depression.

The night was coming, and with it darkness, the hours of uncertainty, the hours when despair is nigh.

But the night is not eternal, and when it is gone, there comes another day, bringing with it a new sun.

ST. MICHAEL OF BELGIUM
By J. J. Shannon, R.A.

By ANATOLE FRANCE
LE ROI ALBERT

IL est né avec l'âme d'un héros et d'un juste. Dès son avènement au trône, il était estimé (j'ai pu m'en assurer) de tout son peuple, respecté de tous les partis politiques et sociaux, et de ceux-là même qui, d'ordinaire, se montrent le moins disposés à s'incliner devant la prérogative royale. Il inspirait confiance à tous. On lui reconnaissait un esprit de droiture, de sagesse, de justice, de douceur. On aimait cette simplicité qui lui était naturelle et qui chez un prince revèle presque toujours un caractère supérieur à la fortune.

Très jeune encore, une terrible épreuve fondit soudain sur lui et sur son peuple et lui fournit l'occasion de donner sa mesure. Quand, par un attentat monstrueux, les allemands violèrent la neutralité de la Belgique, le Roi Albert ne s'inclina pas devant la force et ne se borna pas à protester contre cette violation des traités les plus sacrés. Il tira l'épée et ne se contenta pas d'un simulacre de défense ; il ne jugea pas que l'honneur belge put se satisfaire par une démonstration d'un jour. Sourd aux promesses de l'envahisseur comme il l'avait été à ses menaces, il vit sans pâlir les barbares fondre sur lui, et mettre à feu et à sang un pays coupable seulement d'avoir obéi aux lois de l'honneur. Le Roi Albert opposa aux innombrables hordes du Kaiser la petite armée belge et son épée claire et pure, tirée pour une juste cause. Il se montra digne de son peuple ; son peuple se montra digne de lui. La Belgique tint l'Allemagne en échec et montra ce que peuvent des braves gens qui combattent pour le droit.

Dans cette guerre sainte, le Roi Albert se révéla bon chef et bon soldat. On le vit, dans une batterie à Anvers, pointer lui-même une pièce et atteindre une position qu'on croyait hors de portée. Ailleurs, dans la tranchée, armé d'un fusil, il fit le coup de feu au côté de ses fantassins. Qu'il est beau le spectacle donné par ce jeune prince qui égale en sagesse les meilleurs souverains, en courage les plus rudes troupiers !

Et ces grandes actions du peuple belge et de son roi n'auront pas été accomplies en vain. Ce n'est pas en vain qu'Albert et la Belgique en armes auront fait de Liége les Thermopyles de la civilisation européenne. Ils ont brisé l'élan des barbares, co-opéré puissamment à la victoire des alliés, assuré le triomphe du droit et de la liberté.

Mon pays a contracté envers le Roi Albert et son peuple une dette de reconnaissance qu'il tiendra à jamais pour sacrée. Il y paraîtra quand, de concert avec ses nobles alliés, après le triomphe, il s'efforcera de constituer une Europe harmonieuse.

Anatole France

TRANSLATION by Florence Simmonds
KING ALBERT

He was born with the soul of a hero and of a righteous man. From the moment of his accession to the throne he was esteemed (I say this on good authority) by his whole people, and respected by all political and social parties, even by those least inclined to reverence the royal prerogative. He inspired confidence in all, and the truth, wisdom, justice, and mildness of his spirit were unanimously recognised. His natural simplicity was attractive—that simplicity which in a prince nearly always indicates a character more exalted than his rank.

While he was still quite young, a terrible catastrophe fell suddenly upon him and his people and gave him an opportunity of proving his quality. When Germany violated the neutrality of Belgium by a monstrous attack, King Albert did not bow to violence, and was not content merely to protest against this infringement of the most sacred treaties. He drew his sword, and this with no idea of a simulacrum of defence. He did not think that Belgian honour could be satisfied by a brief demonstration. Deaf to the promises of the invader as he had been to his threats, he did not blench when he saw the barbarians bear down upon him, bringing fire and sword into a country guilty only of having obeyed the laws of honour. King Albert opposed the little Belgian army, and his pure and shining sword, drawn in a just cause, to the Kaiser's innumerable hordes. He showed himself worthy of his people ; his people showed themselves worthy of him. . . .

In this holy war King Albert showed himself a good leader and a good soldier. He was seen at Antwerp in a battery, laying a gun himself, and hitting an objective which was supposed to be out of range. At another point he was found in the trenches, armed with a rifle, and shooting side by side with his infantrymen. How fine is the spectacle of this young Prince, who rivals the best kings in wisdom and the roughest troopers in courage !

These great deeds of the Belgian King and people will not have been done in vain. Not in vain will Albert and Belgium in arms have made Liége the Thermopylæ of European civilisation. They have broken the rush of the barbarians, contributed largely to the victory of the Allies, and ensured the triumph of right and liberty.

My country owes a debt of gratitude to King Albert and his people which they will ever hold sacred. This will be evident, when, in concert with our noble Allies, she will work for the constitution of a harmonious Europe, after our final triumph.

By WALTER SICHEL
To King and People

All the great things have been done by the little peoples.—DISRAELI

Sire, King of men, disdainer of the mean,
    Belgium's inspirer, well thou stand'st for all
She bodes to generations yet unseen,
    Freedom and fealty—Kingship's coronal.

Nation of miracles, how swift you start
    To super-stature of heroic deeds
So brave, so silent beats your bleeding heart
    That ours, e'en in the flush of welcome, bleeds.

No sound of wailing. Look, above, afar,
    Throbs in the darkness with triumphant ray
A little yet an all-commanding star,
    The morning star that heralds forth the day.

Walter Sichel

By ISRAEL ZANGWILL

PARADISE LOST

OCCASIONALLY for me the fog in the North Sea lifts, and through the letters of a young officer on a battleship I get a glimpse of how Britannia is ruling the waves. The precise position of her trident remains scrupulously shrouded—at first even the name was removed from the ship's letter-paper—but the glimpse is enough to reveal the greatness and madness of mankind. It is life at its acme of strain and exaltation : life joyously ready to pass on the instant into death, as some unseen mine is struck, or some crafty torpedo strikes. Everybody sleeps in his clothes, and half the night not at all. The great ship is bared of all save necessities : my young friend's spare wardrobe, with all his miscellany of superfluous possessions, the queer garnered treasure of the years, comes economically home. Why, indeed, sink more capital with the ship than is absolutely inevitable ?

Now and again the tension of this terrible vigilance is relieved, if only by a change in tension. One seeks death instead of waiting for it. There is a grapple with a German cruiser, and those not at the guns crowd cheerfully on deck to watch the match with that wonderful British love of sport. They compare the cannonading, note with lively interest the scores made by the rival shells. Once the rift in the fog shows the return of a raiding flotilla, scarred with glorious battle, and the other vessels of the fleet are dressed to salute its triumph, the bands are playing " Rule Britannia," the crews are cheering and singing.

But none of these peeps has left on me so ineffaceable an impression as the picture of my young friend reading—reading at every break in his grim watches—and reading not the detective stories that unbent Bismarck but—" Paradise Lost ! " For the first time he has had leisure to read that sonorous epic straight through and, unlike Dr. Johnson who questioned if anyone ever wished it longer, he revels insatiably in the Miltonic splendours, and he quotes Addison and the *Spectator* in endorsement of his enthusiasm. Despite the Admiralty decree, you see, he has been unable to regard his books as dispensable : they must sink or float with him. And so in the midst of this waste of white waters and hissing shrapnel, he has found for himself a quiet Paradise of beautiful words and visionary magnificence, and it exists for him out of relation to the tense and tragic actual. And yet what could be apter reading than this epic

> *Of man's first disobedience and the fruit*
> *Of that forbidden tree whose mortal taste*
> *Brought death into the world and all our woe ?*

The very first incident, indeed, recorded after Paradise was lost is a murder, and this fratricidal strife of Cain and Abel has repeated itself in every generation and given to the phrase " the brotherhood of man " a sinister significance. But never in all the long history of blood-lust have so many millions of brothers stood embattled, ready to spike one another's bowels

163

with steel, or shatter their faces with devilish explosives, as in this twentieth century of the Christian era.

Now, whatever be the rights or wrongs of war, one thing seems clear. The weapons are wrong. My young friend, with his fine-spun brain and his spiritual delight in Milton's harmonics, ought not to be annihilated by a piece of raw matter. One does not fight a Sèvres vase with a stone. Bring up your Chinese vase an you will, and let the battle be of beauty. There is a horrible expression, " food for powder "—you will find it in all languages that are really civilised. It implies that the masses are so coarse in texture, are carcasses so gross and sub-human, that their best use is to be thrown to the guns—a providential fire-screen for the finer classes. Democracy will in due time take note of this conception. But in its rude way the phrase shadows forth a truth—the truth that, for all who have passed beyond the animal stage, the war of tooth and claw is antiquated. Our war, if war there be, must be conducted with weapons suitable to the dignity of the super-beast who has been so laboriously evolved, suitable to the spirit which through innumerable aeons has been winning its way through the welter of brute impulses. Not for man the slaver of the serpent, the fangs of the tiger. And shelling is only the ejection of a deadlier slaver, the bayonet only a fiercer fang. It seems futile to have evolved from the brute if our brain-power only makes us bigger brutes. " The man behind the gun "— a 15-inch gun that hurls a ton of metal for twelve miles—is a wilder and more monstrous beast than ever appeared even in the antediluvian epoch, and that he should not be kept safely stuffed in a museum like the ptero-dactyl is an intolerable anachronism. A world in which with one movement of his paw he can kill off a whole congregation of Milton-worshippers is a world which should have been nipped in the nebula. No, if fighting there must be, let my young friend fight against Nietzsche-worshippers—let the lucid lines of the Puritan poet confound the formless squadrons of the Pagan dithyrambist. Brain against brain, soul against soul, thought against thought, art against art, man, in short, against man—there lies the fight of the future. If my young friend were a man of science, he would be kept awake not by the German torpedoes but by the German treatises : were he only a tailor, he should never throw away his yard-stick for a lance but with his good old scissors cut out the Teutonic tailor.

After such civilised fashion, indeed, the Anglo-German contest has long been raging, and the German has been winning all along the line. His patience, his industry, his nice study of his customers, has everywhere swept the Englishman aside. Before his music the Briton fell—in worship ; his drama invaded us triumphantly. Why was Germany not content with this victorious campaign, with this campaign worthy of human beings ? German influence, German *Kultur*—it is spread by peace, not by the sword. To German Universities shoals of Russian students flocked as to shrines, humble feudatories of German scholarship, German thoroughness. To the barbarous regions, where an Ovid might still lament his exile, they

"*Plorans ploravit in nocte: et lacrymæ ejus in maxillis ejus . . . . . Manum suam misit hostis ad omnia desiderabilia ejus.*" [*Lamentatio Jeremiæ Prophetæ. I. 2, 10.*]

By BERNARD PARTRIDGE

LA BELGIQUE: 1914.

carried back German methods, the cult of German science. And to me, on my illiterate island, little German cities, a Munich, a Dresden, where the theatre was classic and inexpensive, and the opera a form of art and not a social display, loomed like models of civilisation. Why must Germany challenge the world on the lower plane of brute matter ? It is only the inferior peoples that need the sword. The Turks have had to rule with a rod of iron—they had no right but might, no gift for the world. Such races must assert themselves in fire and write their edicts in blood. But fire burns down and blood dries up and fades, and the only durable influence is the power of the spirit.

Fatal perversity of Germany—to have misunderstood her own greatness ! Proud in her pseudo-philosophy, she has repeated "man's first disobedience" —she has ignored the divine voice, she has listened to the lower promptings of the serpent. There will never be a Paradise again for man till he bends his ear to a truer philosopher than Treitschke to a prince of peace :

> *Till one greater man*
> *Restore us and regain the blissful seat.*

By EDITH WHARTON

BELGIUM

La Belgique ne regrette rien.

Not with her ruined silver spires,
Not with her cities shamed and rent,
Perish the imperishable fires
That shape the homestead from the tent.

Wherever men are staunch and free,
There shall she keep her fearless state,
And, homeless, to great nations be
The home of all that makes them great.

By COMMENDATORE TOMMASO SALVINI

AL BELGIO E AL SUO RE

AL Re del Belgio, novello Agide Spartano, è dovuta l'ammirazione e l'omaggio di tutti i popoli civili. Un vanitoso coronato invasore, distrusse la tranquilla, laboriosa Nazione Belga, dedita soltanto al progresso intellettuale e commerciale, ricca d'opere d'arte, di classici monumenti e di florida invidiabile industria.

Quella Nazione fu crudelmente straziata, perdendo in una doverosa, eroica difesa, gran parte dei suoi figli, massacrati dal ferro, dal fuoco e dal piombo Teutonico. Oh, quanta promettente energia sacrificata !

E nulla v'era da incolpare né al Sovrano, né al suo popolo !

Il Belgio, essendo neutrale, non poteva permettere il passaggio nel suo stato alle truppe Alemanne, con l'intento di muover guerra alla Francia. Non doveva né doteva permetterlo, e questa fu la cagione dell' assassina invasione della Germania contro il diritto delle genti.

Onta all' invasore e onore alla nazione Belga ed al suo magnanimo Re !

Io sono sicuro che la parte intellettuale e umanitaria della Germania non può che disapprovare il contegno e la condotta del militarismo Prussiano che ruppe con la forza delle armi trattati politici stipulati con le altre Potenze, mancando così a doveri garantiti sul suo onore.

Deploro che l'Italia, la Spagna, la Rumenia, la Grecia e la Bulgaria, non si siano unite alla Russia, all' Inghilterra, alla Francia, al Portogallo, alla Serbia e al Giappone per punire la superchieria e la prepotenza della Germania e dell' Austria-Ungheria.

Vi è però da noi un antico proverbio che difficilmente fallisce e dice : " Dio non paga il sabato." Attendiamo dunque la resa dei conti del buon Dio.

E mentre ci sanguina il cuore pensando al sacrifizio e alla sciagura di quel nobile popolo, alziamo un inno di Gloria al Capo di quell' Armata, che con tanto eroismo e con ammirabile abnegazione, difese i sacrosanti diritti della Giustizia e dell' Umanità.

TRANSLATION (abridged)

All civilised nations offer here their tribute of homage and admiration to the King of the Belgians, that modern Spartan Agis.

A vain-glorious invading monarch has destroyed the peace of the industrious Belgian nation, a nation devoted to intellectual and commercial progress, rich in works of art, in classical monuments, and flourishing by virtue of her enviable industry.

* * * * *

And this was in no wise the fault of the King nor of his brave people. For the Belgians, persisting in their neutrality, could not allow the German troops to march through their country to the conquest of France. They could not and they would not.

Whereupon Germany carried out her criminal and brutal invasion, defying the rights of nations. Shame on the invader ! All honour to the Belgian people and to their noble King !

I feel sure that even in Germany the intellectual and humane minority can but disapprove in the depths of their hearts that Prussian militarism, which by sheer brute force has violated political treaties with other Powers, and failed to keep an undertaking " rooted in honour."

I deplore the fact that Italy, Spain, Roumania, Bulgaria, and Greece have not joined England, Russia, France, Servia, Portugal, and Japan to punish the insolence and treachery of Germany and Austria-Hungary.

But there is an old Italian proverb which is rarely wrong : " DIO non paga il sabato " (" GOD does not pay every Saturday," i.e. He punishes in His own good time.) Therefore we must await the judgment and sentence of our Lord.

* * * * *

SUNT LACRYMÆ RERUM!

BY

PIETRO MASCAGNI

By CONDE DE ROMANONES

LE monde de la civilisation attend avec anxiété les résultats de ces terribles événements, qui lui feront connaître le sort reservé à la Belgique. Cette petite nation, petite jusqu'au jour de son malheur, et de son abattement, mais aujourd'hui d'une grandeur morale qui n'a jamais été surpassée dans l'histoire, ne pourra pas disparaître, ne pourra pas perdre sa souveraineté. Si cela venait à arriver, il faudrait admettre que le bon droit et la justice ne sont plus de nos jours les principes de l'existence des peuples civilisés ; ce serait, en plus, une terrible leçon que ceux-ci ne pourraient jamais oublier. Pourquoi tant de sollicitudes, tant d'énergies depensées à accroître les forces morales et materielles d'un petit territoire, pour le transformer en une nation modèle, digne de tous les respects, de toutes les considérations ! Pourquoi tant d'efforts pour avancer sur la voie du progrès, de la liberté, du respect aux droits d'autrui, si le droit du plus fort doit primer en dernier lieu !

Il vaudrait mieux vivre cette vie d'independence sauvage des peuples qui sont encore en dehors de toute civilisation.

TRANSLATION by Florence Simmonds

The world of civilisation awaits with anxiety the results of the terrible events which will make known the fate reserved for Belgium. This little nation, small until the day of her disaster and overthrow, but now possessing a moral greatness unsurpassed in history, cannot disappear, cannot lose her sovereignty. If such a thing could happen, we should have to admit that Right and Justice are no longer the principles of existence among civilised peoples ; it would further be a terrible lesson that these could never forget. Why should so much care, so much energy be expended in increasing the moral and material forces of a small territory, and transforming it into a model nation, worthy of all respect and consideration—why should such efforts be made to further its advance on the path of progress, liberty, respect for the rights of others, if in the last resort the right of the strongest is to prevail?

In this case it would be better to live the life of savage independence proper to people as yet outside the pale of civilisation.

By DR. LYMAN ABBOTT

WHATEVER may be our various opinions respecting the merits of this terrible war in Europe there can be no question that Belgium, which so far has been perhaps the chief sufferer, is absolutely innocent of any offence. The war has swept over her land, cities have been destroyed, homes desolated and thousands of Belgians killed, because she refused to disregard her own promise but chose rather to battle bravely in a desperate endeavour to maintain that neutrality to which she and the Powers of Europe were pledged. The needs of the Belgians appeal to all lovers of their fellow-men whatever their race, their religious creed, or their sympathies in this war

A STUDY
By Harrison Fisher

By LADY LUGARD

I AM honoured in being allowed to express my profound respect for a nation which has lifted contemporary history in one step from the commonplace to the heroic. The times have suddenly become great. It is the prayer of all our hearts that we may be great with them. For Belgium the prayer is already answered—she has become a great nation. In material ruin she has risen to spiritual conquest so complete that the world lies at her feet. No enemy can deprive her of this triumph. Her young King has reason to be proud and glad. So long as history is told it will be remembered that under his leadership Belgium as an entire nation was ready to face martyrdom for her faith. She has suffered a martyrdom which, by its detail of horror and brutality, seems to be misplaced in the history of civilisation. And the faith for which she has suffered is not her faith alone—it is our faith too. It is faith in honour, faith in truth, faith in courage, justice, liberty—faith in all that renders human relations sacred, tender, and inspiring. For this common faith we are prepared to stand. The nations feel, their Governments have said, that arms cannot be laid down until this faith has been vindicated. With its vindication must come the ultimate victory of Belgium and her reinstatement upon a new and higher plane of nationality.

It has been happily given to England while waiting in confidence for that day to take her part in offering to the stricken Belgian population such help as hospitality and sympathy can give. My own humble part has been to share with others in this work of consolation. It has been at once our comfort and our privilege. We know, alas too well, how little it is, humanly speaking, possible to assuage the unparalleled sufferings in the presence of which we find ourselves. But as we have moved daily in the midst of sorrows which must have touched a heart of stone, and have noted with growing admiration the magnificent fortitude, the simplicity, the gratitude for kindness received with which they have been borne, the hope has become conviction in our hearts that the noble promise will yet again be fulfilled : " They that sow in tears shall reap in joy and he that goeth on his way weeping and beareth forth good seed shall doubtless come again with joy and bring his sheaves with him." " Shall doubtless "—It is for that " doubtless " that I believe our whole nation is prepared to maintain the fight while there is a man or a woman left in the British Empire.

By ROBERTO BRACCO

IN questo momento storico, il Belgio—" la nazione agonizzante "—è la più grande nazione d'Europa.

TRANSLATION
At this historic moment, Belgium—" a nation in its agony "—is the greatest nation of Europe.

169

By MARCEL PRÉVOST

A L'INSTANT tragique où un souverain d'Europe déchaînait la barbarie, un autre souverain s'est levé, qui a déchaîné l'héroïsme. Et soudain l'héroïsme a gagné les peuples, de proche en proche—ces vieux peuples occidentaux qu'on disait trop civilisés pour affronter la mort en souriant. Gloire à Albert, Roi des Belges, qui nous a révélé la valeur de nos âmes !

TRANSLATION

At the tragic moment when one Sovereign of Europe was unleashing the dark powers of barbarism, another Sovereign arose who freed the powers of heroism. And all at once the spirit of the hero permeated the nations—these old Western nations that were thought too civilised to smile at the menaces of Death. Glory to King Albert, King of the Belgians, who has revealed to us the value of our souls.

By JONAS BOJER

We are at last in for an epoch of heroism, the King again taking the supreme place among his nation. The storm has swept away Parliament and speakers, Government and elections, parties and party programmes. Only one thing remains, a monumental thing—the nation and the nation's father.

King Albert, rich when his country was wealthy—happy when Belgium flourished—poor when his kingdom was sunk in ruins—a refugee in his land when his own countrymen were driven away from hearth and home. Brave among the braves, wounded among the wounded, but for ever standing erect as a symbol of the vitality of his people, who had only dreamed to live and work on the plains of Flanders. He was too proud to become a martyr, too strong to ask for pity ; he boldly faced destruction, unconquerable because justice and the future are on his side. There where he shows himself refugees find a home, the fatherless a brother, the homeless a fatherland, the desperate a leader whom they can trust and who is full of faith. He is the man who has given the faded glories of royal crowns a new splendour ; he is the only one in this gigantic fight who bears on his forehead the stamp of divine innocence.

At his side stands his wife, a woman who from being Queen over a realm rises to become the Holy Mother of a nation.

By FREDERIK VAN EEDEN

Homage and sympathy for the Belgians and their King.

170

By LUIGI CAPUANA

HITHERTO it seemed a horrible nightmare from which I could not escape. So I turned to the vigorous novels of my friend Camille Lemonnier, to the delicate melodies of my friend Valère Gille, to the strange but powerful dramas of Maurice Maeterlinck, in all of which I had loved and admired different aspects of a happy laborious Belgium, flourishing in Industry, Commerce, Art, and Letters.

I asked myself : Is it possible ? Is it possible ?

And with feverish hands I turned over the noble pages which *La Belgique artistique et littéraire* of April 1909 devoted to the relief of Messinese and Calabrian sufferers from the earthquake, an outburst of ardent writings and a magnificent series of drawings, beginning with an etching by Her Royal Highness Marie, Countess of Flanders.

My Sicily still remembers this outburst of fraternal charity, and would certainly like to repay it now in the worthiest manner.

Is it possible ? Is it possible ? I still ask myself. In the presence of such a treasure of vitality, love, and compassion, I felt my heart wrung when I recognised, as alas ! I was obliged to do, that I was confronted, not with any horrible hallucination, but with a terrible reality, transcending any monstrous aberration of the human imagination.

Does Belgium no longer exist ?

The arbitrary madness of a Sovereign who believes himself to be in direct communication with God has suddenly let loose a hurricane of fire and iron on her capital, on the richest and most peaceful of her cities, on the most fertile districts of her characteristic provinces, condemning to miserable exile thousands of old men, women, and children, who have fled before the barbarian violence of hordes unworthy of the name of soldiers.

Belgium no longer exist ?

Oh ! it cannot be !

No one could have supposed that this tranquil nation could have had the strength and courage to contest the cowardly German invasion, step by step, to resist continuously, in the face of overwhelming numbers and the gradual decimation of the proud army gathered round her heroic King and her not less heroic Queen.

And none would yet dare to believe that the hour will not soon come when there will be a great reconquest, in which the hated invaders will be driven from the sacred soil of Belgium and he who has not hesitated to expose his own life as freely as the humblest of his soldiers will return to the Royal Palace at Brussels, crowned with a halo of glory.

France, England, and Russia are and will always be proud to contribute to this lofty work of restitution, and I hope to see in the victorious procession with them, my Italy, who cannot and ought not to tolerate the disappearance of Belgium from among the nations of Europe.

And now let us remember again !

The publication of that wonderful number of *La Belgique artistique et*

171

littéraire was followed by a military fête, given by the Brussels garrison in aid of the victims of the earthquake ; proud young soldiers took part in equestrian exercises, and in the evolutions of quick-firing batteries. . . . I think with horror how many of those young figures have disappeared, mowed down by the treacherous war thrust on them by the Germans ; and I think too how many writers like Paul André, Georges Eckland, Henry Davignon ; poets like Emile Verhaeren, Georges Marlon, Auguste Vierset, Théo. Hannon ; painters and sculptors like Edmond Piccard, Xavier Malléry, Ferd. Georges Lemmors, Henry Wautiers ; musicians like Paul Gilson, Emile Mathieu, Victor Ruffin—I take the first names that come into my head—I think how many of these, suddenly transformed into combatants, have paid with their lives for the patriotic ardour of their hearts. Nevertheless, how marvellous is the revelation of that stricken, devastated, and starving Belgium, pressing round her noble King and her gentle Queen, and almost forgetting her own pains in those of the elect couple, those living symbols of a land violated but not vanquished.

And how I suffer at the repression of the Hymn of Praise I would fain pour out to them by the horrible spectacle of the barbarian invasion, which freezes the words on my lips, and confounds my thoughts !

Yet this is powerless to overcome my steadfast faith in the speedy advent of a glorious and complete reconquest.

And with a heart overflowing with this hope, and a hand trembling with emotion I write :

Long live King Albert ! Long live Queen Elisabeth ! Long live heroic— and immortal—Belgium !

By SIR F. CARRUTHERS GOULD

WHEN the story of the terrible European War which is now raging comes to be written in the calm dispassion of impartial judgment, it will without doubt be recognised that no nobler page in history can be found than that which records the heroic self-sacrificing stand which martyred Belgium made, not merely to protect herself against unscrupulous and brutal aggression, but to assert her sacred right to her independence and to protest against being made a passive tool for furthering the wanton and wicked designs of German military dominance over Europe.

War in the twentieth century, and after nineteen hundred and fourteen years of Christianity, seems a monstrous outrage on civilisation, but we in this country, in spite of our hatred of war, feel that Christianity itself would have been still more foully outraged if we had not resolved to draw the sword, and to the best of our power to stand by Belgium and her heroic monarch and his gallant people, and to assert the eternal principles of Justice and Honour.

SHE COMES NOT

WORDS BY

HERBERT TRENCH

MUSIC BY

JOHAN BACKER-LUNDE

By DR. OLINDO MALAGODI (*To represent " La Tribuna," Rome*)

L'ONNIPOTENTE Germania, cercando di giustificare la sua violazione della neutralità del Belgio, alla quale essa stessa era solennemente impegnata, proclamò con le parole del suo Cancelliere :—Necessità non conosce legge. —Con queste parole Germania diminuì la sua stessa potenza, sottomettendola e rendendola schiava di condizioni e circostanze, e ciò facendo umiliò se stessa.

Il Belgio, piccolo e male armato, rispose con la sua eroica difesa, la quale può essere tradotta nella formula opposta :—La legge non conosce necessità. —Con la sua azione il Belgio, mentre veniva materialmente schiacciato, si sollevava alto sul suo potente aggressore, guadagnando una vittoria morale di grande valore per tutto il mondo.

Appunto in questo contrasto si esprime tutta l'epopea gloriosa della difesa del Belgio, che contiene una promessa ed un augurio per l'umanità futura. La Germania di oggi, che non è la Germania di Kant e di Schiller, ha fondata la sua politica sull' assioma :—La forza è il diritto.—Questo assioma corrisponde forse alla realtà presente ; ma appunto per ciò tanto maggior valore acquista qualunque azione che contraddica questa legge di ferro, e la quale, come il sacrifizio a cui il Belgio si è sottomesso eroicamente, contribuisca a preparare una nuova e più umana realtà, in cui—il diritto sia la forza.

Olindo Malagodi

TRANSLATION *by Florence Simmonds*

All-powerful Germany, seeking to justify her violation of Belgium's neutrality, to which she herself was solemnly pledged, proclaimed by the mouth of her Chancellor that " Necessity knows no law." By these words she attenuated her own power, making it the subject and slave of conditions and circumstances, and thus humiliating herself as a nation.

Belgium, small and poorly armed, replied by her heroic defence, which may be translated by the antithesis : Law knows no necessity. Though Belgium has been crushed materially, this deed has raised her far above her powerful adversary and has given her a moral victory of infinite value to the world. *In this contrast all the glorious epic of Belgium's defence is expressed. It holds a promise and an augury for the future of mankind. The Germany of to-day, which is no longer the Germany of Kant and Schiller, bases her policy on the axiom : Might is right. This axiom is perhaps in harmony with actual realities ; but all the more must we value any action which contradicts this iron law, any action which, like the sacrifice so heroically submitted to by Belgium, tends to prepare a new and more humane reality, in which Right will be Might.*

By EARL BRASSEY

THE Belgian people may be well assured that we in England are their true friends. We have felt the keenest sympathy with them in all that they have suffered. We have profoundly regretted our inability to come more promptly to their relief. We have appreciated their exalted patriotism and the dauntless valour of their brave troops. We hope the day is not distant when they will receive compensation for their heavy losses and cruel sacrifices.

Brassey

By ELLEN KEY

SOME months ago Belgium was fertile and fair beyond expression. It was the land of calmly flowing rivers, grand forests, wide fields : beautiful at every time and glorious when wrapped in the golden mists of summer sunset. It was the land of splendid old towns, where the belfries made the heart glad with music, and where great works of art—by masters old and new—filled the soul with joy.

Now Belgium is full of sorrow and misery. The garden is changed into a desert. A great number of the people are dead ; a still greater number are wandering in exile in foreign lands. For the remainder—for King as for beggar—life is a tragedy too deep for tears. This fate has overcome Belgium because the world is still ruled by force, not by justice. *But the name of Belgium is now engraved in the conscience of the world.* Humanity can have no peace in sight of the fate of this people. *That fate must be changed* or we shall witness such a defeat for our higher ideals, such a loss for the great principles which our best men and women have lived or died for, that we ought to resist this defeat and be on our guard against this loss with as much energy as we should use in the defence of our own country.

By LEONARDO BISTOLFI

THE sublime sacrifice of the Belgian people will consecrate the blood-stained earth of its martyrs as an altar reared by the hands of Death to the pure and inviolable beauty of Life.

By LIEUT.-GENERAL SIR ROBERT BADEN-POWELL

IT would be trite to quote David against Goliath in the case of gallant little Belgium standing up to the ogre of Prussian Militarism, but that historic fight had its counterpart recently where a peaceful, hard-working little tailor was set upon by a big, beery loafer. The neighbours, out of pity and sense of fair play, were prepared to run to the rescue, when they stood back to cheer, for the little man stuck up, on his own, to the bully, and punched him and tripped him and held him down till help arrived. In a moment the insignificant little worker had changed into the hero of the village.

There are two things above all others which Britons, down to the very lowest among them, inherently appreciate, and those are Pluck and Fair Play. That is why their sympathy is hot and strong for the plucky little nation which stood up as a champion for liberty and fair play against the overwhelming tide of brute-force.

Robert Baden Powell

176

THE DEATH OF ADMIRAL BLAKE
By A. D. McCormick, R.I.

By SIR JAMES BARR, M.D., LL.D.

SOME EUGENIC IDEALS

AS one of those who do not look upon war as an unmixed evil, and who think that it is sometimes well for a nation to be purified as if by fire, I feel confident that a fine race like the Belgians, who have shown their survival value, will yet rise superior to " German Kultur," and with the aid of their Allies will crush the barbarous monster who seeks to rule the world by brute force. War, no doubt, has played an important part in the evolution of the human race, just as a struggle for existence among lower forms of life occurred' long before the appearance of man on the globe. No doubt this struggle in one form or another will continue for generations yet unborn. The millennium, whatever that may mean, is still in the dim and shadowy future. There is now a vain hope, a kind of blessed assurance, among many peaceful individuals that this is the last great war, that the battle of Armageddon is being now fought, and that men will learn the art of war no more. This is a consummation devoutly to be wished, but one which will not be attained as we are still on the borderland of savagery. I hope the rulers of the allied nations will not be actuated by any such foolish ideas, but will recognise facts and not be misled by lying proclamations of Germany's peaceful intentions—proclamations which contravened facts and the falsity of which should have been apparent to every intelligent being.

I have long recognised that a life and death struggle would be forced on Britain by Germany, but I never thought that it would occur under such favourable conditions for our country. Now that this struggle has occurred it should be the duty of all the Allies to see that the conditions are so altered that it will never recur. As a wise preventive the Hohenzollern and Hapsburg families should be eliminated root and branch, and sane rulers placed in their stead. It should not be left within the power of any series of megalomaniacs to disturb the peace of the world.

The " German Kultur " as manifested in Louvain, and by rapine and plunder throughout Belgium, must be exterminated, and this savage breed as far as possible wiped out, but herein arises an insuperable difficulty. Maeterlinck truly says the Germans are all guilty, any differentiation is a mere matter of degree, and you cannot wipe out 100 millions. Moreover, any such attempt would degrade the Allies to the low base level of German conduct. We must carry on an honourable warfare which will leave no blot on our escutcheon. We must conquer nobly, we must make the Germans pay to their last stiver for the war which they have so ruthlessly conducted. We must weed out the worst of the barbarians, and utterly destroy the princely looters with the rest of the Prussian military gang who have proved themselves a disgrace to humanity. When the Germans discover that dishonourable conduct does not pay, that it has no survival value, then we may eventually get a newer and truer Germany.

Personally, I have no objection to German ascendancy if they produce a finer race than ourselves, but I do object to that ascendancy being attained

177

by brute force. I have never liked German methods, but I have always given them full credit for their perseverance and ability. Unfortunately we have all been too apt to accept the German at the face value put on by himself without carefully examining his intrinsic merit or demerit as the case may be. Germany has produced no genius, there is no scope for individualism, her work is the collective wisdom of commonplace savants, she has never produced nor is ever likely to produce a super-man, there has been no evolution of the higher and nobler nature of man, the race has not received that internal push, as Bergson would say, which has carried life by more and more complex forms to higher and higher destinies. There has been no cultivation of the spirit of altruism, that highest product of human evolution which is shown by sympathy with our fellow-beings in their suffering. On the contrary the worst and most brutal characteristics of the Huns were evolved and developed in the Franco-Prussian War of 1870, and have now been perpetuated in an even more accentuated form in the present war. The German Emperor emulates and out-Herods the conduct of Attila, " the Scourge of God." When, O God, when can such scourges be eliminated ? Surely their existence can be of no value to the higher evolution of the race. The blasphemous speeches of this monarch can have no divine sanction, and should not be allowed to mislead a deluded nation ; the only beneficial effect which they can have may be to lead the guilty to their destruction.

The Allies have shown their manhood and the capacity to rule, we must not therefore rest satisfied with the conquest of Germany, the establishment of peace and the rehabiliment of Belgium, but we must also raise imperial races whose influences will be felt for good throughout the world. We must raise healthy, vigorous manhood and womanhood, men and women who will hold their own in the battle of life with any other nations—we want nations of stalwarts. This can all be rapidly attained by intelligent artificial selection, and the nation which produces the finest, noblest, and most intellectual race will win in the long run. Bacon said : " The principal point of greatness in any State is to have a race of military men." He did not then contemplate the Prussian braggadocio. We are getting more peaceable since Bacon's days. Some are preaching peace, eternal peace, forgetting that there has been a constant and incessant struggle on the earth since the first appearance of life thereon, and the surest way of any nation preserving the peace is to be always ready for a fight. If the Allies had been ready Germany would not have attacked them. The health of a nation is its most valuable asset, and I should like to see every man between the ages of 20 and 60 able to handle a rifle and a bayonet, and, if needs be, take part in the defence of his country.

In King Albert we have a worthy ruler of an imperial race, and I hope he may live long to rule over such a self-reliant and noble people.

By ARMANDO PALACIO VALDÉS
LA LEYENDA DEL REY ALBERTO

En los siglos venideros las madres contarán a sus hijos en las largas noches de inveirno " la leyenda del rey Alberto."

" UNA vez era un rey, hijos míos, que reinaba sobre un pequeño pueblo industrioso, noble y bravo. Y este rey era noble entre los más nobles y bravo entre los más bravos. Cerca de él vivía un gigante temeroso que reinaba sobre un gran pueblo de guerreros. Este gigante mantenía en suspensión y espanto a cuantos le rodeaban y rebosaba de poder y de orgullo. Además poseía un cañón maravilloso, grande como una catedral, con el cual arrasaba los campos y pulverisaba las ciudades. Vecino del pequeño pueblo vivía otro rico y feliz que el gigante codiciaba.

" Déjame pasar por tus estados," le dijo un día a nuestro rey. " Quiero aplastar y reducir a la servidumbre a esa nación que cerca de ti se halla. Si me dejas el paso libre tendrás dinero, participarás del botín que recoja, algunos de los estados de esa nación pasarán a tu poder. Si no me lo dejas arrasaré tu pueblo y seréis todos esclavos.

" No pasarás sino sobre nuestros cadáveres," respondió el rey valeroso. " Mi pueblo, que es uno de los más prósperos del orbe, estima mucho sus fábricas, sus riquezas, sus grandes ciudades, sus hermosos monumentos, pero estima más su honra. Las piedras pueden colocarse otra vez las unas sobre las otras ; pero ¿ quién alzará de sus ruinas el honor derrumbado ? Guarda tu dinero, toma el mío y el de mis compatriotas si te hace falta, arráncanos si quieres la vida, haznos esclavos. No lograrás hacernos viles . . ."

" Entonces el gigante cruel cayó sobre aquel diminuto pueblo, destruyó sus ciudades, quemó sus aldeas, degolló a muchos de sus habitantes y sembró por doquier el espanto y la desolación.

" El rey magnánimo salió de sus estados, pero ¡ caso extraño ! los encontró mucho mayores. Todos se declaraban sus vasallos. Donde quiera que iba se le aclamaba como a un emperador victorioso. Las mujeres deshoja- ban flores sobre su cabeza, los hombres agitaban sus sombreros gritando : ¡ Viva el rey !

" Al fin, rodeado de un puñado de soldados heroicos, penetró nuevamente en sus estados y comenzó la reconquista. Muchos hombres le ayudaron, los unos con su espada, los otros con su pluma, los otros con sus oraciones. Los ángeles del cielo le abrían paso. Y palmo a palmo en lucha tenaz y sangrienta se fué apoderando de su perdido reino. Cuando al cabo logró sentarse otra vez sobre su trono, el universo entero dejó escapar un grito de alegría. Porque la justicia había quedado triunfante, la ley de Dios cumplida y el poder de las tinieblas vencido.

" Hijos mios, este rey fué después dichoso sobre la tierra y ahora lo es en el cielo."

Armando Palacio Valdés

ARMANDO PALACIO VALDES
TRANSLATION by Prof. Fitzmaurice-Kelly
THE LEGEND OF KING ALBERT

In the coming ages, during the long winter evenings, mothers will tell their children " The Legend of King Albert."

" *Once upon a time, my children, there was a King who reigned over a small, industrious, noble and valiant race ; and this King was the noblest of the noble, and the bravest of the brave. Near him there lived a dreadful giant who ruled over a great race of warriors. This giant kept all those about him in awe and fear, and he abounded in power and pride. Moreover, he had a wonderful cannon, the size of a cathedral, with which he made havoc of the country-side and ground cities into dust. This small nation had for its neighbour another state—a rich and happy state, which the giant coveted.*

" ' *Let me pass through your dominions,' he said one day to our King. ' I want to destroy and enslave that nation which dwells nigh you. If you let me through, you shall have wealth ; you shall share the plunder that I get ; some of the provinces of that nation shall come under your sway. Should you not let me through, I will crush your people and you shall all be slaves.'*

" ' *You shall not pass—except over our dead bodies,' answered the valiant King. ' My people, one of the most prosperous on earth, sets great store by its*

manufactures, its riches, its large cities, its handsome monuments : but it loves honour more. You can again pile stones one upon the other ; but, if honour be uprooted, who can raise it from its ruins ? Keep your money ; if that is what you want, take mine and my people's ! Take our lives ! Enslave us ! You will fail to make us base ! '

" *Then the cruel giant fell on that tiny race, destroyed its cities, burned its hamlets, slew many of its inhabitants, and spread fear and misery everywhere.*

" *The high-minded King set forth from his dominions, but—marvellous to tell !—he found them growing larger. All proclaimed themselves his vassals. Wherever he went, he was hailed as though he were a triumphant conqueror. Women scattered flowers on his head ; men waved their hats, and cried— ' Long live the King ! '*

" *At last, surrounded by a handful of heroic soldiers, he made his way once more into his Kingdom, and began to win it back again. Many helped him : some with their swords, some with their pens, others with their prayers. The angels of heaven opened up a path for him. And, after a desperate and bloody struggle, inch by inch, he kept on recovering his lost Kingdom. When, at last, he came to his throne again, the whole world raised a shout of exultation. For justice had triumphed, God's word was fulfilled, and the powers of darkness were vanquished.*

" *My children, this King was happy afterwards on earth, and is now happy in heaven.*"

By PAUL BOURGET
LE ROI ALBERT

LA guerre, à travers tant d'épreuves, et de si affreuses, réserve du moins ce bienfait aux peuples et aux individus qui acceptent virilement sa tragique nécessité : l'éducation par la résistance, en sorte que ce formidable élément de destruction peut devenir un élément fécond de reconstruction. La guerre procure aux gens de cœur un autre bienfait : celui de l'exemple à donner et à recevoir, en sorte encore que cette sanglante ouvrière de discorde l'est aussi d'union. Elle resserre d'un lien plus étroitement noué le faisceau social, à l'heure même où l'on croit qu'elle va le briser. L'exemple, quand il est celui du devoir sur le champ de bataille, rallie d'un tel élan les volontés autour du drapeau ! C'est le supérieur modelant sur lui l'inférieur, le courage redressant la défaillance, la force servant de règle à la faiblesse, l'énergique devenu une prédication vivante. Il montre en lui ce que *peut* l'homme quand il *veut*, ce que vous *pourrez*, vous, son camarade, si vous *voulez*. Et vous *voulez*. — Braver le danger, souffrir, mourir, — ces mots n'avaient pour vous, héritier comblé d'une société heureuse, qu'une signification si lointaine ! La guerre en a fait en quelques jours une réalité terrifiante. Aurez-vous la force de l'affronter ? Vous en doutez. Et voici qu'un autre,

180

By L. RAVEN-HILL

"*You mark my word Jarge ; that there Kayser 'll come to a bad end : I've 'ad my eye on un for many a day !*"

là, devant vous, déploie cette force, froidement, tranquillement. Une contagion émane de son attitude. Ce qu'il a pu faire, vous le ferez. Et vous marchez au danger, vous voulez souffrir, vous savez mourir. C'est le miracle du sacrifice, qu'il se multiplie dans tous ses témoins. Ce miracle, nous y assistons à chaque jour, à chaque heure, depuis ces trois mois. Cette propagation de la flamme sacrée, c'est vraiment la course de la torche dont parle Lucrèce :

Et quasi cursores virtutis *lampada tradunt*,

dirais-je en osant substituer au *vitaï* du texte ce mot de *virtus* que les Romains, ces soldats-nés, chargeaient d'un tel sens !

Parmi ces porteurs de l'héroïque flambeau, aucune figure ne m'émeut autant que celle du Prince pour qui ma patrie la France n'aura jamais une reconnaissance assez frémissante. Je veux parler de ce Roi Albert dont la personnalité magnifique a donné son sens le plus haut à cette dure guerre. Sans lui, sans le peuple belge, elle n'eût été qu'un cataclysme mondial d'une signification indécise. Je lis bien dans des articles et des discours que nous assistons à une lutte entre la Démocratie et la Féodalité, que nous avons repris la tradition des volontaires de 92. Cette phraséologie ne correspond à rien d'exact. Ce n'est pas comme démocrates que nous nous battons. Les Anglais n'ont pas cessé d'être la monarchie et l'aristocratie seculaires qu'ils étaient avant le 2 août 1914, et nous autre Français nous défendons notre sol, tout simplement. L'Allemagne n'est pas davantage une féodalité. Ce n'est pas un groupe de hobereaux que nous avons devant nous, c'est tout une nation de commerçants, d'industriels, de paysans, d'ouvriers. Ne prenons pas au sérieux cette prétendue opposition de la *Sozial Democratie* qualifiée justement par un révolutionnaire plus logique de " philistinisme petit bourgeois." Ce pays veut dominer les autres pays et d'abord conquérir la France, envahir ses champs, ses mines, ses vignobles, ses usines, son argent. Cette lutte brutale pour la vie d'un côté, pour l'hégémonie de l'autre, s'est éclairée tout à coup d'un rayon d'idée. C'est au Roi Albert que nous le devons. Aucune des leçons de cette guerre n'est plus éclatante. C'est l'exemple projetant sa lumière à la fois dans le monde moral et dans le monde politique. Je voudrais dire pourquoi en quelques mots. Je m'excuse de commenter des faits connus de tous. Ils ne seront jamais assez rapportés, parce qu'ils ne seront jamais assez médités.

Voulez-vous que nous reprenions le *Livre blanc*, cette brochure qui devrait être tirée à des millions d'exemplaires et mise entre toutes les mains ? Les pires utopistes y apprendraient à penser juste sur les origines de la guerre. Il contient, on le sait, la correspondance du gouvernement britannique et de ses agents pendant cette crise du 20 juillet au 4 août. Elle se compose de cent soixante et une pièces. Rien que le numéro d'ordre sous lequel s'inscrit la première dépêche relative à la Belgique a quelque chose de pathétique. C'est le cent quinzième ! Les cent quatorze télégrammes précédents se sont échangés entre Londres, Pétrograd, Berlin, Paris, Rome. Les grandes puissances causent entre elles avant d'engager la redoutable partie. La toute petite Belgique est absente de ces conversations. Qu'a-t-elle de commun avec les intérêts en jeu ? Elle entretient, dira son ministre des affaires étrangères, à la date du 1ᵉʳ août encore, " des rapports excellents avec ses voisins et elle n'a aucune raison pour suspecter leurs intentions." Au *Foreign Office* de Londres, on est moins rassuré. Cette dépêche numérotée 114 exprime l'inquiétude de Sir Edward Grey, lequel annonce au ministre anglais à Bruxelles qu'il a " demandé aux gouvernements français et allemand si chacun d'eux était décidé à respecter la neutralité de la Belgique." Celle-ci, résolue elle-même a maintenir cette neutralité, ne s'émeut pas. Elle repose sur la foi d'un traité contresigné par l'Angleterre, l'Allemagne et la France. Le 3 août, le gouvernement allemand lui remet une note demandant le libre passage pour ses armées sur son territoire, moyennant quoi l'Allemagne s'engage à maintenir l'intégrité du royaume et de ses possessions. Sinon la Belgique sera traitée en ennemie. Le Roi Albert a douze heures pour répondre. Devant cet *ultimatum*, il n'hésite pas. Il sait que l'armée allemande est une force terrible. Il connaît l'Empereur Allemand. Il sait que l'orgueilleux, après une telle démarche, ne reculera plus. Son trône est en jeu, plus que son trône : les sept millions d'âmes, — quelle éloquence prennent les vulgaires termes de statistiques dans certaines circonstances ! — qui lui sont confiées : il voit en esprit ce beau pays indéfendable : ces charbonnages, ces carrières, ces usines, ces filatures, ces ports, cette florissante industrie épanouie dans ces plaines ouvertes qu'il ne pourra pas préserver. Mais il s'agit d'un traité où il y a sa signature. Répondre oui à l'Allemagne, c'est trahir ses co-signataires, le Français et l'Anglais. C'est manquer à l'engagement pris, se déshonorer, soi et son peuple, et le Roi dit non. Le reste est connu.

Cet héroïsme de la probité, c'est celui du Régulus antique retournant à Carthage et au supplice pour tenir la parole donnée. Mais c'est aussi celui du commerçant qui ne veut pas être banqueroutier et qui vend tout, maison, meubles, linge, argenterie pour faire face à ses engagements. C'est celui du fils qui se ruine pour payer les dettes de son père. " A quel prix ce pacte aura-t-il été tenu. Y avez-vous pensé ? " demandait M. de Bethmann-Hollweg à Sir Edward Goschen. J'entends le Roi Albert répondre : " Ce n'est pas mon affaire. Il y a là un chiffon de papier, comme vous dites. Mon nom est dessus. Cela suffit." Turenne aussi, comme on lui reprochait un jour de remplir une promesse faite à des voleurs : " Je tiens parole à M. de Turenne," repliqua-t-il. Cette fidélité du roi belge et de son peuple avec lui au " chiffon de papier," qu'elle est simple et qu'elle va loin ! Ce sera l'honneur aussi de l'Angleterre de l'avoir comprise et partager. Il ne s'agit plus là d'une idéologie contestable, comme de savoir si la Démocratie est supérieure à la Féodalité ou le Socialisme au Capitalisme, vaines billevesées à piper le naïf Démos. Il s'agit d'un contrat, et à son propos, de tous les contrats, d'un acte signé, donc de tous les actes signés et, comme

182

¡THE BELGIAN OF TO-MORROW
By WILLIAM NICHOLSON

la propriété repose, par définition, sur un contrat, il s'agit de toutes les propriétés, donc de tous les rapports possibles entre les hommes et du fondement même de la société. Oui, c'est l'ordre social tout entier que le Roi Albert a défendu quand il a prononcé son *non possumus*. C'est l'ordre social tout entier que M. de Bethmann a renié, quand il a craché sur le " chiffon de paper." C'est l'ordre social tout entier que l'Empereur allemand a piétiné quand il a franchi la frontière belge. C'est l'ordre social tout entier que la France a salué au Havre dans les personnes des ministres du Roi Albert. On raconte que cet admirable Prince avait toujours sur sa table, dans son cabinet de Bruxelles, un volume de notre Le Play. Combien ce Maître de la Réforme qui a si fortement insisté sur le rôle essentiel des autorités sociales eut été fier d'avoir un pareil disciple ! Combien ému de voir ce chef entraîner son peuple, et ce peuple le suivre, avec une si généreuse unanimité dans la défense du principe qui est la pierre angulaire de la civilisation !

Le roi Albert a fait plus. Le Premier Anglais l'a reconnu dans un de ces discours, comme les orateurs britanniques en prononcent dès qu'ils se meuvent dans la grande ligne de leur histoire. Il y eut jadis une Europe de petits Etats et dont le morcellement rendait plus difficile un choc monstrueux d'énormes masses humaines, tel que celui auquel nous assistons aujourd'hui. M. de Bismarck fut l'ouvrier, génial et funeste, qui acheva de détruire cette Europe si prudemment aménagée. La Belgique est un des rares petits Etats qui aient survécu. Si nous voulons, la tempête finie, établir une paix durable, c'est cette politique des petits Etats qu'il nous faut reprendre. Un des monarques de la coalition le disait avec bien de la sagesse à l'un de nos meilleurs ambassadeurs : " La tâche des alliés c'est de ramener l'Europe à la période antébismarckienne." La besogne de guérison est là, non pas dans d'inefficaces et chimériques proclamations d'un pacifisme final, non pas dans le redoutable projet d'une plus grande unification allemande sous étiquette républicaine. Il importe à l'avenir du monde civilisé qu'il n'y ait plus une Allemagne, mais des Allemagnes, une mosaïque de petits états et non plus le bloc amalgamé par la main puissante du chancelier de fer. Mais pour qu'une pareille Europe soit viable, la condition *sine quâ non* est que le respect de l'indépendance des petits Etats soit le premier article de son code. C'est cet autre principe, fondement et garantie du futur équilibre international que les Belges ont convié les Anglais et nous autres Français à défendre avec eux, nous ramenant, nous aussi, dans la grande ligne de notre histoire. La vieille monarchie française n'a jamais eu d'autre programme et la vérité politique se trouve rencontrer la vérité sociale dans le geste du roi. Il l'a fait ce geste, si simplement ! Depuis ces longues et dures semaines qu'il a vu ses villes bombardées, ses banques rançonnées, ses sujets massacrés, ses ministres obligés de demander un asile à la France, pas une fois il n'a proféré une plainte, et, correspondance sublime du cœur des sujets au cœur du Prince, pas une parole de regret n'a été entendue qui trahisse une défaillance du peuple envahi. Une volonté invincible au service d'une pensée juste, connaissez-vous un spectacle qui éveille dans l'âme un plus mâle sursaut de respect et, s'il est possible, d'émulation ? Michelet disait de Kléber qu'il avait " une figure si militaire que l'on devenait brave en le regardant." Du Roi Albert, on pourrait dire que l'on devient plus honnête homme, rien qu'en pensant à lui.

Paul Bourget

TRANSLATION (abridged)

War, in the midst of its awful and manifold trials, bestows at least one benefit on the nations and individuals who accept its tragic necessity in a manly spirit : that of education by endurance, which may make this formidable element of destruction a fertile element of reconstruction. War has yet another benefit to offer to " men of good will " : that of the example to be given and received, by means of which this bloody artificer of discord becomes also an agent of union. It binds the social sheaf more closely together, at the very moment when it seems about to scatter it. Example, when it is the example of duty on the battle-field, rallies all energies round the standard with extraordinary vigour! The superior models the inferior upon himself, courage reanimates despair, strength becomes the rule for weakness, the stout of heart is a living sermon. He shows what man can do if he will, what you, his comrade, could do if you would. And you will.—To brave danger, to suffer, to die—to you, fortunate heir of a happy age, these words had such a remote significance ! In a few days war made them a terrible reality. Would you have strength to face it ? You doubted it. But another, close to you, showed this strength, calmly and quietly. His attitude was contagious. What he can do, you will do. You go out to meet danger, you are willing to suffer, you will be able to die. It is the miracle of sacrifice that it multiplies in all who witness it. We have been seeing this miracle every day, every hour for the last three months. This propagation of the sacred flame is really the handing on of the torch of which Lucretius speaks :

Et quasi cursores *virtutis* lampada tradunt,

I would venture to say, replacing the vitaï *of the text by that word to which those born soldiers, the Romans, gave such deep meaning :* virtus !
Among these bearers of the heroic torch, no figure is to me so touching as that of the Prince to whom my country, France, can never be too passionately grateful. I speak of that King Albert whose splendid personality has given the highest meaning to this stern war. Without him, and without the Belgian people, it would have been but a universal cataclysm of no very definite significance.

*   *   *   *   *

King Albert has done more. The First of Englishmen has recognised this in one of those speeches British orators make when they are moving on the great lines of their history. Europe was formerly a collection of small States, the fragmentary nature of which made the monstrous onslaught of immense human masses such as that we are witnessing to-day very difficult. Prince Bismarck was the sinister genius who destroyed this prudently arranged Europe. Belgium is one of the few small states that survived. If when the storm is over we wish to establish a lasting peace, we must return to this policy of small States. One of the Sovereigns of the Coalition wisely said to one of our best Ambassadors : " The task of the Allies is to bring Europe back to the ante-Bismarckian period." The cure lies in this direction, not in ineffectual and chimerical proclamations of definitive peace, nor in the redoubtable project of a greater unification of Germany under a republican label. It is essential to the future of the civilised world that there should be no longer a Germany, but several Germanys, a mosaic of small States, instead of the block amalgamated by the mighty hand of the Iron Chancellor. But to ensure the existence of such a Europe, it is a sine quâ non *that the first article of its code should be the independence of small States. It was this principle, the basis and the guarantee of future international equilibrium, that the Belgians called upon the English and the French to defend with them, thus bringing us too back to the great tradition of our history. The old French monarchy was faithful to this principle, and political truth recognised social truth in the King's action. This action he performed with the greatest simplicity. Throughout the long, hard weeks in which he has seen his towns bombarded, his banks robbed, his subjects massacred, his Ministers compelled to seek asylum in France, he has not uttered a single complaint, and such has been the sublime sympathy between the heart of the Prince and the heart of his people, that not a word of regret has been heard revealing the despondency of an invaded people. An invincible will, serving a true conception—could any spectacle stir the soul to more virile respect and, if possible, emulation? Michelet tells us Kléber had such a martial air that those who saw him became brave. Of King Albert it may be said that even thinking of him makes one a better man.*

184

By T. P. O'CONNOR

"YOU have saved Europe," were the words that came instinctively to my lips when I met my friend, M. Edmond de Prelle, of the Belgian Legation, for the first time after the opening of the War ; and these words still sum up my feeling and the feeling of millions of the peoples of our Empire with regard to the part which Belgium has played in this great tragedy of a European War. Give due praise to the gallant entry of the French Army, to the deathless story of French's retreat ; and still you have to come back to the point that it was Belgium that met and held back the first onrush of the Germans in their invasion of Western Europe. The heroic defence of Liége, followed by similar heroism, obstinate bravery, tenacious defence, in other parts of the Belgians' native land, had the incalculable results on all the future of staying the progress of the war of the Germans ; of turning topsy-turvy their ambitious and well-arranged Time-Table ; and thus of giving to both France and England the full time and opportunity to be ready for the invaders on their belated arrival on the soil of France. If Paris be safe to-day, if the French and British troops are now steadily throwing back the invader, if, in short, the whole tide of the fortunes of battle have turned, it is Belgium that must always have the glory of striking the first and decisive blow which led inevitably to those splendid results.

The heroism of this resistance is made all the greater by the gigantic inequality between the forces of Belgium and those of her powerful enemy ; the greater the disproportion the greater the heroism. It is comparatively easy for one brave army to face another which is about its equal in strength ; but for an army infinitesimal in point of numbers to face the gigantic army of Germany to go into battle was what soldiers call a forlorn hope—that is to say, an enterprise for which only the bravest even among the brave volunteer to undertake. And to Belgium, as to Greece in the days of her ancient struggle against the hordes of Asia, civilisation will always give her infinite gratitude, and Liége will take its place in the same calendar as Thermopylæ.

This resistance then to Germany has put Europe and civilisation under this great debt to Belgium ; but I can add that future generations of Belgians will bless the generation of to-day who by their heroic resistance have placed the liberty and the independence of Belgium on an impregnable rock. Never again will any Power, however powerful, unscrupulous, or cruel, dare to violate the soil or attempt to destroy the national and independent existence of Belgium. The men—the women and the children also—of Belgium who have died, have sealed with their blood the divine right of Belgium for all time to own and rule their own country.

T. P. O'Connor

185

By M. D. MÉRÉJKOWSKY
Translated from the Russian by C. Hagberg Wright, LL.D.

TO THE BELGIAN PEOPLE

WE do not say to you—Have courage. No courage could be greater than that which you have shown. But we say to you—Have faith. Your sufferings have not been in vain ; they have awakened the conscience of the peoples. From henceforth your land, drenched with the blood of your sons, shall be a Holy Land : from henceforth your cause shall be the cause of Humanity. To wipe away the tears from your eyes, to heal your wounds, to restore a hundred-fold that which has been taken from you, *this* the peoples have solemnly sworn—*to this* they have pledged their honour, and that oath will be kept. We desire no solace while you remain desolate, we desire no liberty while you remain in bondage, we desire no victory until you have conquered. In the day when the victors triumph, the first crown shall be yours ; and Humanity shall bestow it upon you. All nations shall make way for you, and in the forefront you shall enter the promised land.

D. Méréjkowsky

By M. TOUGAN BARANOVSKY
Translated from the Russian by C. Hagberg Wright, LL.D.

TO BELGIUM AND HER KING

IN the life of a man as in the life of a Nation, Evil is closely interwoven with Good. Without Evil there would be no Good—for Good is nothing more than the vanquishing of Evil.

From this point of view Evil not only serves Good but is also, as it were, the invariable basis of its activity. Great historical crimes, like those of which we are eye-witnesses to-day, have their place in the triumphant onward march of eternal truth. The more terrible the crime, the more beautiful and the more dazzling the power of that good which overcomes it. Was not the Crucifixion essential to the everlasting victory of Jesus ? And shall not the picture of Belgium ruined and laid waste by her foes be graven for ever on the pages of human history ? Shall not our remote descendants make songs and legends about the glorious country of King Albert which has given proof of supreme courage and unconquerable spirit in the awful hour of barbarian invasion ? And shall not Belgium by her example inspire Humanity throughout the ages to do deeds of heroism and to battle for truth. Henceforth King Albert belongs to all of us, he is our common possession, like one of those spiritual heroes who raise the value of the whole of mankind. And after many, many years, when every trace of the present bloody struggle has vanished, when the names of the battle-fields and the great commanders are forgotten, when all the horrors we are now living through seem but far-off legends, when the proudest temples and palaces of our era have crumbled into dust, the image of the noble King shall still continue to inspire the poet.

By A. KOUPRINE
Translated from the Russian by Henry Bradley, LL.D.

NOT applause, not admiration, but the deep eternal gratitude of the whole civilised world is now due to the self-denying Belgian people and their noble young Sovereign. They first threw themselves before the savage beast, foaming with pride, maddened with blood. They thought not of their own safety, nor of the prosperity of their houses, nor of the fate of the high culture of their country, nor of the vast numbers and cruelty of the enemy. They have saved, not only their fatherland, but all Europe, the cradle of intellect, taste, science, creative art, and beauty; they have saved from the fury of the barbarians, trampling in their insolence, the best roses in the holy garden of God. Compared with their modest heroism, the deed of Leonidas and his Spartans who fought in the pass of Thermopylæ falls into the shade. And the hearts of all the noble and the good beat in accord with their great hearts. . . .

No, never shall die or lose its power a people endowed with such a noble fire of blood, with such feelings, that inspire it to confront bereavement, sorrow, sickness, wounds; to march as friends, hand in hand, adored King and simple cottager, man and woman, poor and rich, weak and strong, aristocrat and labourer. Salutation and humblest reverence to them!

A. Kouprine

By M. D. ANOUTCHIN

WHO now, save the Germans, would not compassionate poor Belgium, small, but at the same time great, utterly devastated and depopulated for this sole reason—that she has dared to remain loyal and to defend her soil against the unrighteous invasion of barbarians.

One would have to be a William II, representing the worst side of Teutonic militarism, to dare name the noble country a traitor. We Europeans admire the heroism of the Belgians and their knightly King.

Let us hope that with the united forces of England, Russia, France, Belgium, Serbia, and Japan, the enemy of good faith and humanity will be utterly broken. In all these emergencies the device " now or never " is not to be forgotten, and the sword shall not be sheathed until the Kaiser acknowledges himself beaten.

By LOUIS COUPERUS

TOWARDS noble Belgium, victim of a world-tragedy, all sympathies stretch out like maternal hands, eager to soothe her quivering griefs. To her noble Sovereigns, King Albert and Queen Elisabeth, a chorus of consolation raises this cry: Despair not, for sooner or later the victim is always avenged by Justice and Destiny.

By HALL CAINE
GREAT BRITAIN *

Not that she's old and full of days, O God,
 Not that she keeps the round Earth's wealth in fee,
 Not that her ships are sovereign of the sea,
Not that her sons, forth from their native sod
Have borne her flag as far as man has trod,
 Not that her arm is feared, nor yet the flood
 Of her avenging wrath, her ancient blood—
Not therefore is she mighty, O my God.

But that as Mother of Nations, strong yet meek,
Her strength is given her to protect the weak,
 And that she cries o'er any child of Thine
At any wrongful blow of any State,
 " Because her soul is outraged she is mine "—
Therefore it is that God made Britain Great.

Hall Caine

   * *Reply to Rossetti's " Refusal of Aid Between Nations."*

By MAETERLINCK
To the Editor of KING ALBERT'S BOOK

IL ne m'appartient pas de célébrer en ce moment la gloire de ma petite patrie. Vous l'avez fait du reste de si admirable façon, avec une éloquence si précise et si belle qu'il n'y a rien à ajouter à votre Introduction. Vos paroles m'ont ému jusqu'aux larmes. Elles nous apportent le plus haut témoignage que l'on puisse espérer dans l'histoire parcequ'elles sont prononcées au nom d'un grand peuple pour qui l'honneur, la loyauté, la fidélité aux engagements solennels, le courage silencieux, tenace et invincible, furent toujours les lois mêmes de la vie. De tout mon cœur, merci !

Maeterlinck

TRANSLATION
It is not for me to sing the glories of my little country at this moment, and indeed you have done so yourself with such a true and noble eloquence that it would be difficult to add anything to your Introduction. Your words brought tears to my eyes. They bear the highest testimony we can hope for in history, for they speak in the name of a great people to whom honour, loyalty, faith to solemn covenants, and silent tenacious, invincible courage have always been the very law of life. With all my heart, thank you !

THE END OF KING ALBERT'S BOOK